(continued from the front flap)

Although our legal system views trials as forums explicitly constructed for persuasive advocacy leading to judgment, they can be organized and interpreted by the media to persuade large public audiences. Thus, as the forensic drama develops through the media, it becomes a means for adjudicating among discourses competing for public stature, and it establishes particular ideas or personae as standard references for public argument. In doing so, it functions for both elite and mass audiences as a means for making political judgments and for rationalizing problematic social practices.

Robert Hariman is Associate Professor of Speech Communication at Drake University.

Popular Trials

STUDIES IN RHETORIC AND COMMUNICATION
General Editors:
E. Culpepper Clark
Raymie E. McKerrow
David Zarefsky

Edited by Robert Hariman

Popular Trials
Rhetoric, Mass Media, and the Law

The University of Alabama Press   Tuscaloosa and London

Library of Congress Cataloging-in-Publication Data
Popular trials : rhetoric, mass media, and the law / edited by Robert
    Hariman.
    p. cm.
    Bibliography: p.
    Includes index.
    ISBN 0-8173-0474-6 (alk. paper)
    1. Trials—United States. 2. Mass media—Law and legislation—
United States. 3. Persuasion (Psychology) I. Hariman, Robert.
KF220.P67   1990
345.73'7—dc20
[347.3075]   89-33736
                                                       CIP

British Library Cataloguing-in-Publication Data available

Contents

Preface

This book began as a proposal for a research seminar convened at the 1985 convention of the Speech Communication Association. Since then the members of that group who stayed with the project have been joined by a few others who heard of their work. The project received funding for editorial assistance from the National Endowment for the Humanities Faculty Development Fund of the College of Arts and Sciences, Drake University. The process has been beset with the inevitable delays accompanying common work, but it has proved to be an economical response to the problems of studying a class of events each of which produces truckloads of data. I would like to express special appreciation to Kathleen Farrell, for her insights regarding the connections between this project and related scholarly programs, and to William Lewis, for his keen criticisms and sure sense of argument. I look forward to seeing this work augmented as other communication scholars recognize the persuasive power and cultural density of popular trials.

Popular Trials

Introduction

Robert Hariman

Scopes, Sacco-Vanzetti, the Rosenbergs, the Chicago Seven—
these names have come to represent bitter conflicts and dramatic moments in our social history. Such popular trials have
provided the impetus and the forum for major public debates,
they have set some of the conditions of belief for those debates,
and they have conferred powerful legitimacy upon particular
political ideas. Yet, despite the high drama of each trial and its
ability to stimulate volumes of commentary in popular, legal,
and scholarly texts long after its time, popular trials have received little attention as a class of persuasive events. This in-
attention today may stem from an understandable skepticism
about the mass media's contribution to public life, or from a
less defensible belief in the autonomy of The Law from more
unruly social influences, but it is not warranted by the historical record. From the trial of Socrates to the dozens of proceedings reported daily in the contemporary press, the popular
trial has been active as a rhetorical form, a social practice, and
a symptom of historical change.

   This volume argues that popular trials should be recognized
as a genre of public discourse. By examining popular trials we
discover rich materials for understanding the texture of a society's public life, and by identifying the conventions of this
genre we can articulate both comprehensive means of persuasion and those elements distinguishing the individual com-

municative event. The following essays provide critical studies of seven trials, as well as two chapters situating this work within genre criticism and media studies. This introductory essay will articulate the perspective informing the volume, discuss the relation of this perspective to relevant fields of inquiry, preview the following essays, and suggest possible applications not elaborated in the essays themselves.

Critical Perspective

In the simplest sense, a popular trial is a judicial proceeding that gains the attention of a general audience, usually through sustained coverage by the mass media. Such coverage typically involves descriptions of the proceedings, biographies of and interviews with the principals, and commentary about both the issues of the trial and the conduct of the trial. Popular trials can be distinguished from judicial proceedings not receiving popular attention (most trials), as well as from reports of and subsequent commentary about judicial decisions having significant legal and social consequences (e.g., *Brown* v. *Board of Education* or *Roe* v. *Wade*). Popular trials also should be distinguished from public hearings, despite the obvious similarities in form and function, for the hearings (such as those regarding the Watergate scandal) often have to establish, rather than presume, judicial authority, and they usually lack the key element of symbolic closure provided by the trial's verdict.[1]

This simple definition needs to be augmented and refined, however, if we are to understand the richness of this class of rhetorical events. For example, popular trials typically have additional characteristics such as the oddity of the crime (e.g., the Lindberg kidnapping, facial mutilation of a fashion model, political charges such as "conspiracy"), great intensity in audience response (e.g., union identification with Sacco-Vanzetti), timeliness (e.g., Rosenbergs and the Red scare) and special media representation (e.g., live coverage of Claus von Bulow's second trial, retail videotapes of Bernard Goetz's pre-trial testimony). In addition, many are political trials, dealing with fundamental questions of the government's power and legitimacy, the citizen's rights and obligations, and the mediating role played by major cultural institutions and texts. (The relationship between popular trials and political trials is discussed further in the next section of this essay.) In every case, the fact of popularization introduces additional dynamics of persuasion and comprehension that shape popular and professional understanding of the trial.

Above all, popular trials are thoroughly rhetorical. First, all trials are forums explicitly constructed for persuasive advocacy leading to judgment. Any type of proof can be brought within the courtroom, from divine revelation to scientific experimentation, but everything must be presented within the context of advocates arguing before an audience; within the courtroom, persuasive speaking is the sovereign means for achieving rational judgment. The popular trial retains this reliance upon persuasion and also amplifies it through dramatizations of advocates pleading and jurors pondering the cases. Second, popular trials are means of persuasion. They supply opportunities and materials for advancing causes, both within and without the courtroom, before, during and after the trial, by the participants themselves and by commentators ranging from the President of the United States to the citizen in the street in Paris. Third, popular trials are composed of powerful persuasive techniques. The courtroom trial possesses inherently appealing means for establishing belief, such as a dramatic format, narrative coherence, and the performance of rationality, and it is structured further by the rhetorical conventions and particular biases of the mass media. The writers in this volume are committed to understanding how popular trials are created by these many dynamics of public communication. The common assumptions of the following essays are that a sound understanding of a popular trial should include in a significant way an account of its persuasive nature, and that scholarship in communication would benefit from the critical study of popular trials as a genre.

Although recognizing the persuasive dynamics of popular trials is an important step toward fully understanding their nature and significance, it also seems to work against us, for the more a trial appears to be a scene or product of public controversy and rhetorical artistry, the less legitimate it appears. As we discover cases where the popularization of the trial interferes with the courtroom proceedings, or where the public discussion extends far beyond the impact of the decision upon the common law, and when such discussion perhaps begins with and continues because of basic misunderstandings about legal practice, then it seems that good law and powerful rhetoric do not mix well, and that one might choose to study one or the other but not both together in the popular trial. I shall argue below that, despite its occasional value, this distinction itself requires largely unrealistic conceptions of both law and rhetoric. For the moment, however, the objection that popular trials must be legally suspect can help us better articulate their richness.

Let us distinguish between legal significance and rhetorical significance. Legal significance means that a case influences subsequent legal argument and legal judgment. Such a case influences lawyers as they decide whether and how to argue, and it influences judges and juries as they attempt to make reasoned judgments in accord with the law. A case has rhetorical significance if it becomes a standard reference in public argument. Thus, the Rosenberg trial could be used in editorials discussing such diverse topics as U.S.-Soviet relations, nuclear weaponry, and the imprisonment of Nelson Mandela. Obviously, many trials that are significant legally never catch the public eye, and many popular trials have considerable rhetorical significance but negligible legal significance. We can better appraise the impact of any trial by considering how it would be placed on a scale using these two measures, the legal and the rhetorical: For example, most trials have little impact upon the common law and are ignored by the media; many decisions issuing from unreported trials have become influential within the legal community and unknown elsewhere; *Roe* v. *Wade* is a famous decision proceeding from a relatively anonymous trial that both has legal authority and serves as a symbol of the liberal state; the Rosenberg and Chicago Seven trials were popular trials that achieved no special recognition within the legal community—save as cautions against the recurrence of similar embarrassments—but remain major symbols of their historical moments; the Baby M trial received extensive coverage and achieved immediate significance both legally and rhetorically. Thus, although a commitment to the norms and autonomy of the legal community might limit analysis of how some trials attain considerable cultural importance, we can improve our understanding without having to disregard the legal context by recognizing that trials can fulfill multiple cultural functions.

The prerequisites for attaining legal significance are familiar subjects of discussion within legal scholarship, but rhetorical significance remains a relatively unexamined topic. Rather than assume that the popular trial is irrevocably a legal proceeding, or ultimately a media event, the better approach is to conceptualize the trials as a class of events constituted by a unique intersection of legal and media practices functioning to maintain a community through persuasive argumentation and judgment. In other words, popular trials constitute a genre of the literature of public life. This literature has many genres, including inaugurals, public hearings, congressional reports, stump speeches, political cartoons, and so forth. Like each of these, popular trials have unusual prominence within public discourse: They occur regularly or frequently, and they have conventional features, a proven appeal, and proven impact.[2] Furthermore, these common traits coalesce to fulfill the functions of public discourse: The popular trials operate as a means for making political judgments and they confer intelligibility upon the practices of living together. In short, popular trials, like all the forms of public discourse, are a "literature as equipment for living."[3] Individuals and groups form their opinions, which are their means for making sense of the world and acting effectively to advance their interests, by interpreting the trials and reaching verdict about the action under trial and about the relevant institutions represented in the trial, including the institutions of law and government. Trials function in this way as forums for debate, as symbols of larger constellations of belief and action, and as social dramas used to manage emotional responses to troubling situations. We can develop this perspective further by considering its relationship with several pertinent areas of scholarship.

Prior Research

Critical study of popular trials as a class of persuasive events allows us to appropriate and contribute to several fields of inquiry, including prior studies of popular trials, legal scholarship, research in legal communication, mass media studies, and the criticism of public address.

Prior work on popular trials involves the many books written about individual trials and those few written to account for trials as a class of events.[4] The accounts of individual trials often are written by principal actors in the drama, defense attorneys being notoriously prolific defenders of their own role. The books are eminently readable, but the objective is generally promotion of the writer or of the institution of the law, and although they serve as engaging studies in strategic thinking they do not lead us toward a more explanatory account of the events themselves. The more scholarly studies are generally contributions to historical inquiry (or political debate) but are not inclined to discuss the rhetorical character of their subject. A notable exception is *Thine is the Kingdom: The Trial for Treason of Thomas Wentworth, Earl of Strafford, First Minister to King Charles I, and Last Hope of the English Crown* by John Timmis III.[5] Timmis uses the conceptual apparatus of neo-Aristotelian criticism to account carefully for how the historical events were structured by the argumentation before the court. Although the writers in this volume do not use his methodology, his book stands as an important precursor for our project. For the most part, however, historians have looked to the popular trial because the trial has conveniently collected the materials of history, but then looked through the trial for the purpose of seeing the historical moment more clearly and so often overlooked how the trial functions according to conventions of rhetorical practice.

Although there have been a number of commercial publications that each present a group of popular trials,[6] the several scholarly books discussing political trials as a class bring us closer to our present interest. *Political Trials*, edited by Theodore L. Becker, and *American Political Trials*, edited by Michael R. Belknap, organize studies of individual trials in order to delineate basic characteristics of the political trial, certainly the most common and significant type of popular trial.[7] Becker roughs out a typology to locate the different ways in which political motives can intrude into the legal process, and Belknap suggests that political trials are symptoms of periods of intensified conflict. A third book, Ron Christenson's *Political Trials: Gordian Knots in the Law*, follows the common orientation of the previous collections but articulates another theme as well.[8] Christenson studies a group of trials in order to discuss the morality of obedience and dissent with the law, and analyzes each trial to strengthen his argument on behalf of the rule of law. Although these collections are valuable source books for the study of popular trials, they suffer from two basic limitations: They overlook many of the persuasive elements in trial format and in press coverage, and their interest in political trials obscures our view of the larger class of all popular trials.

This conventional identification of the two classes has been understandable but misleading. Most, not all, political trials are popular trials; many, not all, popular trials are political trials. By assuming that political trials are the only (or only significant) popular trials, we become disposed to make several mistakes. First, we could ignore or devalue the significance—including the political significance—of other trials, such as the von Bulow trial. Second, we could seriously misread trials, such as the Hinckley trial, that function to redefine events from political to non-political categories. Third, we could overlook important dimensions of explicitly political trials that would be revealed by comparison with more "social" trials (of such political triviality as the Mayflower Madame) and with such social processes as conferring celebrity. The study of political trials, individually and as a class, is likely to continue much as it has begun, but we should not assume either that inquiry governed by that classification is self-sufficient or that that such study will suffice to explain many of the "non-political" popular trials that also have a significant presence in our public culture.

The relationship between the popular trial and legal scholarship is complicated by the role legal ideology plays in both. Popular trials function in great part because they project successfully the authority of The Law, which in turn is supported by such practices as legal education and scholarship. Thus, the low regard for the trial's popularity within legal scholarship—or at least, the fact the legal scholars typically profess indifference to such concerns—issues from the fact that both legal practitioners and legal scholars benefit from maintaining the fiction of legal autonomy. As The Law must be what is not political, not popular, and more complicated than could ever be reported in the press, so the occasional popular trial should receive only the attention merited by its legal significance, and no more.

Although few studies issue from the law schools, the basic insight of legal realism provides a sufficient rationale for pursuing such studies and for incorporating them into the legal curriculum. Because legal discourse functions as the official discourse in our society, the courts inevitably have to function outside the bounds of the legal documents. As Alexis de Tocqueville remarked, "Scarcely any political question arises in the United States that is not resolved sooner or later, into a judicial question. . . . The language of the law thus becomes, in some measure, a vulgar tongue."[9] Karl Llewellyn and others articulated this perspective as a legal philosophy appropriate to modern society: "The court voices, so to speak, as an official organ not only The Law, but, in its sizing up of the situation and the controversy, the court voices also the residual non-expert horse sense of the community in the whirl of this technologically baffling world."[10] Thus, the distinction between legal and rhetorical significance at least partially collapses, and with it should fall the automatic preference for legal expertise. The legal practice has to function with careful regard to the "extra-legal" issues and in a manner allowing a general public to make sense of the world through the interpretation of legal discourse.[11] The question of how much legal autonomy and legal authority exists in any particular argument or ruling often remains a crucial question for determining how and how well the court functioned as a social instrument, but these distinctions should no longer be invoked to dismiss a line of inquiry.

This perspective also parallels the understanding of the law that has been articulated by rhetorical scholars. Classical authors such as Cicero stressed the continuity of law and rhetoric and clearly saw the law as having both technical rules and a general public function. Contemporary theorists stress the necessity of locating persuasive meaning in the act of addressing a situation,[12] the role of persuasive practices in determining knowledge itself,[13] and especially the social knowledge essential for common life,[14] as well as the particular role persuasive practices play in the social construction of reality occurring within any courtroom and so within the law itself.[15] In sum, rather than seeing popular trials as odd or embarrassing moments in legal practice, we should recognize how they provide opportunities to articulate ideas important to our larger understandings of legal interpretation and the role of law in society. In particular, we should recognize how popular trials provide the most audience-intensive approach to using the courts to construct and apply society's common sense.

There is another branch of scholarship regarding legal practice that has a more direct kinship with the critical essays in this volume. The study of legal communication by researchers working in the disciplines of speech and psychology is now a thriving concern.[16] Two orientations prevail here: analysis of technical rhetoric in the trial process and criticism of the relationship between the law and the media in respect to constitutional issues.[17] The technical studies emphasize the minute elements of appeal and assent active in interviewing witnesses, selecting jurors, instructing jurors, presenting evidence, arguing, deliberating as a jury, and so forth.[18] This approach bears two limitations when applied to the popular trial. First, the fixation upon the legal scene and its conventions cannot account fully for how the condition of popularization affects the trial itself or account at all for the use to which the trial is being put by others. Not surprisingly, when scholars in legal communication have studied prominent trials, they often have continued to chronicle the means of persuasion employed and to explain events in respect to the advocates, judges, and juries present, and have treated everything beyond that as a contamination by the media of the forensic process. The technical emphasis need not be at odds with a more comprehensive rhetorical critique, though; they are better thought of as concentric analyses. The second limitation is more serious, however. Typically, the research into legal communication is conducted by or for or in conversation with people also acting as consultants to prosecution, defense, court, or a state commission. Although this alliance need not compromise the objectivity of the individual study, it does influence the agenda and approach to explanation for the community of researchers. The study of legal communication operates comfortably as a "handmaiden" to legal practice. Although this scholarship obviously is socially beneficial, it is equally inappropriate to the need for social critique, including critique of the legal profession, which often is essential for dealing with a popular trial on its own terms.[19]

The second perspective in the study of legal communication involves studying the continuing negotiation occurring within legal practice between the imperatives to provide for both a free press and a legal process insulated from the excesses of popular opinion. Here trials, and often popular trials, receive careful study in respect to the constitutional issues at stake in the First and Sixth Amendments.[20] Here the kinship with the following essays is particularly strong, for free speech research assumes a generally critical stance, even relishing at times the role of watchdog. Ultimately, however, this perspective has its own limitations, for it is bound to a set agenda of issues and the task of appraising one kind of political significance; it, too, is best seen as one approach that contributes to, but does not encompass, a large class of events.

Another relevant area of inquiry is the study of mass communication. The relevance is obvious, and as the concluding essay in this volume is devoted to articulating a relationship between popular trials and media studies, several cautionary notes will suffice here. Media studies are essential to understanding the dynamics of the popular trial, but they bring problems of their own as well. When scholars have examined the effects the media can have upon courtroom deliberation, they have done so in respect to pragmatic questions about pre-trial publicity, the effects within the courtroom of televising the proceedings, and the use of televised testimony or similar innovations in judicial procedure.[21] Although this work helps legal practitioners, it is of little use in accounting for the effects of the popular trial upon a public. On the other hand, when editorial commentators have recognized the role the media plays in the popular trial they have been too quick to fret about "the awesome power of the mass media" and have not been disposed to consider the positive or rational dimensions of popularization.[22] Generally, media studies have overlooked the importance of popular trials within the media, as well as the complexities of the popularization supplied by the media, because media studies have limited their sense of genre to the basic categories of televisual programming. The essays in this volume vary in their emphasis upon the role of the media in popularization, but all assume that the popular trial exists because of though not solely because of the media, that its explanation must come from recognizing its composite origins, and that the techniques of persuasion constitute the common denominator for all the social practices at play in a popular trial.

The remaining area of inquiry directly relevant to this project is the history and criticism of public address. Scholars in public address traditionally studied both great public debates and leading legal advocates, but rarely together and generally with a strong orientation toward valorizing the speakers.[23] This tradition supplies a common background for this project, however. Our basic interest in demonstrating through critical studies how the trials function as forms of public communication is a direct development of the traditional inquiry into public discourse. The following essays vary considerably in critical vocabulary and purpose, but as a group they are consistent with the methodological trends of the past three decades. First, they illustrate how criticism has expanded the basic conception of the rhetorical text. The popular trial is a non-traditional rhetorical text for several reasons: It contains many speakers and voices as well as diverse forms of commentary; it presents some auditors with oral proceedings, others with written transcripts, and most with fragmentary descriptions; and it mixes technical protocols of the law with loose conventions of the mass media. Thus, it exemplifies the kind of text, or kind of critical interest, that has increasingly characterized contemporary rhetorical criticism, in that it is decentered and overdetermined. One of the exasperating features of a popular trial for some is that it does not automatically center our attention in the manner expected of a legal proceeding; in fact, the central focus of the trial is often exactly what the participants are contesting, as when one side tries to keep the trial inside the courtroom while the other strives to move it into the press, each in order to achieve a rhetorical objective. The corresponding multiplying of perspectives during the trial in turn represents the complexity of its composition, as a myriad of social, political, economic, institutional, and other agencies all act to affect its manner and outcome.

This interest in the multiform text in turn justifies the second assumption we share with contemporary criticism, which is that the traditional reconstruction of the persuasive process around the speaker is only one among many approaches to a rhetorical text. Rhetorical critics have been moving away from the speaker orientation since the 1960s, and recent critical studies have provided the impetus to our project.[24] Despite the fact that many a popular trial is portrayed as a contest of celebrity lawyers, not least in their own accounts of the event, the manner in which the trial secures a popular audience is itself a fascinating phenomenon suggesting that the speakers may not be calling the tune.

There is a sense, however, in which contemporary criticism is echoing the more traditional studies it has displaced. After a period of conceptual innovations and methodological arguments, many critics today are returning to the earlier commitment to understand and nurture the conditions required for high quality public discourse. In a similar vein, many academic and popular commentators have bemoaned the decline in the traditional formats of public address, but they then have gone no further than blaming the mass media or, at best, searching for the causes of this decline. Perhaps we need to ask whether other genres of public thought could be waxing. We need to consider how the basic functions of public address may nonetheless continue to be met, albeit in a less pure and more fragmented manner, through the ascendency of other patterns of assertion, commentary, and judgment. If the popular trial proves to be significant in this sense, it certainly will continue to merit scholarly criticism.

The Essays

The following essays conceive of the trials as rhetorical phenomena produced by the interaction of at least legal and journalistic interests; each of the critical studies considers both the discourse within the courtroom and the popular discourse about the trial. The individual essays are partial accounts of different events, but together they present a composite picture of the genre. The essays could be organized in several ways. Typically, discussions of popular trials in the press and in academic settings use a topical format that presents labor trials, treason trials, race trials, anti-war trials, murder trials, and so forth, often in chronological order as well. Because this volume is designed to turn our attention to the common features of persuasion often obscured by the topical format, the essays are arranged to reinforce several emphases developed within our alternative approach.

The critical studies of individual trials are bracketed by two more general essays. My essay on popular trials and social knowledge amplifies the definition of the popular trial as a genre of public discourse. As the trials offer a "performance" of the laws, they enact social knowledge in several senses: The trial is a recognizable social practice; it is constituted by social agreements, including the agreement to recognize voices other than one's own; and it presents and authorizes particular beliefs. Furthermore, the popular trial fulfills an additional public function because it provides the social practice most suited formally to comparing competing discourses. Finally, the popular trial observes specific rhetorical constraints, including (but not limited to) the adversarial format, reliance upon official symbols, the formal closure of a decision, and emphasis upon characterization.

The first critical essay, John Lucaites's analysis of the impeachment trial of Henry Sacheverell in 1709–10, elaborates how a popular trial can contain the major value terms for a community. This trial was conducted in a specially constructed public amphitheatre, received vociferous press coverage, occasioned public riots, and quickly became a mirror of the major problems of political legitimacy dominating English government. Lucaites examines the role of such terms as "Hereditary Monarchy" and "Right of Resistance," and he argues that the trial constituted a "rhetoric of control" for both Whig prosecutors and Tory defenders that determined the range of possible arguments and managed national tensions while legitimating constitutional government.

The so-called monkey trial of John Scopes for teaching evolution in the Tennessee schools was the decisive act of a struggle between populism and progressivism that had been captivating the South and Midwest for decades. Despite its having no influence upon legal doctrine, the Scopes trial had a major impact upon American public discourse. Lawrance Bernabo and Celeste Condit account for the rhetorical significance of the trial by examining how the strategies of defense, prosecution, and the journalists for the national press combined to establish a new consensus about the roles of science and religion in American national life. Their study demonstrates the complexity of a popular trial: The trial provided a national forum for scientific discourse while ruling against its use in the courtroom, the journalists' story of the trial was derived from the legal story yet came to oppose the law, and the prosecution's reliance upon legality handicapped their ability to legitimate their political philosophy.

The trial of the Chicago Seven (or Eight) was the most prominent popular trial of its time, and one that has come to symbolize the cultural turmoil of the 1960s, the antiwar movement in particular, and the American legal system itself. The Chicago Seven defense was explicitly, aggressively interested in making the trial a popular trial that could be used as a forum for public debate about the Vietnam war. Juliet Dee examines the trial to determine how well it served the defendants' rhetorical objective. The trial proved to be a public forum, but one placing significant limitations on the defendants' message, including the normative constraints of judicial storytelling and the political and production constraints of the American press.

The trial of John Hinckley also served as a forum, although not for negotiating the views of the defendant. William Lewis examines the manner in which Hinckley's trial became a dramatic presentation of basic contradictions in our society's ideological structures. For one of the few times in his presidency, Ronald Reagan was forgotten as the trial turned everyone's attention to the problem of appraising Hinckley's sanity, and through that strange filter, our basic conceptions of law, medicine, and the family. The trial provided an active process of negotiation about our institutional "texts" and our corresponding common sense about the social order. Lewis reveals that, contrary to the stock objection that the insanity defense undermines the law, the Hinckley trial reinforced conventional patterns of legal authority, family structure, and medical treatment.

In the next essay, Susan Drucker and Janice Platt Hunold examine the trial of Claus von Bulow to draw our attention to the refracting medium itself. They ask, how is our understanding of this trial shaped by the manner in which it was presented on television? They argue that, contrary to the pretensions of the networks, the medium presented the events according to the conventions of its regular daytime programming—such as soap operas—rather than adhering to a "realistic" portrayal of the content of the trial. By extension, we can see how any popular trial might contain internal contradictions among the values of its several perspectives: say, among the media's values of entertainment, the legal system's values of justice, and the audience's values of public morality.

The last two critical studies emphasize the role popular trials can play within specific communities. Although famous trials are played on the national stage, they also have special import for smaller audiences—as when a Chicago lawyers association banquet included a mock trial satirizing Judge Hoffman. More commonly, trials receiving little or no coverage in the national media have dominated the attention of a smaller community, whether it be a region, state, city, or small but diffused community such as the Catholic left. Larry Williamson examines the trial of Roger Hedgecock, mayor of San Diego. This story of cynical personalities in an urban setting reveals how the biases peculiar to trial coverage by the mass media shape public knowledge. Williamson argues that the San Diego news media, contrary to their espoused standards of objectivity, stylized coverage by linking the trial to other popular trials (without regard to legal relevance) and by portraying the individuals involved as the stock characters of folk narrative.

The trial of the Catonsville Nine, who had burned Selective Service files, had particular significance for the non-geographical community of American Catholics. Justin Gustainis evaluates how the defendants, well aware of the possibilities of a popular trial, committed the crime to use the trial as a means for activating religious opposition to the war. Everything went off without a hitch, yet the defendants were repudiated by both clergy and laity in their own church, although they did become role models within the Catholic left. This story presents some of the paradoxes confronting anyone evaluating the rhetorical efficacy of a popular trial, for the trial contained the potential to be enormously influential and did become very important for a community of activists, yet it also failed to influence its public audience, perhaps because it never escaped the dilemma of having had to offend them to gain their attention.

The last essay returns to a more general discussion of popular trials. The power of the mass media to provide powerful distortions of their subject appears more ominous as we realize that popular trials constitute our primary representation of the legal system and that they review and judge the major issues of the day. Barry Brummett examines the effect the media technologies, as they are situated within certain cultural practices, have upon the social consciousness created through a popular trial. He argues that the trials dispose public understanding of public issues and of the legal system itself to be serial, personified, and commodified, and consequently inferior to the understanding to be gained through other, less mediated participation in our political and legal practices. Brummett's pessimism opposes the optimism in my suggestion that popular trials are often successful means for enacting social knowledge, and these two attitudes mark the range and significance of the genre.

Obviously, other trials and other essays also would have served well;[25] nor has the intention here been to settle disputes about particular trials. Other arrangements would work—perhaps they should be encouraged. Consider how the essays included here could be arrayed according to the following interests: from those essays that focus primarily upon the discourse "within" the trial to those that emphasize the discourse "outside" of the trial; from those essays that see the discourse in the trial as rational argument to those that see it as performative ritual; from those essays focusing on advocates' use of the media to those that focus upon media construction of the trial. These and other relationships offer opportunities for further consideration of the complexity and influence of this genre in our public life.

We hope that such consideration occurs. Three avenues for future work could lead to immediate benefits. First, popular trials are superbly suited for teaching. Their dramatization of historical material already has served historians well. The study of popular trials as distinctive communicative events offers rich material for courses in public address, media studies, legal communication, and the sociology of law. Critical studies of individual trials can serve as models of rhetorical analysis and judgment for classes in rhetorical criticism, as well as for advocacy classes in law school.

Second, the evaluation of these trials can improve media and legal practice, particularly if we surrender the idea of returning to a pristine time when the law was uncontaminated by the intrusions of the public. The trial of Socrates should remind us that the mass media is only a latter-day development of an ancient imperative towards using common judgment as a means for social cohesion, and some of the studies in this volume have suggested how popularization was socially beneficial without being legally harmful. These and other studies also suggest ways in which there is room for improvement, both in the manner in which the media present the trials and in the strategies employed by the defendants, advocates, and witnesses.

Finally, popular trials call for additional research. The trials offer excellent opportunities for developing current research programs in the critical study of the mass media and in the genres of public discourse, and also for expanding the boundaries of the good work being done in legal communication. They also should be particularly appropriate for applying contemporary ideas in social theory, most notably those of Michel Foucault and Jurgen Habermas, because they offer such a prominent combination of the major institutional discourses of our time.

And, of course, the social history never stops: The Baby M trial is receding from view—stories on surrogate motherhood and other related issues are being relegated to the middle pages and the Sunday magazines—but in its place have come trials of American spies, Middle Eastern terrorists, and aged Nazis. We all will continue to watch and read about these and similar proceedings, discuss, dispute, and judge the stories told, constantly adjusting our sense of common identity. And then do so again and again with these and other trials, for they are wells of our public speech, springs of our common life.

1

Performing the Laws
Popular Trials and Social Knowledge

Robert Hariman

In the seventh book of the *Laws* Plato justifies censorship of the theatrical companies by acknowledging that "we are ourselves authors of a tragedy, and that the finest and best we know how to make. In fact, our whole polity has been constructed as a dramatization of a noble and perfect life; that is what we hold to be in truth the most real of tragedies. Thus you are poets, and we also are poets in the same style, rival artists and rival actors, and that in the finest of all dramas, one which indeed can be produced only by a code of true law—or at least that is our faith. So you must not expect that we shall lightheartedly permit you to pitch your booths in our market square with a troupe of actors whose melodious voices will drown our own."[1] Plato tells us that a society reproduces itself through performance before spectators in a public space, where the community comes to be by being brought into the realm of appearance through an act at once aesthetic, ethical, political, and rhetorical. The drama portrays the substance of common life—the values binding the community—for "if your sentiments prove to be the same as ours, or even better, we will grant you a chorus, but if not, I fear, my friends, we never can."[2] The drama has as its text the laws, which are themselves the record of prior dramatizations, and which are altered as well through the act of performance. *The performance of the laws* then becomes a singularly powerful locus of social control, for it is the very means by which the members of the community know who they are.[3]

This passage gives us the conception of the social whole of which the popular trial is the representative part, each the opposing pole of a synecdoche continually active in the reproduction of society. The laws exist outside of performance, yet the performance of the laws is essential for their becoming realized in lawful living. In Aristotle's terminology, the mode is epideictic; according to Hans-Georg Gadamer, understanding occurs through application; following Thomas Farrell, the social knowledge essential for public decision making is grounded in the consensus achieved before and by specific audiences, confirmed by recurrent practices, capable of generating future social practices, and inescapably normative in its implications;[4] in our common experience, the laws are as good as we judge them to be when watching or reading about their performance in court. One week it was Baby M, the week before it was high school textbooks, before that it was the Walker trial, von Bulow, Hinckley, Angela Davis, the Catonsville Nine, the Chicago Seven, the Rosenbergs, Sacco-Vanzetti, Dreyfus, Dred Scott, Tom Paine, Thomas Wentworth, Martin Luther, Socrates. . . .

My purpose is not to review the hundreds of trials that have become signposts in the history of the West, nor to catalog the many more trials that constitute a significant percentage of the daily storytelling by our mass media. The scope of my subject (of performing the laws) is indeed extensive, although our awareness of the rhetorical value of popular trials has been somewhat retarded. In this essay, I will advance three propositions toward the end of understanding how popular trials function as rhetorical processes shaping the social construction of reality: First, popular trials constitute a major genre of public discourse; second, the function of this genre is primarily to adjudicate discourses; and third, the genre fulfills this function by applying specific generic constraints to more diffuse public debates. If we accept these claims, an additional suggestion follows as well, which is that the trials and the laws themselves are more profoundly rhetorical and less autonomously legal than supposed by either rhetorical or legal scholars.

The Genre

I hope I can introduce my terminology without stimulating the anxieties about definition endemic to genre criticism—what Thomas Conley labeled so captivatingly as "the Linnaean Blues."[5] Public discourse is discourse occurring in the public domain—and especially in the news media—about public affairs, agents, institutions, and values. A speech attacking "secular humanism," the report of that speech, the editorial about the speech, and the letter to the editor about the editorial are all examples of public discourse, whereas the dinner table conversation about the speech and the marriage announcements printed in the newspaper are not. A genre of public discourse is an ensemble of communicative conventions having an aesthetic unity and rhetorical efficacy,[6] and a convention is a common, tacit assumption used by speakers and auditors to compose and interpret messages. For example, the eulogy follows the narrative and topics of the deceased's life to honor and never blame the individual while calling the community to live according to its ideals. The trial follows an adversarial format to reach a decision resolving a social conflict.

A genre, then, is a form of social knowledge in several senses. First, it is what people know, in the sense of being what they rely upon when otherwise in a condition of change, disorientation, or trauma. This is why generic forms that have been relaxed during more common periods of routine social exchange predominate in moments of social and political transition; witness how a disaster stimulates pronouncements, prayers, eulogies, addresses, white papers, and other formal offerings that later dissolve back into the welter of conversation characterizing the ordinary business of living together. When speakers are less confident about what they are saying they rely more upon their knowledge of what they are doing— that is, they rely on substantive knowledge when they have it, and emphasize knowledge of the social practice when they don't. Nor is this knowledge of the social practice necessarily "leaner" or inferior to substantive knowledge: For a social practice is essentially teleological, and so intensive participation in a social practice (such as litigating a dispute) can supply just the direction people need to rediscover their bearings.[7] Second, a genre is known socially, in the sense that it is sustained by the agreement of others themselves acting within social relationships. A genre exists only as long as others agree that it exists; the individual's knowledge of the genre must be matched by others' willingness to recognize its forms and authority. Third, a genre is a container for common beliefs: It is built to hold certain types of symbolic material for specific ends.[8] Sonnets hold sentiments in exciting contiguity and inaugurals hold traditional values in secure display. A genre of public discourse is built to hold public knowledge, that is, the common beliefs by which a community defines itself.

The key to elaborating the manner in which popular trials function as social knowledge is to conceptualize the trials as a genre of public discourse. The generic status of popular trials follows from their suitability for social knowing in each of the above senses. First, the popular trial is a well-known social practice which can be relied upon whenever events extend beyond prior community prescriptions. It is no accident that we have turned to the courts to deal with issues such as the production of babies as commodities, the organization of a "counter-culture," or the security requirements of a nuclear power. Substantive public beliefs—our conceptions of who we are, what kind of community we live in, and what we should do—are continually breaking down and so requiring reconsideration and either change or re-affirmation. Our conceptions break because of "external" factors such as economic and technological changes and, more frequently, because our conceptions themselves contain contradictions that eventually rupture our social world. The many labor trials early in this century document the strain industrialization placed upon our conception of equality under the law, and the Baby M case revealed the contradiction between the bourgeois ideology of family life and the increasing commodification of bourgeois society. In every case events have challenged conventional conceptions of the world, which are themselves used daily in countless ordinary persuasive acts, and the trial is convened in the mass media to adjust our sense of things. The reason the *trial* is used, rather than the event (murder, theft, strike, etc.) alone or the many texts (speeches, books, cartoons, etc.) available on the subject, is that it is already a known practice—a stable format, and so a way of interpreting events in a world temporarily become ambiguous.

The popular trial is also an intensively social event amplifying conventional manners of presentation. Today we are well aware of how insistently all the actors play to the audience, as lawyers retain press agents, secure book rights in advance, hold daily press conferences where they display witnesses, and design their courtroom strategies for both the immediate and the extended audiences, but we may lose sight of the fact that this extra-legal, patently rhetorical orientation has always been a necessary part of the performance of the laws. Look, for example, at the scene outside the courthouse in Dayton, Tennessee:

The town, in fact, assumed the appearance of a crowded circus arena. Leather-lunged vendors of hot dogs and lemonade competed with booksellers hawking Bibles and biological treatises among the gaunt, godly hill people who crowded the streets. Journalists, from all parts of the world, vied for news stories. Internationally famous scientists, on hand to testify for the defense, rubbed shoulders with T. T. Martin, the frenzied, white-maned secretary of the Anti-Evolution League of America, and with Deck Carter, "the Bible Champion of the World" and the only person with whom God had communed directly since Joan of Arc. The high priest of irreverence, H. L.

Mencken of the *American Mercury,* mingled freely with those whom he delighted in describing as "gaping primates" and "yokels" from the buckle on the Bible Belt. Darrow's cohort, urbane New York attorney Arthur Garfield Hays, listened with utter disbelief as a group of gyrating Holy Rollers screamed: "Thank God I got no education, Glory be to God." And, of course, the monkey motif was everywhere: children dangled toy monkeys in the streets; a circus man displayed two chimpanzees; and a Coney Island sideshow offered its prize exhibit, Bozo, to the defense.[9]

Here, and here alone, are the many voices of the national theater brought together. The Scopes trail was a superb test case not because of its legal issues—which both sides quickly recognized to be quite limited and quite clear—but because it provided the stage for a performance of the laws. The issues had been debated passionately for decades in part because the speakers spoke so differently and could rarely do otherwise than wholly misrepresent the other positions. Voices reverberating from high church pulpit, Holy Roller tent, or academic tabernacle could not be brought together in those forums, as they had to be brought together if they were to be judged as "rival artists and rival actors." The trial required that people of vastly different perspectives recognize a common forum, while allowing them to keep and project their own voices. The trial was able to proceed as an authoritative practice because it was also an acceptable extension of their more parochial social habits, and particularly their habits of speaking. Even though the speakers within the courtroom spoke within the decorous conventions of forensic speaking, their significance came from their speaking as spokesmen for the different voices clamoring outside the trial.

The popular trial also is a form of social knowing in that it is the means by which we hold what we know. It is a symbolic container allowing symbolic material to be collected and affirmed as social goods—that is, as substantive knowledge. It is a means by which we create, disseminate, judge, and ratify as facts those assumptions about the world and those values of the community that together are supposed to be informing the laws. As the community attempts to be an incarnation of the good life, and the laws a representation of the community, the performance of the laws becomes the moment when these fictions can themselves be put to the test. Popular trials address points of law but they answer such questions as whether American society is a class society and whether the Bible should be the highest moral authority. These and similar questions all comprise the specific concept of social knowledge which, according to Farrell, "comprises conceptions of symbolic relationship among problems, persons, interests, and actions, which imply (when accepted) certain notions of preferable public behavior."[10] Furthermore, the popular trials seem to be particularly suitable for staging knowledge that is explicitly or implicitly implicated in social control. Whether charting the phenomena of wealth and celebrity in a von Bulow trial, or the relation between law and medicine in the Hinckley trial, or the power of the mass media in the Sharon and Westmoreland trials, or the personal uses of government in the trials of Governor Edwards, Mayor Hedgecock, and a host of lesser officials, popular trials often examine those essential connections in the society's means for distributing resources and inducing quiescence.[11]

The full significance of this point is often obscured by over-reliance upon the distinction between the discourse within the courtroom and the popular discourse swirling around the trial in the mass media. From that perspective, there is no "container" and no clear sociological function, for legal discourse isn't designed to do such work and so much of the rest is obviously spurious to the case. Several caveats are necessary here. First, there is no question that there often are rhetorically significant differences between the two realms of discourse, and that the legal discourse often is more rational while the popular discourse carries considerable distortions of the legal issues—often using them as a foil, and more often as a pretext—to activate more emotional and ideological responses to the issues in the trial. Second, contrasting the forensic and popular discourses sometimes can bring the critic to better understand what is happening in the media and in society. Third, at times the distinction is itself at issue on either side, with the trial advancing the use of legal and other kinds of expertise to solve social problems while the media present folk discourse and common sense as the better materials for decision making. Fourth, as the prior observation suggests, the distinction itself is not a neutral marker of objective reality, but a means for the constitution of legal authority; consequently, we can suspect that sometimes it may be enforced for reasons other then advancing our understanding of how people are deliberating about the common good. Finally, as many of the essays in this volume demonstrate, in a number of significant trials this distinction is flat wrong. Even when a popular trial adheres to the stylistic conventions of the courtroom while the media employ all the devices of yellow journalism, the differences between what is said within and about the trial may be far less important than the rhetorical elements common to both forums. At this point, the question of which presentation is really the trial is as academic as asking whether a play really occurs on stage or in the minds of the audience. The better approach is to define the many discourses of a popular trial as a unified rhetorical occasion having generic characteristics, and to consider how the genre allows and constrains a process through which a community defines itself.

Adjudicating Discourses

We could argue that the trials constitute a genre because there are so many of them (which there are) or because they have been so important historically (which they have been) or because they receive such selective attention by the media (which they do), but none of these observations does much to help us explain how particular trials develop or to understand their significance within society. I submit that popular trials function as a genre because their common elements are particularly well suited to supplying the performance of social knowledge required by any society. Whatever one's class, status, or access to people and positions of influence, the need to make sense of an enormously complex social whole requires the selection of exemplars—acts, events, or texts that illustrate the workings of the whole. This common need is the *raison d'être* of the popularized trial. Perhaps any part of the whole can be considered, whether popular song lyrics or Department of Agriculture reports or town hall architecture. But some customs will be *formally* suited to create and disseminate our understanding of our public culture. Thus, the Supreme Court opinion commands our attention because of its convergence of tradition, authority (especially the contemporary authority of expertise), carefully crafted discourse, legality, and finality. But the Court's discourse is known only *post-hoc*, after the process of deliberation has been conducted with little or no popular observation. Although the Court's opinions qualify as a superior literature of governance, or perhaps as the premiere genre within our political literature, they lack some of the dramatic and symbolic characteristics essential for complete engagement of the mass audience. For the complete exemplar of our political culture we need the trial itself, with all its due process, presentational flair, and popular appeal. When we examine the trials as exemplars of the social whole, we discover that they present society as a text, and the text as a collection of discourses.

The popularized trial serves so well as an exemplar of social knowing because it contains explicitly the problem of comparing and evaluating discourses before an audience of ordinary citizens. Some of our discourses are subject to routinized public accountability— so civic meetings are advertised publicly, enter their minutes into the public record, and so on—but most of what we do and say is not monitored so directly. How do we know that we are speaking rightly when we say that criminals can be rehabilitated, or that money corrupts, or that the entrepreneur is the American hero? That is, how do we know that our public beliefs are sound?

A trial is a forum for judging discourses, and contemporary trials increasingly include witnesses brought into the court for their ability to speak in the many special vocabularies of our time. Psychiatrists, physicians, sociologists, accountants, military officers, theologians, and others appear before the jury, who have to weigh simultaneously the evidence and the discourse in which that evidence is presented. And the discourse of the law is itself under study, as juries and commentators alike attempt to discern what is the common rationale in differing interpretations of, say, "malice" and "reckless disregard."[12] Thus the specific character of the trial as a communicative forum emerges: The trial is a social practice for producing authoritative judgments of discourses. This critical function both contributes to the function of rendering verdicts on questions of justice, and operates independently of it. We reach a judgment by determining who is speaking most honestly and accurately and appropriately, and we use the occasion of judging individual actions in order to appraise more pervasive discourses. In the words of James Boyd White, "the law with all its faults has been by far the best and most powerful method of cultural criticism American society has had. Certainly, it has proved more valuable than modern philosophy, sociology, political science, or journalism. The main reason for this, as I say elsewhere, is that the law is in structure multivocal, always inviting new and contrastive accounts and languages."[13]

A prominent example of how trials function to judge discourses publicly is provided by the trial of John Scopes in 1925 for violating the state law forbidding the teaching of evolution in the public schools.[14] Both sides were willing to make the trial a test case of the law, and the clash between prosecution counsel William Jennings Bryan, the great evangelist and conservative populist orator, and defense counsel Clarence Darrow, the avowed agnostic and eloquent progressive, provided all the drama an eager press desired. The climax of the trial came when Darrow put Bryan on the stand to grill him about the contradictions and implausibilities incurred in the literal interpretation of the Bible. The trial had "turned into an argument about the orders of knowledge,"[15] and as Darrow became increasingly aggressive and Bryan increasingly worn, the nation watched the unravelling of a received relationship among its major religious text, its public philosophy, and its educational practices. By the end of the trial the language of fundamentalism had been thoroughly discredited as a form of knowledge and the appeal to Biblical authority had been disqualified from the public domain.

Bryan's death days after the trial provided eerie confirmation of the collapse of the language he had embodied. Despite the fact that the state won the case, fundamentalism was now being routed from government and religious commentary was being replaced by scientific testimony as the authoritative discourse for public decision making.[16] American public discourse continues to be powerfully constrained by this legacy. Stated otherwise, the legal outcome of the trial was of far less importance than its critical function of judging discourses.

This use of the popular trial to adjudicate discourses is particularly pertinent today, as American society witnesses, on the one hand, an increasing predominance of expert discourses in the public realm and, on the other hand, the critiques of this change ranging from academic analyses of expertise and institutionalization to the various reactionary movements amalgamating the symbols of church, school, and family. These contrary attitudes often now are staged in the same trial, as when the Baby M trial featured both approving characterizations of judicial expertise and condemnation of a psychiatric appraisal of motherhood, or when the Hinckley trial adjudicated the discourses of law, medicine, and family.[17] When we recognize that the adjudication of expert discourses is a distribution of powers within society, and that expertise itself is increasingly an object of political conflict, then the role of the popular trial as a means of social formation acquires additional significance.

Generic Constraints

The Scopes trial was one episode in the comprehensive struggle between progressivism and more indigenous political interests. The distinctive contribution of the trial was that it provided the best forum for articulating and judging the competing beliefs. The trial was not the only forum—newspapers, sermons, electoral campaigns, and legislative debates all had dealt with the conflict for decades— but it was the forum that best provided the drama (that press, pulpit, and the assemblies lacked), the extra-political legitimacy (missing from electoral decisions), and the rhetorical context, that is, the explicit attention to the competing forms of speech, that were required for a significant resolution of the issue. People needed to determine what qualified as knowledge and who qualified as knowledgeable among those vying for influence over their schools. Although individuals reach judgments privately, the full legitimacy to be conferred comes not from the aggregation of individual judgments, but rather from the public presentation and explicitly social commentary given by witnesses under oath, judicial pronouncements, and the like. Recall also that most discourse evaluation occurs within the communities "owning" the discourses as physicians judge physicians, psychologists judge psychologists, and so forth. The trial, then, provides the public with explicitly public and authoritative norms for resolving a dispute about what kind of speech should be influential in public affairs. This comparison of discourses does not occur innocently, however, for the genre itself is not equally disposed to every kind of speech, and it advances the interests of the law and the media. Thus, to understand fully the popular trial's function we need to see how it constrains discourses.

The constraints active in any popular trial are likely to fall into three somewhat arbitrary categories: the constraints provided by the legal forum, those provided by media practice, and those indigenous to the social conflict being presented. For example, the Westmoreland trial filtered a review of the Vietnam war through the legal construct of malice aforethought, self-interested coverage of the trial by the media, and still unanswered questions about public accountability in American foreign affairs. Any comprehensive criticism of a particular trial would of course have to consider all such constraints. I will discuss only those general constraints that originate in the procedures and norms of trial practice. These include the adversarial format, use of official symbols, the necessity of decision, and the theme of judging character. The adversarial format is the most obvious, and so most easily underrated, constraint. This practice is the root source of the trial's drama and its means for the comparison of discourses. It also shapes our knowledge of the subjects in the trial: So the counter-culture becomes more credible just by being one side of the Chicago Seven trial, and the role of the contracting agency drops out of sight in the Baby M trial.[18] Note also that these cases, like many others, depend upon the media exaggerating the polarization familiar in legal practice; yet the standard suggestion that the "original" qualifications on that tendency would be restored by focusing solely upon the legal text is both quixotic and blind to the necessity of the adversarial element in the performance of the laws.

The use of official symbols constitutes the basic *mise-en-scène* of the popular trial. Here we include all the decorum activated by the physical setting itself,[19] as well as the general characteristics of legal language[20] and the special use of such symbols as "the Constitution."[21] These dramatic props are the source of the trial's legitimacy—and so counteract the anxieties resulting from adversarial antagonisms. The full import of these elements comes from recognizing how the trial usually is dealing with an issue already debated in a legislature; the legislature makes the laws but the trial provides their more authoritative performance. These symbols also both present actors with resources for persuasion and shape our knowledge of the issues independently of adversarial tactics. In the Chicago Seven trial, the court simultaneously focused a widespread social conflict, elevated the status of that conflict and served as symbol of the official culture; the defendants' violation of its decorum served as a powerful tactic for subverting that culture; the judge's misuse of the official symbols motivated a widespread reconsideration of the official culture; and the spectacle of a courtroom gone awry provided media of the left, center, and right the opportunity and authority to insist that their view of the world had been confirmed.[22]

The necessity of concluding with a decision about the case distinguishes the popular trial from every other public forum. Formal closure provides the genre with both its aesthetic unity and its ability to stimulate and focus debate. One reason trials continue to be the representative anecdotes of issues—as the Rosenberg trial is for treason and Hinckley trial is for the insanity defense, for example—is that they of all the occasions for the controversy result in a decision, whereas all the editorials, white papers, documentaries, public hearings, special reports, books, sermons, and so forth do not. This constraint on the social knowledge enacted by the trial is both a blessing and a curse, for though it often forces the public to move closer to serious consideration of the decision itself, it also supplies a thoroughly artificial resolution. On the one hand, the Catonsville Nine—who with clear premeditation committed the crime to get the trial to get the media coverage to propagate their objection to the Vietnam war, and who did little in the trial to escape conviction—probably were able to influence the Catholic left more because of their conviction than they could have done with more conventional advocacy.[23] On the other hand, the inference drawn by many of us from the acquittal of Angela Davis that justice is colorblind demonstrates how too much can be made of the popular trial's formal satisfactions, for we have allowed that trial to obscure the continuing racial inequities in the American criminal justice system.

The most complicated of the generic constraints active in the legal forum is its fascination with character. From the witness's oath to the character witness to the stock characterization of the judge to the determinations of intent to the essentially ethical cast of judgment itself, the legal setting displays the elements of an inquiry after character, and the media amplify this theme into character studies ranging from laughable to penetrating. In any case, this tendency amplifies both the dramatic nature of the trial, for characterization is a central element in dramaturgy, and its rhetorical disposition, for character (in the classical vocabulary, *ethos*) is one of the three basic modes of proof. The popular trial becomes predominantly a series of character studies, often according to the roles developed in other, model trials. We are familiar with the flamboyant defense attorney and the pedantic prosecutor, are quick to look to see if the judge is a Hoffmann and to scrutinize the biographical sketches of the defendants and witnesses. Notice how the presentation of the Baby M trial revolved around character studies of the several parents (supplied to the press, of course, by the ever helpful attorneys) and of the judge. The great pains taken by the press to assure the public that the judge's character was impeccable—including the assurance that he took good notes—illustrate neatly how these characterizations have direct effect upon attributions of authority and upon the use of authority to manage uncertainty.

The most interesting aspect of characterization is that the discourses being adjudicated in the trials are themselves personified. When Bobby Seale was physically gagged in the Chicago Seven trial, the nation saw in unmistakable terms that the discourse of Black Power was not being allowed into the courtroom; the trial's display of the texts of the counterculture became an affair about and among white folks. This substitution of the speaker for the speech is the means by which we are able to judge discourses at all. Only when Darrow and Bryan faced each other could the public finally decide between scientism and fundamentalism. And so Hinckley became the language of unreason, communism became the Rosenbergs, women's suffrage became Susan B. Anthony, and so forth. One way to assess the significance of this constraint is to consider how it may determine whether a trial becomes popular (and so potentially much more persuasive than otherwise): Class action suits such as the Bhopal case may fail to become popular trials, despite their attention to controversial issues of the day, because they fail to provide characters allowing the public to make judgments of character.

Social Knowledge

By characterizing popular trials as performances of the laws I have placed them within the general theory of the social construction of reality. From this perspective, societies function in part by sharing beliefs that achieve the superior status of knowledge; this social knowledge is dynamic, that is, always being created, tested, changed, and abandoned or amplified; this process by which society reproduces itself while modifying itself is inescapably performative; one form of performance by which our society creates, tests, changes, and judges social knowledge is the popular trial. My discussion of the popular trial as a genre of public discourse has been directed to articulate the larger rhetorical tendencies at work in this performative process, while leaving room for the more particular analyses of persuasive tactics necessary for understanding any particular trial. I have argued that the popular trial produces social knowledge in several senses: It is a recognizable social practice; it is constituted by social agreements, including the agreement to recognize voices other than one's own; and it presents and authorizes particular beliefs. Furthermore, the popular trial fulfills a special social function because it provides the social practice most suited to comparing competing discourses. Finally, the popular trial observes specific rhetorical constraints, including (but not limited to) the adversarial format, reliance upon official symbols, the formal closure of a decision, and emphasis upon characterization.

Much remains to be said, however. Both academicians and legal practitioners need to chart the range of persuasive strategies and tactics available for inducing belief within a popular trial, as well as the limitations imposed upon persuasion by the trials' generic conditions. Another project, and one more closely related to the first than academic studies usually admit, would be to demonstrate the value of the trials for the study of social history. Much could be learned by examining specific trials, now understood to be much more than legal proceedings, in order to understand the particular fund of social knowledge constituting a society.[24] Furthermore, if we are to understand the basic tendencies and limitations in a society's ability to know we need to consider the strengths and weaknesses of the processes within which its knowledge is produced. We need to ask what can and cannot be accomplished in a popular trial, and what biases inform the very form of the trial and its coverage in the media, and whether such trials bring out more of the best or the worst in the institutions (of the law, the media, the military, the university, etc.) that cooperate to produce them. Finally, we need to search for specific examples of interaction between popular trials and other genres, with particular attention to other presentations of the law in the mass media, which now range from conventional courtroom dramas (on both television and film) to situation comedies to such hybrids as "Divorce Court," "People's Court," and a mock trial of Austrian Chancellor Kurt Waldheim.

Yet in looking so far ahead I am overlooking the following critical studies. Whatever the general characteristics of popular trials, the greatest benefits of their study will come from focusing on individual cases. The popular trial is not a Platonic form; it is a concept allowing us to understand actual communicative events that are complex, fascinating, and important. As the following essays demonstrate, a performance of the laws can be a dramatic event rich enough to challenge any critic.

Constitutional Argument in a National Theater

The Impeachment Trial of Dr. Henry Sacheverell

John Louis Lucaites

The impeachment trial of Henry Sacheverell, D.D., conducted by the House of Commons in 1709–10 stands out as one of the more significant events in the relatively brief reign of Queen Anne (1702–14), the last of the Stuart monarchs. The facts of the case are quite simple: On 5 November 1709, Dr. Henry Sacheverell, a High-Church, Anglican Minister, delivered the annual sermon in commemoration of Gunpowder Day to the City Fathers at St. Paul's Cathedral in London. The text for that sermon was drawn from 2 Corinthians 11:26 "In Perils among false Brethren," and its application was to the presence and danger of Protestant dissenters and occasional conformists in the Church and State.[1] Both the temper and tone of the sermon were seditious, vigorously and militantly promoting the traditional Anglican and Tory commitments of "passive obedience" and "non-resistance" to the absolute "Supreme Power," and thus implicitly calling into question the prevailing Whig interpretation of the Glorious Revolution of 1688 founded on the commitments to a "contractual government" and the "right of resistance." The sermon was quickly published on 25 November, and by the end of the year had undergone several reprintings totalling in number no less than 40,000 copies.[2] By 15 December, Queen Anne's ministry, led by Godolphin and the Whig Junto, chose to impeach Sacheverell for "high crimes and misdemeanors" and to take advantage of the trial as a public forum for promoting the Whig interpretation of the Glorious Revolution.

The trial itself was a *public* spectacle unlike any other impeachment trial in England's history to that date.[3] To begin with, it lasted for twenty-five days, more than three weeks longer than the customary three to five days for such proceedings.[4] Moreover, it broke with Parliamentary tradition by being tried before a Committee of the Whole House, rather than solely before the Lords at the Bar. To this end, Her Majesty's Surveyor, Christopher Wren, was commissioned to prepare Westminster Hall to accommodate all of the members of both Houses of Parliament plus as many friends and relatives as possible. By the time he was finished Westminster Hall was converted into an "amphitheater" that held close to two thousand people, including spaces for foreign diplomats and special guests of the Lord High Chamberlain, as well as public galleries to which a limited number of spectators could gain admission for a price.[5] From the beginning of the trial until its end there was hardly ever an empty seat to be found.

The popular response to the trial was equally spectacular. Sacheverell's impeachment was the *cause célèbre* of London newspapers and pamphleteers from its announcement in December to its conclusion in late March.[6] Large groups of supporters and detractors followed the carriages of both Queen Anne and Sacheverell each morning as they arrived at Westminster Hall for the day's proceedings, even though they had virtually no chance of gaining admission. And on the evening of the third day of the trial, March 1st, riots broke out across London conducted under the banners of "The Church in Danger" and "High Church and Dr. Sacheverell."[7] Although there were only several reported fatalities and a relatively small number of injuries, the riots were not inconsiderable: Dissenters' meeting houses throughout the city were taken apart pew by pew and burned in giant bonfires, and roving mobs threatened dissenters wherever they encountered them. Holmes claims that until the famed Gordon Riots of 1780, there was nothing "as destructive or frightening to the government or property-owners of London as the 'detestable tumults' of 1710."[8]

In the end, the Whigs won what appeared at the time as little more than a Pyrrhic victory. Sacheverell was found guilty by the slimmest of margins, by a vote along party lines, and sentenced to a token punishment that consisted of being prohibited from preaching for three years and having his sermons burned in public by the Common Hangmen—a far cry from the general sentiment amongst Whig MPs that he be banned for life from preaching, barred from any future preferments, fined, and imprisoned; some went even so far as to call for pillorying and a public beating.[9] More significant is the fact that he was hailed as a popular hero throughout the nation, as public sentiment swelled in support of the Anglican Church and Tory principles and in opposition to the Queen's Whig ministry. Indeed, popular discontent with the Whigs was so high following the trial that Queen Anne was compelled to prorogue the Parliament on April 5th, although she gave no indication at that time of any intention to change her ministry.[10] By late summer, however, following a highly publicized and celebrated tour of England by Sacheverell, the popular pressure for an immediate general election was overwhelming, and on 7 October a general election was held returning a significant Tory majority.[11] The Whigs had won the impeachment but lost control of Parliament and the Queen's ministry to the Tories.

Tory control of the government and the appearance of their victory was short-lived, however, as George I acceded to the throne in 1714, marking the beginning of a Whig supremacy in Parliament that was to last until 1760.[12] One might thus be inclined to conclude that the Sacheverell impeachment trial was an interesting and unique, albeit minor and relatively insignificant political event in the course of the history of a nation that extends from the Norman Conquest to present day. Such a conclusion, however, would ignore the fact that throughout the Whig supremacy of the eighteenth century, and indeed well beyond it, the arguments and principles of government eventually promoted by the Whig managers of Sacheverell's impeachment became the received explanation of England's Glorious Revolution, and thus served as the public justification and rationale for the principles of the British Constitution.[13] The Sacheverell trial must thus be considered potentially as important in establishing and stabilizing the authority and legitimacy of the eighteenth-century British government as were *The Federalist Papers* and the constitutional ratification debates in establishing and stabilizing the authority and legitimacy of the United States federal government. In order to understand the significance of the Sacheverell impeachment as a public trial, we thus need to focus attention on its specific nature as a "discourse of legitimacy," functioning not so much as to promote the partisan interests of Whigs or Tories, as to assure the fundamental authority of England's constitutional government itself. In what follows, I will discuss the rhetorical nature of discourses of legitimacy, and then examine the ways in which the Sacheverell impeachment functioned in this context as a public trial.

Discourse of Legitimacy

A discourse of legitimacy is a public symbolic effort to manage the contradictions implicit or manifest in a society's ideology towards the end of achieving and authorizing a particular construction of the meaning of its primary public values or commitments-to-community. According to Michael McGee, these ideological values achieve material presence in a community as "ideographs."[14] Ideographs are ordinary and culturally biased phrases or terms that represent, in condensed form, the normative, collective commitments of an ideological community. So, for example, the American commitments to a right to own one's own home, the right to have at least a representative voice in any governmental decision that will result in taxes on one's wages and other holdings, and the right to pass one's holdings on from one generation to the next without intrusive governmental interference, are all condensed and represented by the ideograph ⟨property⟩.[15] A survey of twentieth-century American public discourse is likely to uncover, in addition to ⟨property⟩, such ideographs as ⟨liberty⟩, ⟨equality⟩, ⟨states' rights⟩, ⟨national security⟩, ⟨the right to work⟩, ⟨rule of law⟩, ⟨freedom of speech⟩, ⟨public trust⟩, ⟨the right to bear arms⟩, ⟨law and order⟩, and so on. When taken in their entirety, these ideographs constitute the ideal value structure of American democracy; literally, they are the linguistic "building blocks" of our ideological community, and they identify for us the range of publicly acceptable motives-to-action. As such, they constitute a culturally sanctioned rhetoric of control, establishing *both* expectations and limitations on public behavior, as well as the public rationale that can be used as justifications for past and future public beliefs and behaviors.[16] So, for example, the public expectation is that our leaders will actively pursue ⟨law and order⟩ in the context of the ⟨rule of law⟩. When our leaders choose, for whatever reason, to ignore this relationship, or to stretch it to its furthest limits, it is incumbent upon them to justify their behavior in terms of an intervening ideographic commitment, such as the ⟨national security⟩. To fail to be able to do so in a convincing manner is to risk losing the ⟨public trust⟩. Wise leaders, or at least successful ones, will recognize and accommodate the prior persuasion built into the ideographic structure of their ideological community.

Another important feature of ideographs is their inherent flexibility as cultural signifiers, that is, the agreement to abide by a particular ideograph as the linguistic and material signifier for a particular social or political value or commitment-to-community is not necessarily to agree to any one particular meaning signified by that ideograph. Ideographs, in other words, are polyvalent, and can mean potentially very different things to different members of the community. This is not to say that meanings for ideographs are totally arbitrary or polysemous; there are limits, but they are specifically rhetorically material limits dictated by (1) the range and history of their acceptable usages in the community (a diachronic structure), and (2) their relation to other ideographs relevant to the specific rhetorical situation they are employed to modify or mediate (a synchronic structure).[17] So, for example, in the American experience the ideograph ⟨liberty⟩ comes to mean one thing when linked to the ideographs ⟨free speech⟩ and ⟨law and order⟩ in the controversy over whether or not Nazis should be allowed to march in Skokie, and something quite different when linked to the ideographs ⟨national security⟩ and ⟨public trust⟩ in a controversy over the propriety of a U.S. military invasion of the island of Grenada. The value of this quality of ideographs is that it makes it possible to accommodate a wide range of competing interests in a particular community, because the tie that binds the community is not a commitment to the absolute and universal meanings of key values, but to a set of key terms that are rhetorically consistent, but also flexible enough to be adapted to different situations, circumstances, and interests.

Of course, because ideological communities often strive to accommodate a wide range of competing interests, conflicts do emerge over the appropriate meaning and usage of particular ideographs in particular situations. So, for example, pro- and anti-handgun advocates dispute the meaning of the ⟨right to bear arms⟩, just as pro-choice and anti-abortion advocates argue over whether ⟨liberty⟩ ought to be defined in its relationship to ⟨freedom⟩ or ⟨life⟩. In each case, however, both sides maintain their allegiance to the particular ideographs as fundamental commitments of the community, simply disputing their particular meaning or interpretation in a particular context. The important exception to this is when a controversy develops precisely as a crisis of legitimacy in which the very authority of the state or particular leaders to govern is called into question, or where the foundational narratives of the community itself are disputed, for example, the United States Civil War. Because such crises literally risk tearing a community apart at the seams, prudent leaders on all sides of such controversies strive to negotiate and manage the ideographic competitions that materialize the ideological tension productive of the crisis. Such is the rhetorical purpose and function of discourses of legitimacy.

When treated as a discourse of legitimacy, then, the Sacheverell impeachment trial becomes more than a clash of public personalities, or a simple inter-party dispute, with each side seeking popular support for its position. Rather, it represents a first and most important step in the public rhetorical process through which Whigs and Tories negotiated an ideological consensus regarding the structure and meaning of their shared history and the political vocabulary of acceptable public motives-to-action which it generated. *It be-*

comes, quite literally, the public site for the struggle over the meaning of England's Glorious Revolution, and by extension, for the legitimacy of the British Constitution itself. In order to explain the function of this trial in establishing the spirit of whiggism that was to pervade England in the eighteenth century we must thus examine the rhetorical process through which it unfolded.[18] To that end, I will proceed in three steps. First, I will examine the rhetorical situation which called forth this trial as a specifically public discourse of legitimacy; second, I will chart the ideographic competitions that emerged in the trial; and finally, I will examine some of the argumentative mechanisms through which the public became implicated in the management and negotiation of these ideographic competitions.

The Rhetorical Situation

"The Church in Danger"

Prior to 1688, the Anglican Church managed to secure its power and authority as the established Church of England through a series of repressive Parliamentary Statutes, such as the Test and Corporation Acts, designed to assure the uniformity of religious practices and the absolute exclusion of Catholics and Protestant dissenters from positions of civil and ecclesiastical authority.[19] Following the forced abdication of James II in 1688 and the accession of William and Mary in 1689, the Anglican Church retained its status as the established Church of England, but its political power and authority were clearly under siege. The passage of the "Bill of Rights" in 1688 and the "Act of Settlement" in 1701 combined to alter the succession by virtue of Parliamentary sovereignty, and thus undermined in practice any serious belief in a divine rights or hereditary monarchy, as well as the implicit and heretofore inviolable relationship between the church and the state.[20] At the same time, the passage of what became known as the "Toleration Act" in 1689 indulged the vast majority of dissenting Protestant sects by granting them the right to conduct Nonconforming religious services in their own meeting houses, and thus undermined the Anglican Church's absolute authority in ecclesiastical matters.[21] Perhaps more importantly, it opened the door for the practice of what became known as "occasional conformity"—a letter-of-the-law loophole in the Test and Corporation Acts which allowed dissenters to qualify themselves for civil office by taking the Sacrament in an established Anglican Church at least once in the twelve months preceding their election, leaving them technically free to worship wherever they chose until the next election.

The erosion of the Anglican Church's authority was exacerbated by the Convocation crisis in 1701 which resulted in a formal schism between High Church and Low Church parties that quickly aligned themselves with Tory and Whig constituencies respectively.[22] Although there were a number of ecclesiastical issues that separated High Churchman from Low Churchman, the primary point of contention between them revolved around their opposing answers to the question: What should be done about the proliferation of religious dissent and Nonconformity in the nation?

The issue came to a head between 1702 and 1704 when Tory members in the House of Commons argued in three successive parliamentary sessions that the growing number of Dissenters and Nonconformists had placed "the Church in Danger" and thus attempted to pass legislation prohibiting the practice of "occasional conformity." In each instance they were overruled by the Whig-controlled House of Lords. In 1705 the Tories initiated resolutions in both Houses declaring "the Church in Danger" under the present administration. This too was defeated by the Whigs who sponsored and passed a contrary resolution proclaiming the Church to be in a "most safe and flourishing condition" under the present administration and proclaiming that "whoever goes about to suggest and insinuate, that the Church is in Danger, under her majesty's administration, is an enemy to the queen, the Church, and the kingdom."[23] The purpose of this resolution, of course, was largely symbolic of the power that Whigs and Low Churchmen had achieved in Parliament, and it had relatively little effect on the behavior of the most ardent of High Church clergy who proceeded unencumbered for the next five years to proclaim "the Church in Danger" in their sermons.[24] Unintentionally, however, and far more importantly, it reaffirmed in principle the constitutional significance of the relationship between the Church and the State, for what it implied was an agreement between Tories and Whigs, and High Churchmen and Low Churchmen alike, that if the Church were *truly* in danger, then a national crisis was imminent.

The impact of this became clear in 1709 when the issue of "the Church in Danger" achieved national political prominence once again, this time as a result of rumors that the Whigs intended to liberalize the Test and Corporation Acts so as to allow Nonconformists to qualify for civil office by taking the sacrament in any Protestant congregation.[25] Following its rather considerable defeat in the election of 1708, the Tory Party was in eclipse in 1709, desperately searching for an issue that would allow it the opportunity to fan the flames of national emotion. The influx of Calvinist refugees into England as a result of the Whig-sponsored Naturalization Act provided the issue, and xenophobia provided the emotion. When the Whigs began to make noises about the need to reform the procedures for qualification for public office in order to accommodate these "poor Palatines," the High Church clergy, still smarting over the failure to secure the "occasional conformity" bills several years earlier, rose to the occasion. From January to October the charge of "the Church in Danger" issued forth from virtually every High Church pulpit in the nation, and the primary perpetrators of that danger were the Whigs in Parliament, and the increasing number of Dissenters and Nonconformists, especially those who seemed to violate so freely the strict tenets of the Act of Toleration through the practice of occasional conformity. It was against this backdrop that Dr. Henry Sacheverell was invited by the Tory Lord Mayor of London to deliver the annual Gunpowder Day sermon.

Gunpowder Day is a day of national celebration commemorating the discovery of the plot by the Catholic Guy Fawkes to explode the King, Lords, and Commons on the first day of Parliament in 1605. It took on added national significance in 1688 as it coincided with the landing of William and his army at Torbay, an event which set in motion England's "Glorious Revolution." For eighteenth-century Englishmen, then, 5 November was an especially important day, so much so, that in London it was celebrated annually by law with a sermon delivered before the Church Fathers at St. Paul's Cathedral. Typically, the sermon delivered on that day was encomiastic, praising the virtues of the Glorious Revolution and those who had protected England against the intrusions of Papal interlopers since the days of Guy Fawkes, and blaming the evils of Popery. As we shall see, the sermon that Sacheverell delivered in 1709 violated these expectations by implying that the "church was in danger," and by assailing those who promoted the principles of the prevailing Whig interpretation of the Glorious Revolution as "false brethren." It is highly unlikely that such a violation of expectations in and of itself would have led to his impeachment for "high crimes and misdemeanors" before the highest court in the land. *How* he violated those expectations is another matter altogether, and in order to understand the exigency that invited forth that impeachment we need to examine the way in which he violated those expectations.

The scriptural text for Sacheverell's sermon was drawn from Paul's Second Letter to the Corinthians, "In Perils among false Brethren," and as he began with a direct reference to the Gunpowder Plot it could not have occurred to his listeners that he was about to embark on a potentially seditious discourse. Two moves in the exegesis, however, should have clued his audience to the fact that this would be no ordinary Gunpowder Day Sermon. First, he quickly shifted the focus of the sermon away from the solitary evils of Popery to the specter of Puritan fanaticism by equating the malignity of the Guy Fawkes conspiracy with the regicide of Charles I, and thus identified both Catholics and dissenters as "treacherous False Brethren, from whom we must always expect the utmost perils, and against whom we can never sufficiently arm ourselves with the greatest caution and security."[26] Second, in elaborating the contemporary relevance of the text he paralleled the beleaguered condition of the former Church of Corinth with the present Church of England in elaborate terms that would leave his audience, all too familiar with the premises that he was asserting, with but one enthymematic conclusion: "the Church in Danger." Having already justified a consideration of Dissenters as false brethren, it was no trick to realize that less than one-third of the way through the sermon Sacheverell had carefully turned this celebratory occasion into an opportunity to promote the threat posed by the increasing numbers of Dissenters and Nonconformists and by the practice of occasional conformity.

The remainder of the sermon was divided into three sections, each of which promoted the perception of a national crisis. In the first section, Sacheverell proceeded to identify the false brethren in both Church and State, subtly implying the close, if not conspiratorial, relationship between the Low Church ecclesiastics and the Whigs in Parliament. The false brethren in the Church were those who refused to abide the doctrines and tenets of the scriptures to which they owed allegiance by virtue of communion, and who were willing to tolerate and even accommodate the Dissenters through some form of religious comprehension.[27] His real target, however, were the false brethren in the State who promoted constitutional innovations in the absence of "unavoidable necessity," and in particular the Whigs who sought to disrupt the previously inviolable relationship between Church and State by denying "the subject's obligation to an absolute, and unconditional obedience of the supreme power in all things lawful, and the utter illegality of Resistance to any pretence whatsoever."[28]

Having thus identified the false brethren in Church and State, Sacheverell proceeded in the second section to characterize the specific perils that they posed to each, which ultimately he maintained was to "put it in the power of our professed enemies, to overturn, and destroy the constitution and the establishment of both."[29] The conspiracy he envisions between the false brethren in Church and State strives not only to alter the Church's constituted articles of faith, which in turn will undermine the very structure and stability of the Church—earlier equated with the constitution of the State—and thus promote atheism, or worse, Popery, but also raises the conspiratorial specter of Puritan fanaticism. So, for example, with veiled references to the Parliamentary vote of 1705 declaring the Church "in a safe and flourishing condition," he concludes, "And now we are under no danger in these deplorable circumstances? Must we lull ourselves under this sad repose, and in such a stupid, lethargic security, embrace our ruin? . . . I pray God we may be out of danger! but we may remember the king's person [Charles I] was voted to be so, at the same time that his murderers were conspiring his death."[30]

In the third section of the sermon Sacheverell focuses his attention on the "heinous malignity, enormous guilt, and folly" of the sin of False Brotherhood, emphasizing in particular the violation of sacred oaths and the greed driven hypocrisy perpetrated by men of "character and stations" [the Whig Junto] that leads inevitably to the destruction "of all common honesty, faith, and credit in the world, and in the place of it sets up an universal trade of cozenage, sharping, dissimulation, and downright knavery."[31] The alternative, he suggests in the peroration, is to adhere to the foundations of our government in the inviolable relationship between the established Church and the State, and to "thunder out" against any efforts to the contrary: "Schism and faction are things of impudent and encroaching natures; they thrive upon concessions, take permission for power, and advance a toleration immediately into an establishment; and are therefore to be treated like growing mischiefs, or infectious plagues, kept at a distance, lest their deadly contagion spread. Let us therefore have no fellowship with these works of darkness, but rather reprove them. Let our superiour pastors do their duty in thundering out their ecclesiastical anathemas, and let any power on earth dare reverse a sentence ratified in heaven."[32]

"High Crimes and Misdemeanors"

What was it about this particular sermon that motivated the Whigs in the House of Commons to impeach Sacheverell for "High Crimes and Misdemeanors," the highest possible charge before the highest court in the land? After all, he (and for that matter, numerous other Anglican High Churchmen) had been regularly making similar charges in sermons at least since 1702, and none of those sermons came anywhere near generating the response that "In Perils among false Brethren" engendered.[33] To answer this question we need to locate the sermon and its argument in several different rhetorical and ideological contexts.

To begin with, it is important to recognize that although Sacheverell never utters the phrase "the Church in Danger" in the sermon, virtually everything he says in the sermon is calculated to cause the audience to draw precisely that conclusion. This placed the Whigs in Parliament in a particularly precarious situation. As I have already noted, in 1705 the Whigs had not only declared the Anglican Church to be in a "most safe and flourishing condition," but in doing so had also implicitly established the principle that an endangered Church constituted the conditions for a national crisis, seriously threatening the legitimacy of the government. In an important way, their own actions set the basis for a potent rhetoric of control by conceding the implicit relationship between Church and State, and thus establishing the expectation that threats to the endangerment of the Church be taken seriously by the Parliament. For the Whigs to admit by their silence that the crisis which Sacheverell described existed, and to do nothing to abate it, would be to open themselves up to charges of incompetence; or worse, it might even imply their complicity as "false brethren" in promoting the crisis, a point which Sacheverell subtly exploits in the sermon by linking the "false brethren" in both "church *and* state."

Of course, they could have ignored him, as they had done in the past, and this was a course of action that was given some serious consideration. In this particular instance, however, Sacheverell made it extremely difficult for them to do so. First, he delivered the sermon in especially incendiary terms, on a day of national celebration, in the very seat of national government, and then had it published and 40,000 copies of it distributed in open defiance of the London Aldermen.[34] And if that were not enough, he aggravated the matter even further by including a dedication to the published version of the sermon that seemed to leave little question about his intention to put a stop to the "dangerous and encroaching mischief" and "malicious designs" being employed by "seditious imposters" to "flatter" and "poison" the "deluded people" of London.[35] In the Whig-controlled Parliament there was no question as to whom he was referring.

Second, he went to great pains to apply the Anglican theory of ⟨passive obedience⟩ and ⟨non-resistance⟩ to an explanation of the Glorious Revolution that explicitly contradicted the prevailing Whig interpretation of the revolution and the constitutional settlement that followed it. He had not done this before, certainly not in such provocative and dramatic terms, and in doing so here, on this very public occasion, he underscored the fundamental and nagging question of the legitimacy of the Glorious Revolution that had plagued the Whig oligarchy since 1688. To ignore the question now would not only not make it go away, but would quite possibly encourage High Church ecclesiastics throughout the realm to raise and address it from their pulpits, thus enhancing its presence and importance in the public consciousness.

All of this might lead one to the conclusion that a public response to Sacheverell's sermon was required, but why an impeachment before the Lords for "high crimes and misdemeanors"? The answer here seems easier to conjure. To begin with, Sacheverell's sermon was no ordinary sermon. Its presentation on an extremely important, formal state occasion gave it a public authority that required an equally formal state occasion from which to tender a response. Moreover, insofar as the sermon raised questions about the legitimacy of the Glorious Revolution and the revolutionary settlement, it was essential that his charges be treated in the most solemn and serious manner. Certainly there were few events in seventeenth- and eighteenth-century England short of charges of treason that were more formal, solemn, or serious than an impeachment for high crimes and misdemeanors.[36] On a more practical note, a vote of guilty by the House of Lords, the judges in the highest court in the land, would entail serious sanctions allowing the Whigs to hold Sacheverell up as an example to other "high-flying" clergy who might wish to press the issue of "the Church in Danger"; and on this count the Whigs were convinced from the outset that they had the necessary votes to assure a guilty verdict. What they did not know, of course, and it was to have significant implications for the final outcome of the whole affair, was that the trial would end up being twenty-five days long, not three or four as was customary in such cases, and that the case would not simply be open to the public as witnesses to the event, but that it would end up being argued in a national theater, as much before the court of public opinion as the House of Lords.

Ideographic Competitions

The Sacheverell trial began officially on 27 February 1710, six weeks after four articles of impeachment had been entered before the House of Lords in support of the general charge of high crimes and misdemeanors. Each of the four articles focused attention on a different aspect of the general charge, but as Joseph Jekyll, one of the managers of the impeachment for the House of Commons, acknowledged early on in the proceedings, the focus of the whole charge was the first article in which it was alleged that Sacheverell had impugned the "said happy Revolution" by claiming that the "necessary means" used to bring it about were "odious and unjustifiable," and that "to impute Resistance" to it "is to cast black and odious colours upon his late majesty and the said Revolution."[37] It was precisely this question of how to describe the motivations behind the Glorious Revolution that stood as the main point of ideological tension between Whigs and Tories in general; it was materialized as the focus of the trial as each side interpreted the event within the context of competing ideographic commitments, and thus produced a very different narrative of what happened in 1688.

According to the Whig managers of the impeachment, the Glorious Revolution occurred as a result of the arbitrary and tyrannical abuses of power by James II, which violated the "pact and covenant" between King and people that constituted a commitment to the consent of the governed. When Englishmen supported William in opposition to James II, then, they were simply enacting their natural right of resistance as a last and necessary means of securing their liberty.[38] ⟨Consent of the governed⟩ and ⟨right of resistance⟩ thus served as the ideographic terms that organized the manager's narrative of the Glorious Revolution.

⟨CONSENT OF THE GOVERNED⟩ The ⟨consent of the governed⟩ was a principle of government that first emerged in England in the wake of the tyrannies of James I and Charles I, and was used to argue that the supreme authority in the nation was not a divinely sanctioned, absolute monarch, but the combined legislature of King, Lords, and Commons as evidenced in the ancient constitution. The ancient constitution represented the common law which had been derived from the customs and usages of the English people from their pre-Norman origins to the present.[39] Inherent in the ancient constitution was the doctrine of a "limited monarchy" controlled by the Parliament as the representative of the people: Insofar as the monarch was considered to be the executor of the laws of the land, s/he ruled with the ⟨consent of the governed⟩.[40] Tracing the origins of this doctrine to the *Magna Carta*, seventeenth-century Whigs typically argued that it was the sacred responsibility of the monarch to protect and insure the rights of the people to ⟨life⟩, ⟨liberty⟩, and ⟨property⟩ as guaranteed by the ancient constitution.[41] To fail to preserve these rights, or more significantly, to strive to subvert them, would be to violate the obligation implicit in the "Coronation Oath" to confirm the ancient "laws and customs of the realm."[42] As Robert Howard informed the Convention Parliament at its initial meeting in 1689: "When he acts by his will, and not by the laws, he is no king; for he acts by power and tyranny. I have heard 'that the king has his crown by divine right,' and we (the people) have divine right too; but he can forfeit, if he break that *pact and covenant* with his people, who have right, by reason of election, as well as in the name of Mr. King. This original power, resistance or non-resistance, is judged by the power resolved by people and king. *The constitution of the government is actually grounded upon pact and covenant with the people.*"[43] Under such circumstances, these Whigs argued, it was justified, perhaps even necessary, for the people as represented by the Parliament to resist actively the tyrannies of the Crown.

⟨RIGHT OF RESISTANCE⟩   The ⟨right of resistance⟩ was a corollary to the ⟨consent of the governed⟩, the means by which the people could actively guarantee their ⟨liberty⟩ by demonstrating discontent with tyrannical acts of power. In this sense, at least, the Whig commitment to the ⟨consent of the governed⟩ was significant largely as the standard against which the propriety of particular instances of resistance could be assessed. So, very few Whigs, for example, failed to acknowledge the importance of maintaining a strong monarch to execute the laws of the land, or for that matter, even the necessity of granting the monarch the prerogative powers essential to the performance of that duty.[44] When such prerogative powers were deemed necessary, however, they maintained that the final control of such powers—and hence the assurance of ⟨liberty⟩—was inherent in the authority of the Parliament to revoke and to resist tyrannical usages: "There can be no such thing as setting up a power to oppose him [the King], but by putting a *kind* of Supreme Authority in the Parliament, with a power to oppose, as well by making as was by laws."[45] Thus, while it was the ancient constitution which established the standards of governance through consent, it was ultimately the ⟨right of resistance⟩ which assured monarchal adherence to those standards.

Sacheverell's Tory defense counsel characterized the Glorious Revolution in decidedly different terms. Jacobites and Non-jurists had maintained that the revolution was illegal, a usurpation of the indefeasible, ⟨hereditary monarchy⟩, and a direct violation of the principles of ⟨non-resistance⟩ and ⟨passive obedience⟩. Of course, it was the implicit intention of the Whig managers of the impeachment to demonstrate that Sacheverell's treatment of the Glorious Revolution in his sermons allied him with such an openly seditious claim. To temper this move, Sacheverell's defense counsel maintained the more moderate description of the Glorious Revolution that had typically been adopted by most Tory Members of Parliament: James II had "voluntarily" abdicated the throne, leaving the executive seat of government empty, and thus giving Parliament the right to establish the terms of the revolutionary settlement which officially granted the throne to William and Mary.[46] The effect of this, of course, was to weaken the commitment to an "indefeasible," hereditary monarch, but it at least allowed maintenance of the commitments to ⟨non-resistance⟩ and ⟨passive obedience⟩—the legality of which was to become the heart of Sacheverell's defense—by denying that James II had been actively deposed.[47]⟨Heredity monarchy⟩ and ⟨non-resistance/passive obedience⟩ thus served as the ideographic purpose terms that organized the Tory defense counsel's narrative of the Glorious Revolution.

⟨HEREDITARY MONARCHY⟩   ⟨Hereditary monarchy⟩ was a principle of government that emerged in England in the fifteenth century. Its material function was to dictate in precise terms the line of monarchal succession so as to avoid conflicts and confrontations that would seriously undermine the order of the realm at the time of the death of a monarch. Following the Puritan Revolution it was linked with the theory of the Divine Right of Kings which made it virtually irrefutable by raising it to the level of the sacred. As Robert Filmer wrote in *Patriarcha*, a handbook of arguments for Tories following the Glorious Revolution, the King claims his power "as being substituted properly from God, from whom he receives his royal charter," and "unless we will openly proclaim defiance unto all law, equity and reason, we must acknowledge that in Kingdoms, hereditary birthright giveth right unto sovereign Dominion, and the death of the predecessor putteth the successor by blood in seisin."[48] The Whigs called this principle into question in 1680 with the introduction of the Exclusionary Bill designed to exclude the Duke of York (later James II), Charles II's brother and a known Catholic, from the succession in lieu of the Duke of Monmouth, an illegitimate son of Charles II. The bill failed in the House of Lords, and at least for the time being the commitment to a ⟨hereditary monarchy⟩ appeared in practice to be indefeasible.

⟨NON-RESISTANCE/PASSIVE OBEDIENCE⟩   The commitments to ⟨non-resistance⟩ and ⟨passive obedience⟩ were corollary to the commitment of an indefeasible ⟨hereditary monarchy⟩. To sustain the kind of order and stability supposed by the subjects of an absolute monarch, it was believed to be necessary to assert and emphasize the obligation of every subject of the realm to pledge and obey the monarch's dicta. Occasionally, the commitment to ⟨non-resistance⟩ was instantiated in the statutory law, but in any case, it was considered to be irrevocable and inviolable: Resistance to the sovereign authority of the monarch of any sort could never be tolerated. Of course, even the most fundamentalist of Tories acknowledged the possibility that on occasion the King's law could contravene the moral and natural law of God. Even under such circumstances, however, subjects were limited in their responses to ⟨passive obedience⟩. As one long-standing Anglican directive put it: "An obedience we must pay either Active or Passive: the active in the case of all lawful commands . . . But when he enjoins anything contrary to what God hath commanded, we are not to give him this active obedience, we may, nay, one must refuse to act. . . . But even this is a season for the Passive Obedience: we must patiently suffer what the ruler inflicts on us for such a refusal, and not to secure ourselves, rise up against him. For who can stretch forth his hand against the Lord's Annointed and be guiltless."[49]

As has already been suggested, the ideographic competition between the Whig interpretation of the Glorious Revolution organized around the commitments to the ⟨consent of the governed⟩ and the ⟨right of resistance⟩, and the Tory interpretation organized around the commitments to ⟨hereditary monarchy⟩ and ⟨non-resistance/passive obedience⟩ dominated virtually every juncture of the trial as each side sought to make its case. On the face of it, of course, that case concerned the guilt or innocence of Sacheverell: If the revolution were indeed predicated on the legitimate ⟨popular resistance⟩ of tyrannical acts of monarchal power, then Sacheverell's sermons were seditious, and he was guilty of the charge; if there were no evidence of resistance at the revolution, and if the Tory defense counsel could demonstrate the legitimacy of the principles of ⟨non-resistance⟩/⟨passive obedience⟩, then Sacheverell's sermons were within the bounds of propriety, and he was innocent of the charge.

The guilt or innocence of Sacheverell was only a surface issue in the trial, however, for implicit in the ideographic competition between the Whig managers and the Tory defense counsel was a much larger issue concerning the legitimacy of the structure of England's constitutional government, and it posed problems for *both* Whigs and Tories. The Whig commitment to the ⟨consent of the governed⟩ and the ⟨right of resistance⟩ provided a convenient rationale for deposing James II and establishing the revolutionary settlement through the Bill of Rights in 1689. At the same time, however, it established a potentially dangerous historical precedent. Although they tended to privilege a commitment to ⟨liberty⟩ in their discourse as the central principle of their ideology, very few Whigs were true revolutionaries seeking radically to alter the structure of English government or society. As far as most of them were concerned, the invocation of the ⟨right of resistance⟩ was necessary in 1688 as the most viable means of preserving the Ancient Constitution. Nevertheless, serious doubts lingered: Could this precedent be used capriciously to justify future rebellions? and how would that affect the balance between the national commitments to ⟨liberty⟩ and ⟨order⟩?

The Tory commitment to ⟨hereditary monarchy⟩ and ⟨non-resistance/passive obedience⟩ posed a different, but no less troubling problem. The invitation by a committee of peers to William of Orange on 30 June 1688 to "give assistance" to a beleaguered England was a direct violation of the commitment to ⟨non-resistance⟩/⟨passive obedience⟩, just as the Bill of Rights the following year altered the succession, thus undermining the commitment to an indefeasible ⟨hereditary monarchy⟩.[50] Most Tories privileged a commitment to national ⟨order⟩ in their discourse, and thus it was essential for them to retain some semblance of a centralized national authority. To maintain a staunch commitment to an indefeasible ⟨hereditary monarchy⟩, however, was literally to deny the legitimacy of the revolutionary settlement and the Bill of Rights, and to call the current government into question; to completely concede the commitment to ⟨hereditary monarchy⟩ was to risk undermining the executive power and authority of Queen Anne by making her subordinate to the supremacy of Parliament. The problem, then, was how to maintain some sense of centralized national authority without creating a crisis of legitimacy?

The ideographic competition between Whigs and Tories was thus complicated by the tensions created for each by the nature of an evolving rhetorical situation. Hence, as the trial unfolded it became increasingly clear that the trial argument itself would have to sustain a range of multiple negotiations simultaneously.

Argumentative Mechanisms

Public trials, by their very nature, address multiple audiences. The problem that this poses for attorneys can be significant: Does one address the members of the jury as the representatives of the public who will render the official verdict in the case, or does one address the public itself with attention to the potential moral power that a popular verdict might have on the ultimate disposition of the case? This is not an easy question to answer, particularly when the case involves the social and political legitimacy of a particular law, the constitutional structure of the state, or the specific behaviors of public leaders. The reason for this is not only that the public's interest in such cases is eminent, or that the outcome of such cases has a more direct effect on the relationship between individuals and the state than does the ordinary criminal or civil case, but, more important, that the public's opinion is an essential barometer in measuring and determining social and political legitimacy, and the advocates on both sides of the controversy are typically the ordinary trustees of legitimized state power. Thus, the advocates in such public trials who appear to ignore the public presence risk not only their own authority as political spokespersons, but the legitimacy of the particular trial itself as a ritualistic forum for determining public morality or immorality, an issue which, in such cases, is often more important than the cut and dried issue of guilt or innocence.

This seems to have been the case in the Sacheverell impeachment trial. The public presence at the trial was unprecedented in the history of English impeachment trials; nevertheless, the very fact of its presence invited its participation in the judgment to be made. In one sense at least, this had been the original intention of the Whigs in Parliament who had urged a public trial in order to make a showcase of their interpretation of the principles of the Glorious Revolution. Their notion, however, had been that the public would stand in as a "witness" to the event, not as a jury. Once the trial took on the dimensions of a "national theater," and mob violence broke out in support of Sacheverell and High Church principles, it became clear that the public's participation in the trial had far exceeded Whig expectations, threatening not only the Whig case against Sacheverell, but Tory commitment to the maintenance of public ⟨order⟩ as well. As such, the trial took on a public life of its own, equally if not more important than its role as formal, Parliamentary procedure, and it demanded that the advocates on both sides of the bench contribute to the construction of a more or less unified "public" by mediating the competition between the key ideographs that had separated Whigs and Tories since 1688. Thus, while Whigs and Tories were still concerned to establish the guilt or innocence of Sacheverell with respect to the articles of impeachment, the very public nature of the trial required especially close attention by both the Whig managers of the impeachment and the Tory defense counsel to the issue of the legitimacy of the Glorious Revolution, and the need to arrive at some ideological public consensus as to how to interpret that event.

As I have already indicated, the chief ideographic competitions separating Whigs and Tories were the Whig commitments to the ⟨consent of the governed⟩ and the ⟨right of resistance⟩, and the Tory commitments to an ⟨hereditary monarchy⟩ and ⟨non-resistance⟩/⟨passive obedience⟩. The construction of a unified public conception of the Glorious Revolution would require at least an implicit agreement on how to manage the tension between (1) the ⟨consent of the governed⟩ and an ⟨hereditary monarchy⟩, and (2) the ⟨right of resistance⟩ and the commitment to the principle of ⟨non-resistance⟩/⟨passive obedience⟩—both of which, on the face of it, appeared to be contradictory oppositions. To understand how this accommodation occurred, we need to examine how both the Whig managers of the impeachment and the Tory defense counsel addressed these tensions in the context of arguing the articles of impeachment.

The Whig Argument

The focus of the Whig managers' attack in the first article of impeachment was Sacheverell's announcement of the "utter illegality of Resistance upon any pretence whatsoever," and the characterization of anybody who insinuates the presence of resistance at the time of the Glorious Revolution as "casting black and odious colours" upon both the revolution and William and Mary.[51] Sacheverell's claims were of course polarizing in their effect, and the Whig managers went to great lengths to demonstrate that there had in fact been a resistance of monarchal authority promulgated at the revolution, that it was the primary means by which the revolution was effected, and that it was indeed a legal resistance. So, for example, Joseph Jekyl noted that "[the] doctrine of unlimited Non-Resistance was implicitly renounced by the whole nation in the Revolution, so divers acts of parliament afterwards passed, expressing that renunciation."[52]

Jekyl's words in the quotation just cited are important, not only because they assert (and go on to demonstrate with specific citations from the statutory law) the presence and legality of the ⟨right of resistance⟩ at the revolution, but also because they appear to oppose diametrically the Tory commitments to ⟨non-resistance⟩ and ⟨passive obedience⟩. As the Whig argument unfolds in subsequent speeches throughout the trial, however, it becomes clear that they do not intend the ⟨right of resistance⟩ to be understood as an absolute right, but rather as a right the exercise of which must be grounded in "necessity."[53] The point is made most forcefully by Robert Walpole:

Resistance is no where enacted to be legal, but subjected, by all the laws now in being, to the greatest penalties; it is what is not, cannot, nor ought ever to be described or affirmed, in any positive law, to be excusable: when and upon what never-to-be-expected occasions it may be exercised, no man can foresee, and ought never to be thought of, but when an utter subversion of the laws of the realm threatens the whole frame of a constitution, and no redress can otherwise be hoped for: it therefore does, and ought for ever to stand, in the eye and letter of the law, as the highest offence.... The doctrine of unlimited, unconditional Passive Obedience, was first invented to support arbitrary and despotic power, and was never promoted or countenanced by any government that had no designs some time or other of making use of it: what then can be the design of preaching this doctrine now, unasked, unsought for, in her majesty's reign, where the law is the only rule and measure of the power of the crown, and of the obedience of the people?[54]

The ⟨right of resistance⟩ is thus established by the Whigs in the trial ultimately as a conservative commitment of community. It is clearly not as restrictive as the commitments to ⟨non-resistance⟩ and ⟨passive obedience⟩ promoted by the Tory defense counsel, but it is carefully characterized as a right that can only be exercised as a last resort against the worst sorts of tyranny, such as was in evidence during the reign of James II, and then only when intended solely for the purpose of preserving the "rights and liberties" guaranteed by the ancient constitution and instituted through a commitment to the ⟨rule of law⟩. It thus comes to signify as a preservative right that accommodates the Whig concern to guarantee ⟨liberty⟩ in opposition to "tyranny," and the Tory concern to guarantee ⟨order⟩ in opposition to "anarchy."

The Tory Argument

Sacheverell's defense counsel responded to the charge of the first article of impeachment in two different ways, first by establishing the propriety of his claim to the principle of ⟨non-resistance⟩ and ⟨passive obedience⟩ as a general rule of society, and second by demonstrating that, strictly speaking, he was correct in indicating that there had been no resistance at the time of the revolution. On the face of it, both of these arguments address the possibility of Sacheverell's innocence; again, however, it is important to attend to the implications of the specific articulation of these arguments for a unified public conception of the legitimacy of the Glorious Revolution.

The first argument maintained that Sacheverell was correct in asserting the principles of ⟨non-resistance⟩ and ⟨passive obedience⟩ as "general rules" of society, and in any case as explicitly promoted by the Church of England, and by the acts of both Houses of Parliament. The argument was evidenced through the rather laborious process of introducing specific testimony from the *Book of Homolies* and numerous sermons and pamphlets, as well as a number of Parliamentary Statutes, and William III's "Declaration" establishing the basis of his invasion of England.[55] More to the point, was the claim that Sacheverell had never committed himself to an "*unlimited* passive obedience and non-resistance," but to the general rule of "non-resistance" which naturally admits of "exceptions" in the face of "great necessity." Thus notes Simon Harcourt, "I humbly apprehend, my lords, that extraordinary cases, cases of necessity, are always implied, though not expressed, in the general rule. Such a case undoubtedly the Revolution was, when our late unhappy sovereign then upon the throne, misled by evil counselors, endeavored to subvert and extirpate the Protestant religion, and the laws and liberties of the kingdom. The general rule ought always to be pressed; but the exceptions of extraordinary cases, or cases of necessity, are never particularly to be stated. To point out every such case before hand, is as impossible, as it is for a man in his senses not to perceive plainly when such a case happens."[56] That Sacheverell's words could be reasonably understood to include the "exceptions" such as would be "necessary" to have justified violating the rule of ⟨non-resistance⟩ at the time of the Glorious Revolution is a dubious claim at best, and in any case could not be clearly proven one way or the other from the text of Sacheverell's sermon. What is important about this argument, however, is that it represents a position that is almost identical to the conservative Whig interpretation of the ⟨right of resistance⟩. As such, it provides a justification for the Glorious Revolution that would be acceptable to most Anglican High Churchmen as well as, implicitly at least, to most Whigs.

The second argument advanced by Sacheverell's defense counsel was that he had never exactly claimed that there was "no" resistance at the revolution, but that there had been no resistance to the "supreme power." The argument was predicated on the claim that Sacheverell had made regarding the "utter illegality of Resistance on any pretence whatsoever to the supreme power," and of course hinged in particular on how one understood the phrase "supreme power." Again, Harcourt initiated the defense position: "He has, indeed, affirmed the utter illegality of Resistance on any pretence whatsoever to the supreme power; but it cannot be pretended, there was any such Resistance used at the Revolution. The supreme power in this kingdom is the legislative power; and the Revolution took effect by the Lords and Commons concurring and assisting in it. Whatever therefore the Doctor has asserted of the utter illegality of Resistance, his assertion being applied to the supreme power, cannot relate to any Resistance used at the Revolution."[57] Just as with the first argument in response to the ⟨right of resistance⟩, so here, Harcourt's interpretation of Sacheverell's meaning of "Supreme Power" is dubious. But once again, the text of Sacheverell's sermon was just vague enough to allow for the plausibility of such a construction. And at the same time, it created the conditions for managing the tension between the commitments of the ⟨consent of the governed⟩ and an ⟨hereditary monarchy⟩ towards an acceptable ideological consensus.

By conceding the legitimacy of the Revolutionary Settlement which settled the crown on William and Mary, Tories were likewise forced to concede that the absolute supreme authority of the nation no longer resided with the monarch, let alone with an indefeasible ⟨hereditary monarchy⟩. Nevertheless, they generally refused to give up their commitment to some kind of absolute, centralized authority and were absolutely adamant in their refusal to accept any kind of radical ⟨popular sovereignty⟩ as the functional equivalent of the ⟨consent of the governed⟩. By locating the Supreme Power in the legislature, however, they were able to retain a centralized authority while simultaneously accommodating a limited ⟨hereditary monarchy⟩ to a commitment to the ⟨consent of the governed⟩. Thus they maintained that the Supreme Power in the nation resided specifically in the King or Queen-in-Parliament.[58] The position was thus one that could be accepted in general by Whigs and Tories alike. For Whigs, it was consistent with their notion of ⟨parliamentary sovereignty⟩ as an authority grounded in the ⟨consent of the governed⟩. For Tories, it made it possible to view the Revolutionary Settlement in terms of an attempt to balance the relationship between an ⟨hereditary monarch⟩ and Parliament as a commitment to the ⟨rule of law⟩, as well as to maintain that the sovereign legislature ruled with God's blessing and sanction as a divinely remanded authority.

Taken together, the Whig and Tory arguments concerning the first article of impeachment functioned to produce the public arguments necessary to manage the ideological tensions created by the various interpretations of the Glorious Revolution of 1688, and created the conditions for producing a unified public conception of the legitimacy of that event.

Conclusion

I began this essay with a concern for understanding how the impeachment of Henry Sacheverell could result in two very different public reactions, one embracing the principles responsible for convicting him of high crimes and misdemeanors, and thus promoting an ideological consensus regarding the foundations of the British Constitution; and the other apparently rejecting those principles, embracing Sacheverell himself as a national hero. By examining the rhetorical nature of the public trial in which Sacheverell was impeached as a discourse of legitimacy we are now in a position to consider how such a phenomenon could occur.

To begin with, it is important to bear in mind that the trial itself was apparently conceived to serve at least two different rhetorical functions. First, it was designed by the Whigs in Parliament to punish Sacheverell for his blatant and incendiary attack on the Whig ministry led by Godolphin, and to stand as a severe warning to other High Church Anglican ministers who might consider using their pulpit as a political forum from which to question the motives of the Whig dominated Parliament. Second, it was designed to give the Whigs in Parliament the opportunity to present systematically their interpretation of, and thus legitimize, the Glorious Revolution in a formal and legal forum. And when the Whig managers of the impeachment decided to make the trial public, and indeed, to create the conditions for a national theater, it was their assumption that the public would stand in as passive witnesses to the event, in the same way that civilized patrons of the theater are passive spectators to the production that they witness, and thus lend an added air of legitimacy to their actions. What the Whigs failed to take into account, of course, was that the key ideographic commitments that would serve to organize their interpretation of the Glorious Revolution—⟨consent of the governed⟩ and ⟨right to resistance⟩—sent a very different message, implying the public's right to be actively involved in determining the outcome of the trial as a discourse of legitimacy.

When riots ensued on the evening of the second day of the trial, and when public opinion forced the proroguing of Parliament and Queen Anne's change of ministry shortly after the trial, the Whigs were horrified. Their worst fears regarding the radical tendencies in their democratic commitment had been realized, in apparent confirmation of Tory predictions, as the "people" became a wild and raving mob forcing its desires on the government. Initially, one might be inclined to conclude that the Whigs were hoist on their own petard, victimized by their own ideology. Yet closer examination of the dual rhetorical functions of the trial as a discourse of legitimacy should give us pause to reconsider such a conclusion.

In the formal trial itself, the Whigs were big winners. Even though the impeachment of Sacheverell himself was only marginally successful, they had managed to achieve important concessions from the Tories, who pretty much abandoned the commitment to a ⟨hereditary monarchy⟩ subsequent to the trial, and accepted the people's limited ⟨right to resistance⟩ under unusual circumstances. Thus, in terms of the public vocabulary, an ideological consensus had been achieved that privileged the Whig interpretation of the Glorious Revolution, and by extension the foundation of the government in the ⟨consent of the governed⟩.

The Whigs were also winners as regards the popular response to the trial. Of course, the reaction of the popular mobs throughout England both during and following the trial stood in opposition to the Whig's impeachment of Sacheverell. However, this particular avenue of popular response did not mitigate the Whig claim that government was and should be legitimized by the ⟨consent of the governed⟩ and that the people had a ⟨right to resistance⟩. Thus, in a curious way, the very behavior that motivated and produced a change in government, placing the Whigs in opposition, stood in practice as *prima facie* evidence of the ideological consensus that was achieved in the trial. Once the public furor over Sacheverell died down, the ideological consensus that had become instantiated in the public vocabulary remained, and gave a jump start to the spirit of Whiggism that was to pervade and dominate eighteenth-century British politics.

Studying this particular trial as a discourse of legitimacy leads me to conclude that public trials, at least in liberal democratic societies committed to ⟨popular sovereignty⟩ and the ⟨consent of the governed⟩, may well serve important social and political functions that require more careful attention to the rhetorical process in which they emanate. Prior to the Sacheverell trial there had been no expectations regarding the people's *direct* and *active* involvement in the adjudication of such issues as we have seen here. Subsequent to that trial, however, such expectations were circumscribed in the Whig ideological consensus, and there was a very clear recognition that the advocates in public trials need at least to appear to address the public's interest. To fail to do so was not only to risk incurring the wrath of the "people," but perhaps more importantly, to risk the legitimacy of the principles and institutions of government under contention. To the extent that social and political legitimacy becomes a function of the ⟨consent of the governed⟩, there needs to be the appearance of such consent. By allowing, and indeed, on occasion by promoting, public trials, the public's consent for such a process is ritualistically invoked at the same time that the potential warranting conditions for the ⟨right of resistance⟩ are ritualistically eliminated. And in the process, the public's desire for active involvement in the decision making process, is sublimated in its ritualistic status as spectator, ironically constructing a passive and uninvolved mass public.[59] The future study of public trials might thus benefit from careful attention to the ways in which they function as a dual rhetoric of control, simultaneously assuring that public leaders and advocates operate within the context of the ideological consensus of the community, and that the public's desire for involvement in the decision making process is sated short of the violent public outbursts which shook London in 1709–10.

Two Stories of the Scopes Trial

Legal and Journalistic Articulations of the Legitimacy of Science and Religion

Lawrance M. Bernabo
Celeste Michelle Condit

The 1925 trial of John Thomas Scopes for teaching evolution remains a vivid landmark in America's distinctive sociopolitical history.[1] Although the verdict established no important legal doctrines and was muted eighteen months later by an appeals court decision, the case continues to symbolize the dominant American consensus about the legitimate roles of religion and science in national life.[2] The trial stands as a potent cultural image of the boundaries between science and religion because, as a special type of legal event, it provided the locus for the negotiation between these powerful, competing social forces. To understand the way in which this popular trial functioned to reapportion the public arenas in which religion and science could legitimate public argument, we explore the Scopes trial through a theory of social process and with careful attention to the particularities of the discourse of both the trial and the journalistic coverage of the case.

Theoretical Framework

Whatever the lessons of sociology and materialist history about the character of massive social forces that constitute social change, at some point, given the American system of government, these forces must meet overtly in public discourse.[3] It is only through public articulation that the relationships among competing social forces can be *recognized* in a manner that allows government officials and "the public," together, to regulate or respond to such conflicting pressures through law, custom, and policy. Even where "dealings in secret" dominate *decision* processes, the necessity of engaging public support or compliance eventually produces public rhetoric.[4] In other words, it is public articulation that "makes present" social forces in a way that allows them to be directly responded to by a nation as a collectivity.[5]

Public discourse functions as an effective mediator, allowing *compatible* articulations of competing social forces to develop, because in such debate the meanings assigned to the agents, tools, purposes, acts, and scenes that constitute such forces are negotiated before a range of public judges. Inherent in this process of building consensus about meanings is the development of a consensus, among the politically empowered of the nation, about the legitimate character and place of such social forces in public life.[6] In this country, the arenas for such rhetorical combat and construction are generally either the legislature or the judiciary. When the issues arise in the courts, these dramatic upheavals frequently generate "popular trials."[7] The process of mediation through popular trials is an extremely complex one, involving massive quantities of persuasive discourse from many social actors.

At the Scopes trial, thousands of words went into the rhetorical process of constructing a new public understanding of the legitimate realms of "religion" and "science." More words were relayed from Dayton during the trial than from any other comparable event in the nation's history. Chicago radio station WGN broadcast live from the trial, while more than one hundred newspaper reporters from all parts of the country and two from London were in Dayton. Twenty-two telegraphers sent out one hundred and sixty-five thousand words a day on the trial.[8] Before the year was out a complete stenographic report of the trial, an edited version of the transcript by Leslie H. Allen, and Bryan's posthumous *Memoirs* were published.[9]

Precisely because this was a popular trial, this extensive verbal mediation of agonistic social forces was conducted in two different discursive forums—the legal and the journalistic. Because these forums share subject matter, much language, and some history, they are inter-textual. Because they address different audiences, function with field-dependent argumentative rules, and serve different purposes, they mediate such conflicts in different ways.[10] Consequently, two related but different accounts of the relationships among science, religion, and the public schools were constructed by the speakers in the Dayton courtroom and by the media coverage of them.

This major episode of public storytelling was further complicated by the fact that the subjects of the stories were themselves "fields of discourse." What we call "science" is a set of social practices, resources, and persons—a powerful "field" of human endeavor—which is articulated in a particular discourse of its own. Likewise, "religion" is a set of social actors and activities, a field with a unique vocabulary that historically has been operative in different regions of the country, depending on the scope of social legitimacy it is granted.

In 1925 these two fields of discourse employed the law and the press to engage in a public contest for control of the public schools. In this particular case, the tale told by the journalists—a narrative that ridiculed and limited religion and placed scientific discourse as "taken-for-granted"—became more important historically than the account constructed in the courtroom. The journalistic or popular discourse, however, was a derivative of the courtroom story and so, to understand how the trial of John Thomas Scopes came to legitimate science over religion in the public schools and in much of public life, we begin with the legal discourse.

The Background of the Trial

The Tennessee anti-evolution law, which formed the legal basis of the controversy, had been proposed by John Washington Butler. The law declared, "That it shall be unlawful for any teacher in any of the Universities, Normals and all other public schools of the State which are supported in whole or in part by the public school funds of the State, to teach any theory that denies the story of the Divine Creation of man as taught in the Bible, and to teach instead that man has descended from a lower order of animals."[11] On 28 January 1925 the lower house passed Butler's bill seventy-one to five; the vote in the Senate on 13 March was twenty-four to six in favor. Dismayed that the legislature had passed the bill, but needing the support of rural legislators like Butler for educational reforms, Governor Austin Peay signed the Butler Act into law on 21 March 1925 with the hopeful observation that "Probably the law will never be applied."[12] Legislator Butler later declared: "I never had any idea my bill would make a fuss. I just thought it would become law, and that everybody would abide by it and that we wouldn't hear any more of evolution in Tennessee."[13]

Butler's naïveté about the social forces with which he was tinkering was monumental. Neither he nor the governor could so easily fiat the contest, because the discourse of state legislatures is not the sole arena in which power is allocated. The American Civil Liberties Union was well aware of the alternatives and decided to raise a special fund to finance a test case, employing the press to launch its challenge by sending a story to Tennessee newspapers announcing that it sought a teacher willing to cooperate in a court test of the legislature's ruling.[14] A group of Dayton businessmen and lawyers, arguing about the Butler Act, aware of the ACLU's offer, and seeking to advertise their town, approached the high school's substitute science teacher, John Thomas Scopes, about testing the case. Scopes agreed and the members of the group set out to grab their respective roles in history.[15]

This small party was to be the immediate, technical cause of the trial proper, although their significance extended little further than providing a legitimate battleground for larger social forces. In their exuberant effort to put Dayton on the map, they neglected to determine the facts of the case, thereby failing to learn that Scopes was an inappropriate defendant since he had probably never even taught evolution. After the trial, Scopes confirmed that he had never committed any contestable legal violation when he indicated that, as the high school sports coach substituting for the regular science teacher, he had planned football plays, never getting around to the evolution lessons. At most, Scopes had reviewed material covered by the regular instructor. During the trial, Darrow had to coach the schoolboys on their testimony and Scopes was not allowed to take the stand for fear he would reveal his ignorance on the subject he was indicted for teaching.[16]

Scopes, never intending to mislead anyone, had simply told the group gathered in Robinson's Drugstore, "If you can prove that I've taught evolution and that I can qualify as a defendant, then I'll be willing to stand trial."[17] Because both sides wanted the juridical test, this most fundamental issue of fact in the trial was never disputed. Had it been, the public purpose for the trial—the negotiation of major social forces—would never have been able to occur.

If the subject of Scopes's trial was far larger than the actions of a single teacher, then it was necessary that the trial be peopled with characters larger than the real-life townspeople of Dayton. A three-time Democratic nominee for President and a famous criminal lawyer provided ideal antagonists for the drama. Their personal biographies and public personas crystallized the ineradicable entanglement of the courtroom with the larger sociopolitical scene.

William Jennings Bryan volunteered his services to the prosecution only shortly before the state was about to invite him to join them.[18] Bryan's involvement in the issue of evolution went back many years. In the early period, he had held a relatively conciliatory position. In his "Prince of Peace" Chautauqua lecture, which he delivered some three thousand times beginning in 1908, he argued that different theories of creation "all assumed something to begin with." Bryan chose God and the creation account over Darwin and evolution, indicating he would stand on Genesis until he found a theory that went farther back than "the beginning." In his estimation, evolution did not "solve the mystery of life or explain human progress." Across the country, Bryan had repeated the pragmatic reason for his choice: "I object to the Darwinian theory, until more conclusive proof is produced, because I fear we shall lose the consciousness of God's presence in our daily life, if we must assume that through all the ages no spiritual force has touched the life of man or shaped the destiny of nations."[19]

After the World War, Bryan became more vitriolic. Paolo E. Coletta, Bryan's most comprehensive biographer, argues that, "Blaming the chaos, crime, materialism, and sin of the postwar era upon the drift away from God . . . [Bryan] began to flay evolutionists and atheists, particularly Friedrich Nietzsche, in a 'Back to God' speech which he never tired of delivering."[20] In 1922, Bryan went so far as to offer a prize of one hundred dollars to any professor who could reconcile evolution with the Bible.[21] When Professor R. C. Spangler of West Virginia University avowed he could, Bryan sent one hundred dollars, but the interchange, which aired with wide publicity, quickly escalated to a series of charges and countercharges between the two.[22]

Bryan's anti-evolution crusade had had some limited political success prior to Dayton. After Bryan addressed a joint session of the Kentucky legislature in January 1922, a bill to prohibit the teaching of "Darwinism, atheism, agnosticism or evolution" was proposed, only to be defeated by one vote.[23] Oklahoma became the first state to outlaw the use of textbooks sympathetic to the theory of evolution in June 1923, although the provision was repealed the same year it went into effect.[24] Anti-evolution bills were defeated in Georgia (again, the legislation was proposed following a Bryan speech to the legislature), Alabama, and North Carolina, although Florida did pass a joint resolution against evolution written by Bryan.[25] By early 1925 Bryan was actively pursuing the adoption of such legislation, but none had succeeded except for the Butler Act in Tennessee.[26] Two months before the Dayton trial, anti-evolution bills were pending or about to be introduced in ten states from coast to coast.[27]

In the narrow, technical arena of the courtroom Bryan's ostensible opponent was Randolph Neal, dean of the University of Tennessee law school and the "local" lawyer. The actual strategy was planned by the triumvirate of Clarence Darrow, Dudley Field Malone, and

Arthur Garfield Hays. As far as the public was concerned, Clarence Darrow was the key gladiator. The fitness of Darrow as opponent was indicated by journalist H. L. Mencken, a crucial mediator of the event, who had played a role in talking Darrow into taking the case, telling him, "Nobody gives a damn about that yap schoolteacher. The thing to do is to make a fool out of Bryan." Mencken insisted that Darrow was the logical opponent for Bryan; Darrow was not only famous for his defense of Leopold and Loeb the previous year, but was also both an agnostic and an avowed public adversary of Bryan.[28]

The political entanglements of the two were long-standing. Darrow ran for Congress the same year that Bryan's "Cross of Gold" speech had won him the Democratic nomination. Darrow and his political mentor, Governor John Peter Altgeld of Illinois, went down in defeat along with Bryan. Darrow biographer Kevin Tierney argues that while Darrow originally blamed the corrupting influence of Republican gold for his defeat, "Increasingly, he came to see Bryan as a weak, shallow candidate, who, instead of elevating the people, spoke at a level of unconscious mediocrity, without a vision of the future to inform his policies."[29]

In their public duels prior to Dayton, Bryan and Darrow had clashed over the subject of evolution. Darrow had attempted to debate Bryan two years earlier after Bryan's argument with Edward Birge, President of the University of Wisconsin.[30] When Bryan's attack on science was published in the *Chicago Tribune*, Darrow replied in a letter, printed on the front page, containing fifty questions which attempted to find out whether Bryan thought the biblical account of creation was literally true or a poetic allegory. Bryan refused to respond to Darrow's challenge, proclaiming that he did not quarrel with agnostics.[31]

As the legal teams developed, the Dayton trial featured two publicly opposed characters, each deeply embroiled in the discourses of religion and politics, meeting in a forum that would declare one of them victorious. Their public characters intensified the conflict, increasing its importance to the point that the trial of a single teacher could serve as a national battle between two powerful institutions.[32]

The Legal Story

The arguments advanced by the two sides in *The State of Tennessee* v. *John Thomas Scopes*, 154 Tenn. 105 (1925), were manifold. It is impossible to summarize accurately the precise complexities of three hundred pages of legal discourse in a few pages. Nonetheless, we can suggest that both sides of the case offered a technical, legal argument, which was entwined with a second, social argument. The interplay of these two sets of claims and the subsequent decisions of the judge and jury produced the legal version of the trial story.

The narrow legal argument offered by the prosecution was that Scopes's guilt was a matter of incontestable fact and syllogistic logic: The state had outlawed the teaching of evolution, Scopes admitted publicly that he had taught evolution, therefore Scopes was guilty. Following the dictates of their leader, circuit Attorney General A. T. Stewart, the prosecutors worked hard to keep the issue to this technical, legal matter. They rested their case for religion on the legitimacy of the acts of the legislature, thereby allowing the historical fact of presumption to preserve the legal dominance of religion over science. By avoiding sociopolitical debate through narrow legalism, Stewart hoped to forestall the scientific community's bid for increased power in the secondary schools.

Stewart designed the prosecution's argument to preserve political control over the schools exclusively within the state legislature—the camp most favorable to religion and hostile to science. When that effort was threatened by a clever defense strategy, Bryan added a second line of attack: the preferability of religious accounts over scientistic/evolutionary accounts. Bryan's argument, admittedly much more of a rhetorical appeal than a legal argument, was that adherence to science as the basic mode of understanding resulted in a devaluation of human (godly) morality. By assailing the theory of evolution for replacing humankind's linkage to God with a linkage to animals, Bryan asked the public to choose religion as a more comforting and morally productive discourse. In short, employing the test of moral fitness, Bryan argued for the retention of an "origin myth" that preferred moral fitness over human knowledge.

Stewart's strategy and Bryan's position held a powerful advantage in the inherently conservative court system in Rhea County, Tennessee. Not only was the legal system predisposed to Stewart's narrow arguments that preserve that status quo because of its foundation on precedent and prior statute, but the popularly elected judge and the pool of prospective jurors in this case were predisposed by their local biases to accept Bryan's larger, sociopolitical argument.[33] However, Judge Raulston was at least sensitive to the larger role the trial was playing in the sociopolitical system and chose not to cut off the larger dialogue completely. He was influenced toward this decision in part by the wily rhetoric of the defense.

The defense team's primary objective was to introduce the issue of the proper roles of science, state politics, and religion into the national legal system. The ACLU believed that, ultimately, the Supreme Court would rule that scientific discourse had a legitimate place in the public schools. Consequently, the defense worked assiduously (if, in the end, unsuccessfully) to avoid any legal errors that would prevent the case from eventually being heard on appeal to the Supreme Court. After the trial, the defense attorney Arthur Garfield Hays summed up the defense position as representing three clear issues: "First, that the law was unconstitutional because it attempted to make the Bible the test of truth; second that the law was unconstitutional because in the light of present-day knowledge of evolution, to be adduced from scientists, it was unreasonable; and third, that the evidence of Mr. Bryan and other students of the Bible would show not only that there was no inconsistency between an acceptance of the evolution of man and of the Bible, but would also show that the law was indefinite as well as unreasonable because no two persons understand the Bible alike."[34]

Because of a series of unfavorable decisions by Judge Raulston, the defense task evolved into a complicated, three-stage effort. In the first stage they outlined the broad, constitutional grounds for altering the law. In the second stage they worked to overcome the narrow constraints of the trial's legal argument to introduce the broader sociopolitical issues. The final stage moved beyond the legal argument altogether to fan the popular discourse which would ultimately, without even court approval, re-adjust the public presumption between religion and science.

Stage 1: Constitutional Issues

The defense team set up the constitutional issues on 13, 14, and 15 July through a motion to quash the indictment which included thirteen different subpoints. Hays opened the case by noting the indefiniteness of the indictment as drawn. Pointing up the multivocality of religious discourse, he contended that even expounding the theory of divine creation could reasonably be construed as violating the law, given the latitude of interpretation allowed by the wording of the Butler Act. Implicitly resting his case on the validity of science, Hays then ridiculed the act as an unreasonable exercise of police power. To illustrate his point, he drafted a hypothetical law in which teaching that the earth is not the center of the universe, in contradiction of the Bible, would be punishable by death. Such a law would clearly be unreasonable, and so, Hays insisted, the judge had to let the jury hear about the scientific and religious views on evolution "in order to pass" on whether the Butler act was likewise reasonable or not, that is, whether "it tended in some way to promote public morals." Hays concluded, "To my mind, the chief point against the constitutionality of this law is that it extends the police powers of the state unreasonably and is a restriction upon the liberty of the individual" (55–57).[35]

In rebuttal, prosecution attorney Ben McKenzie did not deny science legitimacy as a public discourse directly, but he argued that the schools were bound to the political realm, not to the scientific. Therefore, the politicians had the right to exclude scientific discourse from education. He declared, "We cannot teach any religion in the schools, therefore you cannot teach any evolution, or any doctrine that conflicts with the Bible. That sets them up exactly equal." McKenzie also played to popular political sentiments, setting up the battle between the local rights of Tennessee and the national vocabulary by accusing the defense of importing "foreign" lawyers. He also emphasized the univocity of the local discourse when he replied to the claim that the law was vague by insisting that any 16-year-old boy in Rhea County could understand the law. Finally, the state's position was that Scopes or anyone else could believe in evolution or teach it on the street, but that freedom of speech and religion did not extend to teachers the right to teach the doctrine in the state-supported schools and that the police power of the state allowed the state to control its schools.

Closing the argument on the motion to quash the indictment, Darrow followed the wedge opened by Hays's attacks on indefiniteness, going after the discourse of religion on internal grounds. He sought to demonstrate that religion was varied and inconsistent and that therefore, if the state adopted one particular religious discourse in its laws, it could only do so by establishing one religion over others. As an example, he indicated that the law was "giving preference to the Bible" rather than to another book, such as the Koran. Stewart, virtually dumbfounded by this argument, countered that Tennessee had recognized the King James version of the Bible, and that "The laws of the land recognize the Bible; the laws of the land recognize the law of God and Christianity as a part of the common law." In other words, the prosecution admitted that the state, in fact, had preferred one religion over others and that it was entitled to use its police power to enforce that religion. The hegemonic position seemed so natural and necessary to Stewart that he could not recognize its ideological or political partiality. Hence, when pushed on whether the law preferred the Bible to the Koran, Stewart could only snap, "We are not living in a heathen country, so how could it prefer the Bible to the Koran [sic]?" (66). When Malone made the issue of religious domination even more explicit by asking why the state did not simply require teaching divine creation, Stewart could only deny the stasis of the issue, insisting "it is not a religious question" but merely an issue of police power.

Darrow insisted that the Butler Act ultimately attacked not only evolution, but every competing religion, Christian as well as non-Christian, that did not accept the fundamentalist interpretation of the literality of Genesis. Darrow noted that this besieged group included "the intelligent scholarly Christian, who by the millions in the United States, find no inconsistency between evolution and religion" (75–77). Maintaining that no legislature could determine what was divine, he argued for a replacement of religion. Darrow suggested the legitimate location for the Bible was outside the public realm and its laws, and within the province of private religion and morals. Bolstering his argument by indicating the inherent unsuitability of religion as a critic of science, Darrow pointed up the inconsistencies and shortcomings of biblical accounts of areas covered by scientific discourse, citing specifically the two conflicting stories of creation in Genesis to emphasize the inadequacy of the Bible as a textbook on chemistry, geology, biology, or astronomy (77–78).

In response to the police power argument, Darrow agreed that the legislature had the right to fix the courses of study, but denied the state could pass a criminal statute rather than making an effort to prescribe a course of study (86). In a fiery conclusion, Darrow returned to the issue of pluralism and accommodation, warning that "If today you can take a thing like evolution and make it a crime to teach it in the public school. . . . At the next session you may ban books and the newspapers. Soon you may set Catholic against Protestant, and Protestant against Protestant, and try to foist your own religion upon the minds of men. If you can do one you can do the other. . . . After while, your honor, it is the setting of man against man and creed against creed until with flying banners and beating drums we are marching backward to the glorious age of the sixteenth century when bigots lighted fagots to burn the men who dared to bring any intelligence and enlightenment and culture to the human mind" (87).

We can see how in making this case Darrow was addressing the issues of the "legitimate place" of various discourses quite directly and forcefully. Darrow denied the legitimacy of religion as a primary discourse for public life by presenting the pragmatic impossibility of maintaining religion as a dominant public discourse. He indicated that the discourse of religion was inconsistent, incomplete, and offered no widely shared meanings; as such it was unworkable as a vocabulary for vital, shared public territory, where consensus and consistency were crucial.[36]

However, we must also notice that to some important extent, this attack works only for a national audience, with its "millions of intelligent Christians." On the narrower stage of Tennessee, the problems of pluralism may not have arisen. Where judges, juries and prosecutors—along with every "16 year old Rhea County school-boy"—share a more uniform religious discourse, the challenge would be less telling. Hence, the battle between the local arena and its discourse and the national arena and its discursive concerns constituted one key factor in the trial.

The reactions to these arguments were split equally along national and local lines. The national press replayed Darrow's arguments with gusto.[37] Meanwhile, back in Dayton, Judge Raulston's ruling on the motion to quash essentially paraphrased the arguments Attorney General Stewart had made, denying the defense motion on all thirteen points. Declaring that the law was not vague, Raulston found that the police power was not intrusive because it allowed teachers to teach what they believed outside the public schools and did not require anyone to teach against their own beliefs. Most crucially, Raulston, like the prosecution, ignored the argument that the religious discourse itself was unreasonable and established one religion over others. Raulston focused on the "free exercise clause" of the constitutional protections on religion. His admitted inability to conceive of how the law might violate freedom of religion was premised on the fact that the law forced no one to teach a particular religion nor prevented them from teaching what they wished outside the school. Raulston ignored the defense's emphasis on the "establishment" clause of the First Amendment because he shared the prosecution's naturalized assumption that Christianity was the only legitimate religious possibility. Consequently, he could not understand how citing the Bible in the law violated religious freedom by establishing one religion over others.

In effect, for those inside a singular, univocal religious discourse and those legally tied into the prior relationship between law and Christian religion, the law seemed neither vague, intrusive nor unreasonable, because the religious discourse appeared to offer adequate shared meanings. It would require an arena where the overriding legitimacy, adequacy, and univocity of Christianity was not taken-for-granted for the challenge to Christian religion to be potent. The defense had laid the case for two such arenas, namely the attentive national audience and the United States Supreme Court, and then moved on to their next rhetorical task.

Stage 2: Evolution and Genesis

After the Judge's ruling against the motion to quash, the defense pleaded Scopes not guilty and both sides were instructed to provide the court with opening statements in which they would briefly out-line their "theories" in the case (112). The task of arguing and linking the heart of the immediate case (Scopes's culpability) and the heart of the broader sociopolitical cause (the territory to be allocated to religion and to science) fell to Dudley Field Malone, by trade an international divorce lawyer.

When Malone arrived in Dayton, his two biggest liabilities were his status as a divorced, "backsliding Catholic" and his complete ignorance of evolutionary theory—the crucial issue of the trial.[38] Out of these shortcomings, a remarkable transformation developed: Malone became the personification of the devout Christian who could accept the tenets of evolution without shaking his religious beliefs. To the courtroom audience, Malone served as the embodi-ment of the oxymoron of the Christian "Evil-utionist."[39] By the end of the trial, Malone was receiving the loudest, longest, and most frequent applause from the spectators.

Early in the trial, Malone began to establish his persona. When Stewart made reference to the "agnostic counsel for the defense," for instance, Malone replied, "Whereas I respect my colleague, Mr. Darrow's right to believe or not to believe as long as he is as honest in his unbelief as I am in my belief, as one of the members of the counsel who is not an agnostic, I would like to state the objection from my point of view." Malone then proceeded with an argument that the daily opening prayer had become increasingly argumentative to the point of constituting inadmissible propaganda. When Stewart retorted to Malone that "this is God fearing country," Malone re-plied, "And it is no more God fearing than that from which I came" (90). Later, when the prosecution referred to the defense as repre-senting a "force that is aligned with the devil and his satellites," Malone pitched his persona even more forcefully, angrily declaring, "I have a right to assume I have as much chance of heaven as [the prosecution] have, to reach it by my own goal, and my understanding of the Bible and of Christianity, and I will be a pretty poor Christian when I get any Biblical or Christian or religious views from any member of the prosecution that I have yet heard from during the trial."[40] Having established his character in the first stage of the trial, Malone articulated the argument compatible with that image in the second stage.

The defense's problem, one widely shared in political trials, was to come up with some means to introduce the larger, social contro-versy as a legitimate legal element in the trial. If winning the trial were all that was at stake, Darrow and his associates could have merely denied that Scopes ever taught evolution.[41] Instead, they claimed that Scopes had taught evolution, but had not taught a theory in contradiction to the Bible. This allowed them to argue that the introduction of both scientific and biblical testimony about the relationship between evolution and creation was necessary for determining the guilt or innocence of Scopes. In short, they found a narrow, technical, legal argument which necessarily brought into the legal forum, the larger, sociopolitical issues.

Consequently, in outlining the defense's "theory" of the case, Malone contended that "to convict Scopes, the prosecution must prove that Scopes not only taught the theory of evolution, but that he also, and at the same time, denied the theory of creation as set forth in the Bible" (112–13). The defense's "two-act theory" concerning the Butler Act insisted that the law required two acts—teaching evolution *and* teaching something which opposed the Bible—before a legal violation had occurred. Since Scopes had only done the former, they insisted he was not guilty. The presence of that key "and" in the first section of the Butler Act thus gave the defense a legal opening for advancing all of its broader argumentative positions. The defense could introduce testimony on the validity of evolution, Genesis, and on their potential relationships to each other, because at the very least it would be necessary for the court to decide whether the defense's two-act theory was a plausible one. The judge and jury would presumably need to hear evidence about the compatibility of the two discourse fields.

Bryan, in what proved to be his only extensive speech of the trial, responded to this theory on behalf of the state. Following Stewart's strategy, Bryan attempted to restrain the case from the broader grounds opened by the defense's legal wedge, primarily by ignoring their core argument. He argued that the proposed scientific testimony was neither competent nor proper, given the legal issue in the case, which he insisted was simply whether Scopes had taught evolution in the Rhea County High School. Ultimately, Bryan fell back upon the position taken in the first stage of the trial, denying that the questions were matters of religious expression, insisting that they were simple political issues about "what the people of Tennessee desired and intended and did declare unlawful," adding that the issue "needs no interpretation" (170–71).

Bryan, not only baited by the defense's wedge but also eager to work in elements of his anti-evolution speeches in the record, offered a counterattack against science. Through a sustained and biting wit, which entertained the courtroom audience, he challenged the legitimacy of the scientific discourse. For example, Bryan chastised evolution for teaching children that humans were but one of (precisely) thirty-five thousand types of mammals and bemoaned the fact that human beings were descended "Not even from American monkeys, but from old world monkeys" (174–78).

Malone, who had served under Bryan in the State Department,

responded to Bryan in a speech that has almost universally been considered the oratorical triumph of the trial.[42] Certainly the speech was responsible for linking Malone's name with Darrow in the historical record of the trial.[43] Scopes himself declared Malone's speech to be the dramatic high point of the entire trial, including Darrow's celebrated cross-examination of Bryan:

Malone's triumph over his former boss in the State Department was as stunning to the townspeople as it was to Bryan. All of his followers in Dayton showed shock. Whether it was from seeing their infallible hero cut to pieces or whether it was from first realizing that the things they believed might not be absolutely true, creating a shock within themselves, I do not know. . . . Bryan was never the same afterward and if there were any turning points in the trial that day was one. Dudley Field Malone had shattered his former chief's unbounded optimism, which Darrow is commonly credited with having done later in the trial. Bryan had reached his peak before Darrow ever got him on the stand. If anything, Malone's debilitating coup probably made Bryan want to go on the stand, in the vain hope of regaining some of his tarnished glory.[44]

Malone began this powerful speech with a reassertion of the legal issue: the two-act interpretation. He moved on to defy anyone to believe that the trial was not over a religious question after listening to Bryan's speech (184). His tour de force, however, was the reestablishment of the legitimacy of science (recharacterized as learning in general) and his insistence on territorial limitations on religion, which would give scientific discourse a right to be dominant (in the schools). Malone first aroused fear of "inquisitions" in the crowd by recounting the traditional story of the burning of the library of Alexandria by Arab conquerors. With this potent image as backdrop, he urged the heart of the accommodationist position—for which his persona had been so precisely built. He argued that the Bible should be preserved, but separately, in the realm of theology and morality, and not put into a course of science:

But these gentlemen say the Bible contains the truth—"if the world of science can produce any truth or facts not in the Bible as we understand it, then destroy science, but keep our Bible." And we say "keep your Bible." Keep it as your consolation, keep it as your guide, but keep it where it belongs, in the world of your own conscience, in the world of your individual judgment, in the world of the Protestant conscience that I heard so much about when I was a boy, keep your Bible in the world of theology where it belongs and do not try to tell an intelligent world and the intelligence of this country that these books written by men who knew none of the accepted facts of science can be put into a course of science. (185)

Malone's speech vividly articulated the scientific value of "truth." The term had been implicit in Hays's continued use of "reasonableness" in the constitutional arguments during the first stage of the trial. Now it became a direct claim that truth and faith were separately derived, yet compatible.

When Judge Raulston questioned Malone on his opinion that the theory of evolution was reconcilable with the story of divine creation taught in the Bible, Malone took the opportunity to present the "accommodationist" position in yet one more form, arguing for the embodiment of the position even within the persons of scientists themselves. He pressed the court for admission of the testimony of the scientists, all of whom were "men without question who are God-fearing and believe in the Bible and who are students of the Bible and authorities on the Bible and authorities on the scientific world" (185–86).

In his gale-force conclusion, Malone declared that Bryan's "duel to the death" against evolution should not be made one-sided by a court ruling that took away the chief witnesses for the defense. Malone promised, instead, that there would be no duel because "There is never a duel with the truth" (186–88). Scopes recalled that the courtroom went wild when Malone finished, "The heavy applause he had received during the speech was nothing compared to the crowd's reaction now at the end." Scopes related that after the courtroom had cleared, only Malone, Scopes, and Bryan remained. Heaving a sigh, Bryan said in a low voice, "Dudley, that was the greatest speech I ever heard." Malone replied: "Thank you, Mr. Bryan. I am terribly sorry that I was the one who had to do it."[45]

Malone's speech received wide attention in the national press, but again, the local, legal forum was more circumspect. In the wake of Malone's triumphant oration, Darrow told the scientists who had come to Dayton to testify, "Today we have won, but tomorrow the judge will recover and rule against us."[46] Darrow was correct. The following day Judge Raulston, holding that the court did not have to "decide and determine which is true, the story of divine creation as taught in the Bible or the story of the creation of man as taught by evolution," ruled that the meaning and intent of the Butler Act was clear enough that the court did not need to seek the aid of expert witnesses. The testimony of the scientific witnesses, the judge offered, using language that directly refused the key metaphor of the enlightenment, "would shed no light on the issues" (201–03). Raulston was simply continuing his effort to insist that the contest be settled on strictly narrow, legal issues, denying the relevance of scientific truth to the courtroom or the legislature. In doing so, he sought to maintain the public territory of the discourses of both religion and law, in the face of the threatening encroachments of science.

Most considerations of the Scopes trial agree with L. Sprague de Camp's assessment that Judge Raulston's ruling in excluding experts from providing scientific testimony on evolutionary theory the morning of the sixth day of the trial, "left the defense with no case at all."[47] Capturing this opinion was the *New York Times's* headline the next morning: "Judge Shatters the Scopes Defense by Barring Testimony of Scientists."[48] When Hays entered the obligatory exception to the judge's ruling, Stewart laughingly told the defense attorneys, "You are already hurt as much as you can be hurt" (203). Hays read a few condensed statements from the defense experts on the Bible and filed the statements of eight scientists into the record, having already multigraphed copies for the press (227–80).[49] Only one scientist, zoologist Maynard M. Metcalf, had briefly been allowed to testify as the first witness for the defense, with the jury excluded (133–46), before the prosecution made its motion to exclude the evidence (147–48).

Virtually everyone could see the obvious: Unless the law recognized science as a legitimate discourse, able to speak within the realm of law, the appeal of science to displace religion would not be *legally* legitimated. Legally, the case was completed.[50] Over the weekend, Darrow publicly admitted that Scopes was as good as convicted.[51] Mencken packed his bags and headed home, reporting: "All that remains of the great cause of the State of Tennessee against the infidel Scopes is the formal business of bumping off the defendant."[52] However, Mencken had made a grave error. Although the technical, legal case was essentially closed, the trial was to continue, and the popular (hence, journalistic) story was to be provided with a startling climax.

Stage 3: Darrow's Cross-Examination of Bryan

Although Hays was to claim in his autobiography that the cross-examination of Bryan was unplanned, Darrow spent the night before in preparation. The scientists and Charles Francis Potter, a modernist minister who had lost a public debate on evolution with the fundamentalist preacher John Roach Straton, prepared topics and questions for Darrow to address to Bryan on the witness stand.[53] Darrow even had Kirtley Mather, chairman of the geology department at Harvard and also a devout but somewhat open-minded Baptist, pretend that he was Bryan and answer questions as he believed Bryan would.[54]

The next afternoon, Raulston reconvened court on the front porch of the Rhea County Courthouse because of fears the second-story courtroom could not accommodate the hundreds of spectators. There a well prepared defense sprang the trap, calling Bryan as a witness on the Bible. Eager to refute printed charges that he was an ignorant bigot and to counter the damage done by Malone's speech, Bryan readily agreed to take the stand, insisting only on his right to examine the defense attorneys in turn (226–27, 284). Stewart, who had masterfully controlled virtually every key legal aspect of the trial up to that point, was unable to stop Bryan from falling into the trap. Bryan later claimed he had no choice, contending that any refusal to defend his beliefs in public would have resulted in a disaster greater than anything that might come of answering Darrow's questions.[55]

The trap was brutally effective. Decades of success on the Chautauqua lecture circuit had done nothing to prepare Bryan for the rigors of a cross-examination by any competent lawyer, let alone Clarence Darrow. Bryan's experience as a lawyer was practically confined to the period prior to his election to Congress in 1890.[56] For the most part, Bryan tried to evade Darrow's probes: What would have happened if Joshua had indeed made the sun stand still? Bryan answered that he had never investigated that matter (285–88). More than once Bryan tried to preempt Darrow's attacks, volunteering that the days of creation were not twenty-four hour days (298–99, 302–03).

Eventually, Darrow cornered Bryan into giving answers: Was Jonah really swallowed by a big fish? Yes, Bryan affirmed, God could make man and fish do what He wanted (285). How old was the earth? Bryan finally used Bishop Usher's calculations that the earth was 5,929 years old as of 1925, as well as calculations for the dates of the flood and the Tower of Babel, allowing Darrow to confront Bryan with scientific evidence of civilizations considerably older. Bryan, however, simply refused to accept such evidence (288–91, 295–98). In the face of the public relations disaster that was developing, Stewart objected, demanding to know the legal purpose of Darrow's questioning. Bryan, correctly gauging the effect the session was having, snapped that it was "to cast ridicule on everybody who believes in the Bible." Darrow, with equal precision and vehemence, described the underlying political issue in his quick retort, "We have the purpose of preventing bigots and ignoramuses from controlling the education of the United States" (299).

A few more questions followed in the charged open-air courtroom.

Darrow asked where Cain got his wife. Bryan answered that he would "leave the agnostics to hunt for her" (302–03). Slowly, Bryan began to reclaim his ground, as he inched his way out of the scientific discourse of biological and empirical fact by drawing Darrow into the religious labyrinth of textual interpretation. When Darrow addressed the issue of the temptation of Eve by the serpent, Bryan insisted that the Bible be quoted verbatim rather than allowing the agnostic Darrow to paraphrase it in his own, scientistic terms. Before Bryan could gain much ground, however, the drama came to a sudden close. After another angry exchange, Judge Raulston banged his gavel, adjourning court (303–04).

Later, we will examine in more detail the public portrayal of these events, but for now it is enough to emphasize the legal irrelevance of the cross-examination, the public focus on this event, and finally, the reason for its outcome. Darrow had "caught" Bryan in cross-examination precisely by employing the discourse of science. By asking empirical questions and demanding consistency (especially about the "laws of nature"), Darrow revealed the insufficiency of the discourse of *faith* to answer some kinds of questions. Rigid, Biblical literalism simply could not stand up to that challenge. Bryan played the role of Biblical literalist quite well—he refused to answer questions that could not be answered within the faith structure or answered with literal Biblical answers. In doing so, he made evident the limitations of his religious discourse. The power of the scientific discourse was therefore publicly articulated in a vivid fashion and its legitimacy in certain areas of public debate was established. At the same time, the illegitimacy of religion in certain areas, especially public education, was also established.

The next morning, safely back in the courthouse where Darrow could be more easily protected from the hill folk who were threatening to shoot him for his attack on Bryan, Raulston again returned the trial from the scientific discourse to the legal idiom; he struck the cross-examination from the record (305–08). Bryan, consequently, would have no opportunity to question Darrow. However, the war of words would continue after the trial.[57] Darrow condescended to answering a series of questions from Bryan on the subject of the Christian religion. Darrow essentially answered that he did not know and would not presume to guess about such matters.[58] Ironically, such answers were quite similar to those that Bryan provided on the witness stand and which served to condemn him as an ignorant bigot in the eyes of the world. The different response to Darrow was a sign that the presumptions about the importance of scientific knowledge and the univocity of religion had indeed changed in the nation.

Perhaps more significantly, Bryan subsequently lost the opportunity to articulate his counter-position in the summation speech he had been crafting for three months, because both sides reached an agreement essentially to direct the jury to return a verdict of guilty so the case could begin the appeal process. By foregoing their own closing argument, the defense forced the prosecution to follow suit. Stewart's insistence that the prosecution adhere to the letter of the legal discourse ultimately deprived Bryan of the opportunity for a major articulation of the public place of religious discourse. Bryan was able to say a few words when the various participants made their farewells to the court, eloquently arguing that, however the issue was to be resolved in the end, truth and justice would prevail (316–17), but the great oratorical defense of religion was to go unvoiced. Within the week, hours after he had completed arrangements for the publication of his oration, Bryan was dead.[59]

The legal story of the Scopes trial is one which ends with the clear defeat of the scientist's bid for legitimacy and political control of the public schools. The defense lost the constitutional issues. It lost the right to have its expert witnesses heard when it failed to gain legitimacy for its "accommodationist" interpretation of the law. It also lost the verdict. The strongest portions of the defense's case were stricken by the judge (e.g., the cross-examination) or were never heard by the jury (which was out during the discussions of the "theories" of the cases as well as the constitutional issues and which did not read the attachments of scientific experts). Moreover, until the Tennessee Supreme Court heard the defense's appeal, the case had little legal impact, generating only a few new bills against evolution. No other Tennessee teacher was ever prosecuted under the provisions of the Butler Act. However, as we have hinted throughout, the political impact of the case was in the exactly opposite direction. To understand this reversal, we must scan the public portrayals of the trial which blanketed the newspapers.

The Journalists' Story

The press coverage of the so-called monkey trial was overwhelming. The front pages of newspapers like the *New York Times* were dominated by the case for many days.[60] News magazines, Christian magazines, and political journals all paid great attention to the trial over its course. Generally speaking, press coverage of the trial fell into two camps, represented roughly by newspapers/reportage and magazines/editorials. "News reports" from Dayton focused on the dramatic exchange between the personalities in court and the circus-like atmosphere surrounding the trial (a mood which they themselves had helped to create). However, editorials and essays on the trial usually deplored the entire situation, dismissing the participants and their rhetorical indulgences while advancing the idea that no fundamental conflict between evolution and Christianity existed.

We can offer the generalization that while the "working" press tended to constitute the first camp, the second position was usually maintained by the "intellectual" press. While the working press was essentially represented by daily newspapers (*New York Times*), weekly news magazines (*Time, Literary Digest*), and humor magazines (*Life, Judge*), the intellectual press included religious journals (*Commonweal, Christian Century*), political magazines (*Forum, Outlook, New Republic*) as well as academic journals for groups especially interested in the trial (*Science, School and Society*). More importantly, as we shall see, the two positions match up with the stances taken respectively by Darrow in his assault on Bryan and the fundamentalists, and Malone, in his articulation of the lack of conflict between science and religion. Bryan's position and the position of Judge Raulston although "reported" briefly, went largely without amplification or endorsement.

Ridicule

The dominance of ridicule as the primary mood and theme in the working press served to delegitimate the trial even before it began. Anticipating that Scopes would be found guilty, the working press fitted Scopes for martyrdom and assailed the proponents of "religion." After the trial, Hays responded to a fellow ACLU attorney who had suggested "the case should be brought into the realms of respectability," by demanding to know "Why?"[61] Denied a legal victory in the court system, the pro-evolutionary forces would work for a public victory through an onslaught of ridicule.

The efforts at ridicule were widespread and colorful. *Time*'s initial coverage of the trial focused on Dayton as "the fantastic cross between a circus and a holy war." *Life* shared the portrayal, adorning its masthead with monkeys reading books, and proclaiming that "the whole matter is something to laugh about."[62] Hosts of cartoonists added their own portrayals to the attack.[63] Both *Life* and *Literary Digest* ran compilations of jokes and humorous observations garnered from newspapers around the country. Overwhelmingly, the butt of these jokes were those aligned with the prosecution: Bryan, the city of Dayton, the state of Tennessee, and the entire South, as well as Fundamentalist Christians and anti-evolutionists. Rare exceptions were found in the Southern press, where the fact that Darrow had saved Leopold and Loeb from the death penalty continued to be a source of ugly humor, and in those papers across the country that dismissed the efforts of both sides.[64]

This predominance of humor served three functions. First, it popularized the trial. Those who had planned the trial in Robinson's Drugstore received national publicity exceeding their wildest dreams, although they certainly must have felt the tone left much to be desired. Second, of course, it was presumably good for circulation. Since both sides were taking humorous shots at each other, some semblance of fairness was maintained. Third, given the widespread assumption that Scopes would be convicted, it allowed the press to forestall an interpretation of that conviction as a legitimation of a religious-political hegemony that excluded science. Although the press could control neither the outcome of the trial nor its legal discourse, it could attempt to limit the trial's impact by casting the entire event as a "circus" rather than as a significant social battle. E. S. Martin seems surprisingly explicit about this effort when he attaches to his ridicule the warning that, while the lawyers were well qualified on questions of law: "if these gentlemen are to operate as experts either on evolution or the Bible, they are much less imposing. One looks to them mainly for entertainment, and wonders if they will give a good show."[65]

Delegitimation of the outcome of the trial was thus accomplished through a general ridicule of the trial. It was accompanied, however, by fairly strong ridicule of the location and agents of the trial. Attacks on Bryan were predictably frequent and nasty. For example, Life awarded Bryan its "Brass Medal of the Fourth Class," for having "successfully demonstrated that by the alchemy of ignorance hot air may be transmuted into gold, and that the Bible is infallibly inspired except where it differs with him on the question of wine, women and wealth." The medal featured a caricature of an open-mouthed Bryan with a "Blah" sounding forth, with a flip side showing Bryan with an arm around an ape under the legend "Pals."[66] Such attacks not only delegitimated the trial, but also served to reverse the rhetorical verdict of the trial, anticipating Darrow's ridicule of Bryan in cross-examination. Although Bryan's sudden death brought such ridicule to an immediate halt, forcing several magazines to pull articles and cartoons attacking Bryan or to apologize to readers for being unable to stop their publications from hitting the stands, the damage had already been done.[67] At the end of the trial Bryan had lost the opportunities to examine Darrow and deliver his closing summation because of the machinations of Stewart, Darrow, Hays, and Raulston. By dying, Bryan was deprived of any future opportunities to respond, left only with the posthumous publication of his anti-evolution speech and an essay in *Collier's*.[68]

The most widespread form of this ridicule was directed at the inhabitants of Tennessee.[69] By portraying the state as an "unfit" place and its citizens and courts as unfit agents, the journalists further created a presumption both against the trial and against the collection of interests represented by the prosecution.[70] *Life* described Tennessee as "not up to date in its attitude to such things as evolution."[71] *Time* related Bryan's arrival in town with the disparaging comment, "The populace, Bryan's to a moron, yowled a welcome."[72] Throughout its coverage, the magazine continued this bias, covering the urban-rural tensions in detail, while reducing the issue of constitutionality to a single unsubstantive comment.[73] The press as a whole gave great attention to a wide variety of incidents that further substantiated this image. For example, they reported fully the case of the "free thinker" who was held by the town's sole policeman because "He wasn't talking right, and I was afraid some of the boy's take hold of him." The free speaker was held for disturbing the peace.[74] Those reporters who arrived in Dayton only to discover that the townsfolk were relatively open-minded, simply shifted the focus of their attacks to the Holy Rollers gathered in the hills outside of Dayton or the state of Tennessee as a whole.[75]

The master of vituperative, however, was the literary gadfly, H. L. Mencken, for whom the "hellawful South" had been the subject of a verbal campaign since the 1920 publication of his most scathing essay, "The Sahara of the Bozart," which decried the literary poverty of the postbellum South.[76] Before heading off to the trial, Mencken published an essay in the *Nation* declaring the Butler Act to be constitutional by every known precedent. Arriving in Dayton, Mencken shared this view with Bryan, who declared "This Mencken is the best newspaperman in the country." Mencken's biographers are split on whether Mencken intended his essay to be taken seriously.[77]

Mencken's syndicated columns from Dayton for the *Baltimore Evening Sun* drew vivid caricatures of the "backward" local populace, referring to the people of Rhea county as "Babbits," "morons," "peasants," "hill-billies," "yaps" and "yokels." He chastised the "degraded nonsense which country preachers are ramming and hammering into yokel skulls." About the nicest thing Mencken managed to say about the community was that "The Klan has never got a foothold here, though it rages everywhere else in Tennessee."[78] Aided by his friend Edgar Lee Masters, Mencken attempted to perpetuate a hoax, distributing flyers for the Rev. Elmer Chubb. But the claims that Chubb would drink poison and preach in lost languages were ignored as commonplace by the people of Dayton, and only the *Commonweal* bit.[79] Mencken's most venomous assault was his withering obituary of Bryan, "In Memoriam: W. J. B," in which Mencken became one of the few people ever to accuse Bryan of insincerity.[80] Years later Mencken did question whether dismissing Bryan "as a quack pure and unadulterated" was "really just," but the damage could hardly be undone.[81]

Mencken's columns made the Dayton citizens irate and drew general fire from a sensitive Southern press.[82] The *Daily Oklahoman* gave in to outraged subscribers who demanded Mencken's columns be dropped, informing its readers that "Mr. Mencken in his attacks on intolerance himself went beyond the limits of reasonable and tolerant criticism."[83] Years later Mencken published a collection of clippings reviling him, of which two dozen choice excerpts came from Tennessee papers during the Scopes trial.[84] Mencken's portrayals, however sustained and excessive, were nonetheless reflective of the general direction of the press coverage as a whole. They also reveal the fundamental "lines of battle" drawn in the sociopolitical war.

The attack on the "locals" articulated the central motive behind the national press's tendency to side against the judge, the prosecution, and religious fundamentalism. The national press simply did not share the native discourse of the Tennesseans. To begin with, they were not submerged in a vocabulary of naturalized Christianity; the derogation of foreign ways is an all too normal response to difference. In addition, they were highly sympathetic to the case of science. As a national press they had recently come to honor Darrow's values—"truth" and "objectivity"—as part of their credo.[85] Finally, and crucially, their very survival was dependent upon upholding national discourses over local ones; a national press can only succeed where there is a national idiom. No wonder then that the journalists articulated their preference against "the local."

The depiction of the scene of the trial and the home ground of the prosecution as local rather than national and as backward rather than progressive vividly constructed the religious case as a subjective and limited one, pitted against the "universal" political value of progress. The fear of being caught in ignorance or "backwardness"—outside of progress—was pervasive. The fervor of the concern with intellectual progress is evident not only in the news accounts, but in the two sorts of stories that responded to these accounts. Southern papers fretted about how their region was being portrayed, the *Savannah News* asking "Is it Genesis or Tennessee on trial in Dayton?"[86] The Southerners did not disown the value of (intellectual) progress, but rather wished to deny their own failure to meet that standard.

A second reflection of the widespread endorsement of "education" and "progress" over "backwardness" is found in the sensitive American reaction to the European press. Foreign reporters indicated that Europeans were amazed that an American state would attempt to prevent the teaching of evolution, a matter that had been settled in Britain "long ago."[87] Even the London *Times* characterized the trial as an attempt by the defense to establish "Darrow and Malone's Dayton University."[88] In response, the *Outlook* observed, "In European countries there are constantly recurring educational and religious questions from which America is immune. To Americans they seem often queer and crude." The magazine pointed out that America had no counterpart to England's established church.[89] George McCready Price, chief proponent of the "deluge" theory of geology, an early form of scientific creationism, wrote the London *Times* to declare that average Americans knew more about evolution than their British counterparts. Of course, Price added that Americans were "also much better prepared to say that the evolution idea is at best only a theory," a comment attacked on the *Times*'s letter page.[90]

Almost universally, the press accounts displayed a basic consensus clearly absent in the narrow local scene of the trial. It was the scientific definition of human progress, with its emphasis on truth, not the religious preference for morality, which predominated in the articulated national consciousness by 1925. Bryan, recall, had attempted to portray the bend to evolutionism as a move toward moral decline, a linking of human beings with "backwards" animals rather than with the "higher" moral being of God. The newspapers completely ignored that linkage. In a complex reversal, it was Bryan who was usually portrayed as "the pal of the monkeys" in numerous editorial cartoons.[91] Because the "intellect" was designated as the feature that, by allowing "progress," *distinguished* humans and monkeys, Bryan's refusal of scientific "truth" and the value of intellect placed him in the "backward" set with pre-humans, even though it was precisely that link his origin tale denied. Images of morality as the central human goal had been subordinated to images of scientific or intellectual progress. Consequently, in the journalistic discourse, the vocabulary and concerns of religion lost ground to its scientific counterparts. Bryan's case, dominant in the local scene of the trial even without full articulation, went virtually unarticulated in the public arena.

However, to understand the new positions of science and religion, we must review the context. Religion was not eradicated by these rhetorics, for indeed, we are talking about a court trial in which science was attempting to gain a first legal hearing. The excoriation of religion, therefore, was not for the purpose of eliminating religion, but in order to push it back enough to give room for scientific discourse to operate. This is most evident in the second major type of journalistic discourse on the Scopes trial—the accommodationist editorials.

Reconciliation

While news coverage of the trial tended towards ridicule, editorial essays on the Scopes trial almost uniformly articulated the accommodationist position presented by Malone in the trial. E. S. Martin penned one well-reasoned version of the view in *Life,* suggesting that "in evolution they have found the architect's plans which have been followed in Genesis. They do not say the world made itself. They say, nowaday, that God made it and this is how He did it." Martin insisted, "The story of Genesis, intelligently read, matches up with evolution to an extraordinary extent."[92] It is clear in such editorials that science was not seen as replacing religion, but merely joining it, with each to keep to its own territory. For the majority of the public rhetors, the matter was a simple one of granting science legitimacy in addition to religion. While direct attention to the political control of public schools did not occur, the general acceptance of the scientific story meant increased support for the propagation of scientific discourse in these public territories.

The force of the accommodationist position was amplified by the fact that a huge number of its proponents were religious figures. Because the trial started on Friday, the major point of coverage for the *New York Times* over the weekend was not in Dayton, but rather in the pulpits of New York. The *Times* carried reports on the sermons of many prominent ministers who focused on the Scopes trial and the issues involved. Although both sides of the issue were represented, the left-to-right organization of the *Times* reports and sheer numerical preponderance provided a decidedly pro-evolutionary stance, expressed in the idiom of reconciliation. Bryan was depicted as betraying freedom, while evolution was presented as a relatively minor matter, and the Dayton trial was ridiculed as a "silly performance." Several ministers argued "evolution does not contradict the fact of creation." Only one minister was reported as assailing Darwinism as evil, avowing that no Modernist could be a Christian.[93]

This position was similarly espoused in the Christian press.[94] The *Christian Century,* a self-professed nondenominational journal of religion, provides one example of the way in which ridicule and an emphasis on progress combined to provide the backdrop of the accommodationist position. The journal editorialized that "The controversy over evolution had been settled for at least fifty years" and dismissed the trial as a local deviation, resulting from the fact that "Ideas travel slowly."[95] Bryan and the other fundamentalists were disparaged as a part of the "static mind throughout history"—contemporary versions of the prosecutors of Copernicus, Bruno and Galileo.[96] The *Christian Century* also repudiated the trial process itself, declaring that "Matters of scientific nature are not determined by the eloquence of orators or the devices of attorneys."[97] Significantly, the independent legitimacy of science—independent even of legal discourse—could be recognized only outside the courtroom. The editors concluded by directly legitimating scientific discourse and performing their own assignment of territories: "there is such a discipline as natural science, and that, whatever may be the reverence felt by men of intelligence for the Bible as a guide to morals and religion, they do not employ it as a text-book on history and the laws of nature."[98]

The dominant "story" told by the press about the Scopes trial, thus grew from and shared features with the "legal story," but its conclusion was contradictory. The press ridiculed fundamentalist religion, the locale of the trial, and the prosecution team, while producing an accommodationist position that would legitimate science and add it to the legitimate vocabularies that might exert power in certain public areas.

Impact of the Stories

Of course, it is impossible to demonstrate the precise effects of the legal and journalistic stories, painfully articulated through the popular trial of John Thomas Scopes. We ought briefly, however, to trace the legal, historical, and popular legacies of the trial's rhetorical constructions.

Legal Legacy

When his lawyers pleaded him guilty, Scopes was fined $100 (303–13). Two months later, the Tennessee Supreme Court, *Scopes* v. *Tennessee*, 154 Tenn. 105, 289 S.W. 363 (1927), ruled three to one on appeal that the law itself was constitutional—the state had a right to guide the actions of its paid agents. However, the Court unanimously held that Judge Raulston had erred in assessing Scopes the minimum one-hundred-dollar fine possible under the provisions of the Butler Act, thereby violating the provision of the state constitution that any fine over fifty dollars must be imposed by a jury. Consequently, even though the law was upheld, Scopes and the ACLU were denied the opportunity to appeal the case to the United States Supreme Court.[99]

The ACLU sought another test case, but they were unsuccessful in their search for a volunteer. No one else would be tried under the Butler Act.[100] The ambiguity of the legal outcome on the national level was reflected in subsequent legislative history. In the wake of Dayton, at least forty-one bills, riders, or resolutions were introduced into the state legislatures on the subject of limiting the teaching of evolution.[101] As Ferenc M. Szasz has pointed out, "Instead of serving as the apex of the anti-evolution crusade, the Tennessee law and the Scopes trial actually provided a model for it. The situation in the Volunteer state showed that a law could be passed and upheld."[102]

Most of these bills failed to pass. In Rhode Island the bill was referred to the Committee on Fish and Game; the Delaware bill died in the Committee on Fish, Game and Oysters.[103] A Missouri anti-evolution bill, introduced as a joke to liven up a dull session, almost backfired. Urban legislators proposed humorous amendments, such as setting the penalty for imprisonment "for not less than thirty days nor more than forty nights in the St. Louis Zoo." Other amendments postponed enforcement of the law until the year 2000 or limited the bill's applicability to only those communities whose citizens believed "that the earth is flat, that the sun travels around the earth, that the storms of the sea are caused by the fury of the monsters of the deep." When the laughter died away, the vote was close, only sixty-two for the anti-evolution bill, eighty-two against.[104]

However, the record was mixed in a variety of ways. Mississippi and Arkansas both put anti-evolution laws on their books that would outlive the Butler Act.[105] California permitted the teaching of evolution only as "theory," and textbooks were censored in North Carolina. Outside the legislative realm, Governor Miriam "Ma" Ferguson personally saw to it that evolution was eliminated from the school textbooks of Texas.[106] The Los Angeles Police Chief declared that no one would be allowed to "deny the existence of God on the plaza," and Anthony Bimba, a Lithuanian labor editor, was prosecuted in Massachusetts for "exposing to contempt or ridicule the Holy Word of God," a Puritan blue law enacted in 1697. Scientific textbooks were burned in Jewell County, Kansas and Morristown, New Jersey. By 1926, laws required the daily reading of the Bible in the public schools of eleven states, despite the protests of Jews, Catholics, Unitarians, and Quakers.[107]

The constitutionality issue was not decided by the United States

Supreme Court until 1968. In *Epperson* v. *Arkansas*, 393 US 97 (1968), the court, relying on the prohibition of the *establishment* of religion (which neither Raulston nor the prosecution had seemed to comprehend), held that the Arkansas Rotenberry statute prohibiting the teaching of the "Doctrines of ascent or descent of man from lower order of animals" was unconstitutional.[108] The battle between the interests of religion and science has not, even now, however, abated.[109] The Scopes trial, rather than being a decisive legal point, was simply part of a seesaw battle.

Historical and Popular Legacy

The historical output about the trial has been decidedly more one-sided. Darrow, Scopes, Mencken, Hays, and Potter all wrote autobiographies which dealt with the trial at varying lengths.[110] Major treatments of the trial have tended to accept their defense-oriented versions, in spite of the unreliability of some portions of their accounts.[111] In contrast, Bryan died shortly after the trial and his wife, who finished his memoirs, declined to discuss the trial in detail. Early biographers of Bryan, surrendering their ability to control interpretations, tended either to ignore the Dayton trial or to deal with it in an abbreviated fashion, while later scholars usually characterized it as an aberration at the end of a long and distinguished public career.[112] By default, if nothing else, history has subsequently recorded Bryan as supporting the "wrong" side, winning the battle while losing the war.

Books written specifically about the Scopes trial serve to reinforce this image and to reinforce the spirit of ridicule. L. Sprague de Camp prefaces his account of Darrow's cross-examination of Bryan with an excerpt from Lewis Carroll's *Through the Looking Glass*, wherein the Queen responds to Alice's belief "one *can't* believe impossible things" with the declaration: "Why, sometimes I've believed as many as six impossible things before breakfast."[113] The result is a concise, if not overly critical description of Bryan's testimony in court, foreshadowing it as absurd.

The historical record matches the memories in the popular culture. The most influential popular interpretation is undoubtedly Jerome Lawrence and Robert E. Lee's 1955 play, *Inherit the Wind*. The 1960 film version and the 1988 television movie have probably provided most Americans with most of their "knowledge" about the Scopes trial. It was not until after the play opened on Broadway that the *Encyclopaedia Britannica* began to carry an entry on the Scopes trial.[114] The drama also paved the way for the 1958 publication of Ray Ginger's account of the trial, *Six Days or Forever?*

In *Inherit the Wind*'s fictional depiction, Darrow (as Henry Drummond) is transformed into a clear hero over the antagonist Bryan (Mathew Harrison Brady). For example, whereas the real Bryan had not wanted there to be any penalty attached to anti-evolution bills, Brady-as-Bryan demands that the court mete out more drastic punishment in order to make an example of the "transgressor" to the world. Likewise, the cultural enactment sanctifies Darrow, going so far as to transfer his unkind comments (e.g., that Bryan died of a busted belly) to the mouths of others (e.g., E. K. Hornbeck, the Mencken character).[115] In NBC's 1988 television movie version, the play was rewritten in an attempt to be more sympathetic to Bryan/Brady. But the portrayal of the character as more of a fundamentalist preacher served to counter such changes in the script.[116]

Ultimately, *Inherit the Wind* attacks not merely the fundamentalist belief in Genesis and its corresponding denunciation of Darwinian evolution, but a stereotyped "hellfire and damnation" style. The fictionalized Scopes, for example, denounces Brady/Bryan in court, angrily crying out "Religion's supposed to comfort people, isn't it? Not frighten them to death!"[117] The impact of the play/film/television movie can be found even in academia. The college history textbook, *American History: A Survey* devotes two paragraphs to the anti-evolution movement and the Scopes trial, relating how: "At first, Bryan insisted that God had created the earth in exactly six days, just as the Bible said, but later he admitted that a 'day' in Biblical terms might mean many thousands of years."[118] Although this is the climax of the drama's cross-examination scene, Bryan had anticipated such a challenge by Darrow and had willingly volunteered that particular position.[119] The disclaimers of its authors that *Inherit the Wind* "is not history" aside, public perception continues to be that the play is indeed an accurate dramatization of history.[120]

Where the legacy of the legal story generated within the Scopes trial left no legitimation of science, and hence, a continuing legal struggle, the popular and historical version is quite different in its outcome. The assumption of the legitimacy of science has enjoyed widespread public acceptance. "Progress" has become scientific progress rather than moral development, and the distinctiveness of humankind has been reinterpreted as being a place "above animals" (because derived from them, but differentiated by intellect) rather than "below God." The practices in our schools, technological industries, and military reflect clearly this story. The popular account of the Scopes trial was not the sole creator of that story, but because of the wide national attention the trial garnered in a "legitimate" legal arena, the event served to articulate, amplify, and solidify it in the public consciousness. We remember the Scopes trial as the triumph of religion over science.

Conclusions

Popular trials such as the Scopes case are important and complex sociopolitical events. They generally feature contests of major sociopolitical forces, often represented through competing discourses. Because these trials are "popular" (and, with appropriate circularity, they are popular because of the scope of the forces and interests at issue), the contests are mediated both in the judicial realm, with its attendant legal discourse, and in the public realm, through a variety of discourses dominated by journalists but joined by politicians, historians, and movie makers, among others. The legal discourse creates a "story" and makes a conclusion based on one set of rules and procedures—those inherent to the law.

The outcomes of legal stories are, as we have seen, heavily dependent upon the character of legal discourse and its prior alliances with other social forces. This set of procedures is legitimated in and drawn from the socio-political realm and hence has the power, if the situation is right, to adjudicate the contest exclusively in its realm. In cases such as *Roe* v. *Wade*, that power is awesome. The courts nonetheless face limitations. Often the decision from the courtroom is outflanked—by legislatures, by the process of appeal and legal precedent, by biographies of participants, by television movies of the week, and so forth. Especially in these cases where the legal outcome is limited in its impact, the public story may be more definitive. The public tale created by the national mass-media is derivative from the legal tale, but that does not prevent its conclusion from being opposite of the legal verdict. The journalistic accounts, like those of the courts, are strongly influenced by the values and interests embedded in the discourse rules and vocabulary of its rhetors (the national journalists). In the specific constellation of "popular trials" therefore, we find multiple negotiations of meanings that rhetorically produce the stories with which our nation lives.

In the case of the Scopes trial, the process of negotiation is particularly evident. The trial allowed the defense attorneys to articulate scientific discourse in a legitimate public realm, indicating its utility for answering many kinds of questions and indicating the inadequacies of its chief rival for the territory of the public schools. The defense relied directly on the terms (truth, reason) and practices (empirical questioning) of science to bring the discourse legitimacy. Hence, the word *articulation* is quite literal in its application. Although the legal discourse was not willing to give up *legal* ground to allow science formal legitimacy within the courtroom (e.g., Raulston's ruling against the admission of scientific experts and expunging of the "cross-examination" from the legal record), it did provide the forum for an adequate hearing before a largely sympathetic national audience. This audience was formed and reached by a national press hostile to both the legal idiom and the local idiom of the trial. The outcome—a publicly shared doctrine about the "accommodation" of religion and science—assigned new territory to scientific discourse and ridiculed the competence of the law to do otherwise.

Although the active role of the national press in this rhetorical construction should not be understated, we should note as well the role of passivity by the prosecutors of science before the national audience. Under the leadership of Attorney General Stewart, the defenders of fundamentalist religion and the status quo in Tennessee acceded to this outcome by resting their faith solely in the local legislature and court—relying on legal formalism to protect them from national discursive battles. By choosing, at several points, not to give full articulation to their insistence on "morality" or "moral progress," they acquiesced to the exclusion of the religious and local idioms in the growing national definition of "progress" as a strictly intellectual matter. Local agents in a national arena may not be able to dominate public definitions, but they can have a share of influence through good rhetoric of their own, if they recognize that the arenas and audiences for public rhetoric are always multiple ones. By insisting so narrowly upon their myth of origin and the sole legitimacy of local law, they gave up any chance to define the terms with which a forward-hurtling nation would proceed in the future.[121] In the final analysis, it was not that Darrow bested Bryan in personal combat in Dayton. Rather it is more accurate to say that in the long run Malone's accommodationist position triumphed in the popular arena over Stewart's short-term success in securing Scope's conviction in the courtroom.

Constraints on Persuasion in the Chicago Seven Trial

Juliet Dee

Two decades have passed since the infamous Chicago Seven trial sparked heated public debates about prosecuting citizens for their "intent" and about the need for "decorum" in the courtroom. In those fifteen years, most Americans have forgotten the details and even the outcome of the trial, although they may remember the dramatis personae with nostalgia or revulsion, depending on their political outlook. Twenty years after the trial, American jurisprudence has survived despite the defendants' antics during the trial, the United States has withdrawn from Vietnam, and at least some of the Chicago Seven have become yuppies.[1]

In 1969, however, the Chicago Seven defendants were, according to James Ely, "anxious to use the trial as a political forum for their views" on Vietnam,[2] and to enlist support for their opposition to the Vietnam War. But because the media "framed" the trial in terms of whether the federal antiriot statute was constitutional, and whether the defendants received a fair trial, the defendants were less successful in making the trial a significant forum for debate on the larger question of U.S. involvement in Vietnam.

In attempting to persuade the public that they had not conspired to incite riots at the 1968 Democratic Convention, that the charge against them was politically motivated and corrupt, and most important, that the U.S. should withdraw from Vietnam, the Chicago Seven defendants faced certain constraints on their ability to communicate their messages. These constraints are outlined as follows:

(1) *Normative constraints*: Certain "norms" or standards of story-telling were incumbent upon the prosecutors and defense attorneys to persuade the judge, jury, and ultimately the general public of the truth of their competing stories.

(2) *Political constraints*: The defendants' primary message, their opposition to the Vietnam War, was lauded, sometimes reported, or completely ignored by the left-of-center, center, and right-of-center press respectively, in a textbook illustration of agenda-setting and selective perception by the press.

(3) *Production constraints*: The court limited and prohibited testimony and the media tend to emphasized the highly visual or deviant, which conferred celebrity status upon the defendants (an advantage) but at the expense of deliberative debate on Vietnam (a disadvantage).

If the Chicago Seven trial is examined in light of the defendants' crucial dependence on the news media to convey their message, one can find clear explanations for their courtroom antics. If they had merely tried to state their views without the antics, there was the risk that the press would simply ignore them. Thus, although the defendants could not completely overcome the restraints which this popular trial placed upon their speech, their attempts to exploit the persuasive resources provided by the media merit not only respect but closer examination.

By analogy, the wind is a constraint on sailing, and the difference between a good sailor and a sailor who curses the wind is that the former uses the wind to his/her advantage. It would be equally foolish to curse the political biases in the press, as the press is as necessary to our politics as the wind to the sailor; the cursing masks a rhetorical failure. This chapter comprises an analysis of how the Chicago Seven defendants worked within the constraints outlined above to convey to the American public their opposition to the Vietnam War.

The defendants in the 1969–70 Chicago Seven trial included representatives of the major antiwar groups, the youth counterculture, the campus protest movement, and the Black Panther party, making the trial a microcosm of the politics of protest against the Vietnam War. Many contemporaries viewed this trial as the preeminent example of the era's political repression and ultimate evidence of the oppressive character of the U.S. government.[3] Others thought it exemplified the destruction of law and order by a burgeoning radical movement.

The case of *U.S.* v. *Dellinger et al.*[4] grew out of antiwar protests during the 1968 Democratic National Convention. The organizers of the demonstrations of ten to fifteen thousand protestors in August 1968 were David Dellinger, Tom Hayden, and Rennie Davis, leaders of the National Mobilization Committee to End the War in Vietnam (often referred to as "Mobe"); Abbie Hoffman and Jerry Rubin, leaders of the Youth International Party (who called themselves "Yippies"); John Froines and Lee Weiner, antiwar academics; and Bobby Seale, national chairman of the Black Panthers. *Time* magazine described them as representing "virtually every brand of insurgency that challenged U.S. politics. . . . "[5] Although they negotiated and finally sued the city of Chicago for permits to assemble in Lincoln Park, their permits were denied, thus giving the police legal "justification" to disperse the demonstrators with tear gas and clubs in what the Walker Report later referred to as a "police riot."[6]

Although U.S. Attorney General Ramsey Clark was interested in prosecuting the police for brutality, he was succeeded by Nixon's Attorney General John Mitchell, who, as *New York Times* reporter Anthony Lukas wrote, "was publicly proclaiming his eagerness to go after radicals with every instrument at his disposal."[7] In subsequent books about the Chicago Seven trial, both Random House vice-president Jason Epstein and Lukas strongly implied that the real conspiracy was among John Mitchell, Richard Daley, U.S. Attorney Thomas Foran, and Judge Julius Hoffman, who presided at the trial.[8] When Daley realized that Ramsey Clark wanted to prosecute for police brutality, he was outraged. He had been stung by widespread criticism of his hard-line tactics during the convention, and wanted vindication and revenge on those who had dared to challenge him. Lukas summarizes, "So the Daley machine ground smoothly into operation. . . . Judge William Campbell, long a close friend of the mayor, summoned a grand jury and instructed it to look specifically for violations of the antiriot law. Mr. Foran, who owed his appointment directly to the mayor, came up with supporting evidence, and on 20 March 1969, the jury returned indictments against eight demonstrators."[9] With encouragement from Mitchell and Daley, U.S. Attorney Thomas Foran charged the eight antiwar leaders with "conspiracy to incite" the convention riots and with violating the federal anti-riot statute of the 1968 Civil Rights Act, which makes it a crime to cross state lines with intent to incite a riot. On 26 September 1969, the trial began.

Although the trial began with the eight defendants named above, Black Panther Chair Bobby Seale did not wish to be defended by William Kunstler and Leonard Weinglass, preferring Charles Garry, whom he knew and trusted. Garry was unfortunately in the hospital and Judge Hoffman refused to postpone the trial until Garry had recovered. Since Seale could not have Garry as an attorney, he requested his Constitutional right to defend himself, but Judge Hoffman insisted that Kunstler and Weinglass represented Seale and refused to allow Seale to speak for himself. As David J. Danelski writes in *Political Trials,* although the newspapers stressed Seale's disruptions, "the record shows that he seldom spoke unless statements were made about him."[10] But after four weeks, Judge Hoffman could no longer tolerate Seale's calling him a racist, a fascist, and a pig and ordered Seale bound and gagged. Seale still tried to speak for himself through the gags for about a week; then Judge Hoffman declared a mistrial for Seale and sentenced him to four years in jail for contempt.[11] At this point the Chicago Eight became the Chicago Seven.

Normative Constraints: Competing Stories of Prosecution and Defense

In a highly publicized trial, both the prosecutor and defense attorney attempt to motivate the judge, jury, and journalists who report the competing stories of the prosecution and defense to the public. The following discussion will thus examine storytelling in the Chicago Seven trial.

Stories, Frames, and Burke's Pentad

Lance Bennett and Martha Feldman explain that because jurors have no formal legal training, criminal trials are organized around storytelling.[12] Any criminal case can be reduced to the simple form of a story. Various scholars[13] have selected Kenneth Burke's dramatistic pentad as a good story model for enabling jurors to judge the credibility of a story. According to Burke,[14] we organize stories about social action around the five elements of *scene, act, agent, agency,* and *purpose.* This pentad provides a framework for jurors to judge a story's completeness, consistency, and ambiguity.[15] But jurors cannot fit disparate bits of evidence into a meaningful frame if there are too many ambiguities: As the number of ambiguities increases, the chance that jurors will accept a story as true decreases.[16] Through storytelling, advocates must prove an action (or story) through a clear set of actors, scenes, agencies and purposes; a trial generates competing versions of realities.

The jurors know that both stories cannot be true; thus, their task is to find the one that assimilates the undisputed facts more completely and consistently.[17] The chart below illustrates the competing versions of the story told by prosecutors and defense attorneys in the Chicago Seven trial:

	Prosecution	Defense
Actor	Defendants (are dangerous; "evil men")	Defendants (are responsible citizens exercising right to demonstrate)
Scene	1968 Democratic Convention	1968 Democratic Convention
Purpose	Intended, conspired to riot	Nonviolent protest of Vietnam War
Agency	Conspired to speak	Speeches by defendants
Act	Incited riots	Were victims of a police riot

One can see agreement on the scene of the action (the 1968 Democratic Convention), and usually on the identities of the defendants. There is vehement disagreement, however, on the characters of the defendants, their purpose in organizing the antiwar demonstrations, the agency (whether they *conspired* to make speeches, although obviously they had spoken) and the cause of the ultimate act of rioting: Was it the police or the defendants who really incited the riots?

IDENTITY AND CHARACTER OF THE ACTORS.   To demonstrate the dangerous character of the defendants, the prosecution called on police undercover agents who testified that Abbie Hoffman had told a crowd to gather up bottles, rocks, sticks, branches, bricks and "golf balls with nails pounded into them, so when you throw them, they will stick."[18] Prosecutor Thomas Foran described the defendants as highly sophisticated, educated "evil men."[19] The defense attorneys argued that Abbie Hoffman was a clown but not a threat to society, and that Hoffman had been responsible enough to be a psychologist at a state hospital after graduating from Brandeis. When prosecutors accused John Froines and Lee Weiner of making stink bombs, defense attorneys pointed to their respective doctorate and master's degrees from Yale and Northwestern and their strong beliefs in nonviolence. When prosecutors accused Tom Hayden of letting the air out of a police car tire, defense attorney Len Weinglass pointed to Hayden's civil rights work for which he had been beaten and locked up in Southern jails, and described Hayden as "a man who confers with Averell Harriman" and "a man who has travelled in the company of Robert Kennedy."[20] When prosecutors claimed that Rennie Davis urged people to fight the police, the defense pointed to Davis's 4-H background and belief in nonviolence. The prosecution termed fifty-four-year-old David Dellinger the "chief architect" of the convention conspiracy; the defense showed that Dellinger was a Yale graduate who had been studying for the ministry when World War II broke out. As a seminarian, he could have had a draft deferment, but refused to register and was jailed for a year. The defense underscored Dellinger's conviction: "On his release, he again refused to register and was sent back for two more years (and promptly staged a sixty-day hunger strike)."[21] He protested the Korean War and Bay of Pigs invasion, and then became chairman of the National Mobilization Committee to End the War in Vietnam. Thus, whereas the prosecution attempted to portray the seven defendants as dangerous characters, their defense attorney William Kunstler tried to portray them as dedicated and responsible citizens exercising the rights of free speech and freedom of assembly guaranteed in the Constitution.[22]

SCENE AND PURPOSE.   While both prosecution and defense agreed that the scene was the 1968 Democratic Convention, there was intense disagreement over the purpose of the Chicago Seven defendants. When the prosecution attempted to prove that defendants had conspired to riot and asked Abbie Hoffman if the seven defendants had agreed on plans for the demonstrations, Abbie said, "Conspire, hell. We couldn't agree on lunch."[23] When the conspiracy charge was combined with the antiriot statute, the legal issue was taken one step further from what happened in the streets. In effect, the defendants were charged with "an intention to intend" that riots should occur. But the government was not able to prove any conspiracy: The prosecutors even admitted that the eight "conspirators" never met together as a single group before the convention. Bobby Seale had never met any of the others. And even with regard to the five main figures, the government never proved a common intent linking Yippies Hoffman and Rubin with the Mobilization—Hayden, Davis, and Dellinger.

When the prosecution claimed that the defendants had crossed state lines with the intention of inciting riots, the defense attempted to introduce two articles by Abbie Hoffman and a long paper by Rennie Davis and Tom Hayden in 1968 on their strategy for Chicago, which clearly stated that the demonstration should be nonviolent and legal, and to show instead that "the government is the real source of crackpot thinking and violence."[24] Judge Hoffman excluded this document from the evidence as "self-serving." Anthony Lukas commented that if Davis and Hayden's paper "had proposed bomb-throwing or killing policemen, the government could certainly have introduced it as proof of the charges in the indictment. But because it urged just the opposite it was deemed 'self-serving' and inadmissible. How, I wondered, could a defendant prove his intent if he could not introduce evidence of that intent?"[25] Although the defendants tried to publicize the fact that Judge Hoffman had excluded the paper insisting on nonviolence from the evidence, none of the media reported this except the *New York Times*.[26] Except for some readers of the *Times*, the general public may not have been aware at first of Judge Hoffman's strong bias against the defense.

AGENCY.   The "agency" of their crime was, according to the charges, not only the speeches they gave, but their conspiracy to make these speeches. Judge Hoffman certainly did not question the constitutionality of the underlying conspiracy laws, and the court of appeals did not consider the question because the jury did not convict them on the conspiracy charge.

In addition to being charged with the conspiracy to speak, the defendants were also charged with "inciting riots." Although both prosecution and defense agreed that the defendants had given speeches, they obviously disagreed on their interpretations of those speeches. During the first month of the trial, before Bobby Seale was granted a mistrial, the prosecution confronted Seale with taped recordings of two speeches he gave during the demonstrations, in which he said: "Pick up a gun. . . . if you shoot well, all I'm gonna do is pat you on the back and say keep on shooting. . . . If the police get in the way of our march, tangle with the blue-helmeted motherfuckers and kill them and send them to the morgue slab."[27] (Seale was very different from the other seven defendants: His rhetoric was far more inflammatory and specific in its call for violence against the police than was the rhetoric of the others.) Furthermore:

Over and over we heard testimony about those speeches: Jerry Rubin in Lincoln Park saying, "The pigs started the violence, but tonight the people aren't going to give up the park. We have to fight them. They have guns and sticks so we have to arm ourselves with rocks, sticks and everything we can get." Rennie Davis yelling over a bullhorn in Grant Park: "Take the hill. Take the high ground. Don't let the pigs take the hill." Tom Hayden telling the crowd from the Grant Park bandstand: "If blood is going to flow, let's make sure it flows all over this stinking city." Dave Dellinger telling the same crowd a little later, "I'm sure we'll do mobile tactics tonight."[28]

If the defendants had been tried individually under state law for incitement to riot, the state would have had to prove there was a "clear and present danger" that their speeches might cause the demonstrators to riot. But in this trial, the government contended that the connection between speech and action was irrelevant. The speeches were important only as proof of intent.

The prosecutors called one undercover agent after another who insisted that the defendants had plotted to take over hotels, firebomb an underground parking garage, clog streets, break windows, and generally disrupt the city with "hit-and-run guerrilla tactics." *New York Times* reporter Anthony Lukas was nearly convinced by the undercover agents until he began to wonder why the prosecutors had not found a single defector from the ranks of the demonstrators. "If the defendants had been so manipulative . . . why wasn't there at least one disillusioned kid willing to come forward and testify against them? Why this wholesale reliance on law-enforcement officials?"[29]

In other words, one problem for the prosecution was that there was no "ideal criminal," normally a necessary requirement in a conspiracy trial. Hugh Duncan describes the ideal criminal as one who "from the ruler's view . . . not only confesses to the crime of disobedience but admits that he was wrong to disobey authority. That is, he must not only confess, but recant, and he must be willing to recant before publics significant to those in power."[30] But none of the Chicago Seven defendants would play this role; instead of regretting or recanting their actions, they were proud of leading the antiwar demonstrations. Because there was not even one "disillusioned kid" to testify against the Chicago Seven, the prosecution lacked an important means for establishing the credibility of their story.

ACT: Finally, there was vehement disagreement over who was really responsible for the act of rioting. The prosecution of course claimed that the defendants had incited the crowds to riot. But the defense pointed to a reporter's description of what occurred: "At first, the police stepped forward in unison, jabbing in an upward motion with their nightsticks. . . . Suddenly they stopped the unison and began flailing with their clubs in all directions. . . . People scattered. . . . some went down, screaming. . . . I saw a number of women . . . literally run over. In the wink of an eye, the police appeared to have lost all control."[31]

Thus, the major points of disagreement between the competing stories of the prosecution and defense were not over the scene or the agency of speech but over the actors' characters, their purpose, and the question of whether the speakers or the police were really responsible for the riots. As it turned out, eight jurors believed the prosecution's story and wanted conviction on all counts; four believed the defense and wanted complete acquittal.[32] The four who favored acquittal believed that the federal antiriot statute was unconstitutional, but did not realize that a hung jury would have been almost as much of a victory for the defendants as an acquittal. They were afraid that a hung jury would result in a retrial and perhaps conviction on all counts, so, after four days of deliberation, and after already being sequestered for nearly five months, the jury was intimidated into reaching a compromise verdict by Judge Hoffman and a marshal who told them that the judge could keep them there as long as he saw fit. "All this," contends Helene Schwartz in *Lawyering*, "arguably gave the jurors the impression that they would be kept indefinitely until they reached a verdict."[33] Thus, the jury acquitted all seven defendants on the conspiracy charge. But it convicted five of the defendants (Hoffman, Rubin, Dellinger, Hayden, and Davis) of crossing state lines with the intention of inciting a riot.

One explanation why the defendants' case failed in part is offered by Janice Schuetz and Kathryn Snedaker, who analyze the trial by analogy with a burlesque drama: "Even though the burlesque drama partially worked, it also harmed the credibility of the New Left as a responsible and orthodox movement of dissent because the public viewed the performances as too bizarre and offensive. By failing to play their designated roles, produce legitimate legal scripts, [and] give believable performances, . . . the advocates tainted their credibility as legitimate performers on the stage of the judicial system."[34] No doubt Schuetz and Snedaker are correct in assuming that a more conventional performance would have resulted in a more conventional response from the public. But the defendants' performance was in response to the rhetorical attack of the prosecution.

Viewing the trial with regard to the defendants' larger purpose of communicating their opposition to the Vietnam War, it seems that the conventions of storytelling were effective in advancing the individual celebrity of the defendants but far less effective in advancing discussion of the Vietnam War. The defendants' strategy of using the trial to protest the war was inhibited because their defense attorneys were obliged to expend so much time and energy countering the prosecution's narrative and disputing the prosecution's version of the defendants' characters, purpose, and actions. Because so much effort had to be spent establishing the credibility of the defendants, the narrative conventions of the trial itself, more than any individual capriciousness, limited the defendants' persuasiveness. The conventions of storytelling thus became constraints on the defendants' attempts to persuade the public to oppose the war in Vietnam.

Political Constraints: Right-Center-Left Biases in the Press

The Chicago Seven trial provides a textbook illustration of selective exposure among the media that commented on it. Selective exposure is "one of the most widely accepted principles in sociology and social psychology" and has been defined as "any systematic bias in audience composition."[35] In other words, people "tend to see and hear communications that are favorable or congenial to their predispositions; they are more likely to see and hear congenial communications than neutral or hostile ones."[36] The predispositions referred to include political attitudes, of course. "Exposure is always selective; . . . a positive relationship exists between people's opinions and what they choose to listen to or read."[37] In other words, "most people expose themselves, most of the time, to the kind of propaganda with which they agree to begin with."[38]

The strongest form of the selective exposure proposition is that people prefer exposure to communications that agree with their preexisting opinions. Thus people are thought to seek out material that supports their opinions and to avoid material that challenges them. The Behavioral Sciences Subpanel of the President's Science Advisory Committee felt that the proposition was sufficiently well documented to be accepted as established social science fact: " . . . individuals engage in selective exposure. . . . If a new piece of information would weaken the existing structure of their ideas and emotions, it will be shunned . . . if it reinforces the structure, it will be sought out. . . . "[39] "Most people, most of the time, adults and children, erect high tariff walls against alien notions; they become free traders only when exposed to congenial ideas and values."[40]

Selective exposure occurs not only among consumers of the mass media; it occurs, more importantly, among the disseminators—reporters, columnists, editors and publishers—as well. Newspapers may embed in the "same" factual reports different perspectives on the actors and actions.[41] A controversial event such as the Chicago Seven trial, is thus colored by at least two stages of selective perception: (1) the reporters who cover the trial for the public (and their editors, who may strengthen or weaken a reporter's bias), and (2) the readers, who buy newspapers or magazines that are aligned with the readers' previously held conceptions. This essay will concentrate upon the first process, assuming that although selective perception need not dominate reader interpretation,[42] it can do so at times and has to be considered for both a speaker-centered and an audience-centered explanation of selective perception.

Right-of-Center Media

During the year before the trial began, the conservative media were already generating an enormous amount of hostile coverage of the Chicago Seven defendants, some of which merits consideration here.

PRETRIAL PUBLICITY. On 9 May 1969, defense attorneys William Kunstler and Leonard Weinglass moved for a continuance until July 1970 because of pretrial publicity.[43] With the motion they presented over 200 pages of newspaper articles related to the 1968 Democratic convention disorders, its aftermath of investigations, reports and hearings, and the indictments of the defendants. Newspaper articles harped on the theme that a violent invasion was being planned by various political groups, which necessitated the formation of "battle plans" by the authorities in order to "protect the public." The Chicago Seven defendants were the targets of a continuous campaign of vilification.[44] The Chicago press referred to the defendants as "revolutionaries," "anarchists," "militants," "troublemakers," "agitators," "wild men," "notorious spreaders of disorder," "fomenters of convention week rioting," and "potentially dangerous people" with "no scruples about abusing the law" and whose activities were "merely camouflage for organized violence." Tom Hayden was called "Hanoi's disciple"; Dave Dellinger was called "the self-styled non-Soviet Communist."[45]

The Chicago press was very successful in arousing public opinion against the demonstration leaders before the 1968 Democratic Convention even began: "A public poll taken right before the convention reported that 48% of all Americans thought that the political demonstrations had been 'organized to disrupt the convention and create riot conditions in Chicago.' Even more frightening was a report in a Chicago newspaper on the day the convention opened; according to it, 90% of those polled supported the policy that authorities should 'shoot to kill if agitators make trouble.' "[46]

The public outcry against Dellinger, Davis, Hayden, Hoffman, and Rubin escalated when Mayor Daley's office issued a self-expiating report entitled "The Strategy of Confrontation." The report endorsed the police action against the demonstrators and named the defendants as the "fomenters of convention-week rioting." Headlines in the *Chicago Tribune* screamed "Blame Riot on 5." Congressman

Roman Pucinski denounced the defendants as part of a "conspiracy to destroy this nation."[47]

Despite the overwhelming pretrial publicity, Judge Hoffman denied the defendants' motion for a continuance. On 27 August 1969 the defendants again moved for a continuance because of publicity about Bobby Seale's arrest on charges of murder in Connecticut. Judge Hoffman again denied the motion for a continuance. Concerned about pretrial publicity, Kunstler and Weinglass moved for questioning each venireman out of the presence of the others during the voir dire to select the jury. Judge Hoffman denied this request, as well as a later request to reopen the voir dire to "include questions . . . concerning the exposure of the veniremen to press, radio and TV reporting" about the case.[48] Indeed, Judge Hoffman refused to ask any questions during the voir dire to determine whether prospective jurors might be biased against people who demonstrated against the war and racism, how they felt about long hair, or whether the jurors had friends or relatives who were police officers, for example.[49] So inadequate was Judge Hoffman's voir dire that it did not uncover the fact that one juror was engaged to and later married a member of Mayor Daley's administration.[50]

On appeal, the defendants claimed that the court breached its duty in conducting an adequate voir dire to protect them from "the barrage of prejudicial pretrial publicity."[51] The U.S. Court of Appeals for the Seventh Circuit agreed with the defendants' position, concluding that since Judge Hoffman refused to grant a continuance, he did indeed breach his duty to ask veniremen about pretrial publicity on voir dire.[52]

CONSERVATIVE MEDIA COVERAGE DURING THE TRIAL. The conservative publications considered here are the *Chicago Tribune*, William F. Buckley's *National Review*, and *Commentary*.

The *Chicago Tribune* generally took the most extreme position against the defendants, with the exception of a few pro-Seven articles which the editors hastened to point out were the opinions of columnist Bob Cromie: "Our columnist, Bob Cromie, has taken a generally critical position toward Judge Julius J. Hoffman and the outcome of the trial of the Democratic convention rioters. The *Tribune*, in its editorials, has taken a generally approving position. In its news columns, the *Tribune* has tried—successfully, we think—to report the news fairly and without prejudice. . . . We firmly believe that our judgments on Judge Hoffman and the trial are correct. . . ."[53] More typical than Bob Cromie's columns[54] was the editorial run at the very beginning of the trial which described the defendants as "long-haired hominoids" and "frenzied aberrants of the human species."[55] The editorial was equally uncomplimentary toward the 68-member National Committee to Defend the Conspiracy, which included Leonard Bernstein, Julian Bond, Judy Collins, Jules Feiffer, Allen Ginsberg, Joseph Heller, Elia Kazan, and I. F. Stone, to name a few. But these prominent Americans who were attempting to raise money for the Seven's defense were dismissed as "bellicose pacifists" and "rich loafers." The editorial ended with "If this is a political trial, then the prosecution of a revolutionary for murder, arson, or any other crime that might be politically motivated would likewise be a political trial."[56]

On the first day of the trial, Judge Hoffman ordered defense attorneys Michael Tigar and Gerald Lefcourt jailed for contempt merely because they withdrew from the case by telegram before the the trial.[57] When 150 lawyers from across the country traveled to Chicago to demonstrate against Judge Hoffman and thirteen members of the Harvard Law School faculty asked the Illinois Bar Association to investigate the judge's actions, the *Chicago Tribune* described the 150 attorneys as "Hooligan Lawyers" and called for their disbarment or at least censure.[58]

When 700 demonstrators led by the Students for a Democratic Society clashed with police on the first day of the trial, the *Tribune* ran two front-page pictures showing police being injured by demonstrators. Its story detailed injuries to nine policemen but said that the "number of demonstrators injured was not known."[59] The entire article seemed to be based on a police account sans any account whatsoever from a demonstrator's viewpoint.

Two weeks into the trial, the *Tribune* suggested that "patriotic citizens fly the American flag daily throughout the trial."[60] As the trial progressed, the *Chicago Tribune* replaced the term Chicago Seven with "Riot 7" in all its headlines referring to the defendants, although it always used the term "Chicago 7" when referring to Judge Hoffman as in "Chicago 7 Trial Judge Given High Praise."[61] At the end of the trial, the *Tribune* objected to

the attempt . . . to attack the American system of justice by taking the case out of the courtroom and seeking to try the whole judicial system in the court of public opinion. A room was made available in the Federal building for press conferences, and only the defense employed it. The trial judge and the federal prosecutors could offer no rebuttal to the constant stream of propaganda emanating from the press room, because it would have been improper and prejudicial for them to do so. In consequence, the defense had a field day. . . . the press became an accessory to defense purposes by faithfully reporting the press conferences, speeches and demonstrations. . . . The total effect was to implant a reasonably widespread belief that the state and the law are repressive, that racism and the war in Viet Nam will persist, and that justice does not exist.[62]

A week later the *Tribune* applauded Judge Edwin Robson's order forbidding defendants, counsel, witnesses and court personnel to make out-of-court comments about a trial of "15 radicals accused of breaking into and destroying the records of a draft center."[63] It defended the order which, it explained, was necessitated by the out-of-court activities of the Chicago Seven defendants: "Judge Robson has shown how to prevent inflammatory extrajudicial activities by defendants and their lawyers. We may have to enlarge our prison facilities, but the revolutionaries can be contained."[64]

At the end of the trial the *Tribune* conducted a poll of its readers and reported that 84 percent approved of Judge Hoffman's conduct of the trial, and 93 percent approved of the jury's conviction of Dellinger, Davis, Hayden, Rubin and Hoffman for violation of the federal antiriot statute.[65] One is tempted to observe that such high percentages favoring Judge Hoffman and conviction could reflect the percentage of *Tribune* articles taking these positions. On the other hand, the theory of selective exposure[66] would suggest that already conservative readers would select the *Tribune* as providing an outlook most consistent with their own world view.

Like the *Chicago Tribune* editors,[67] William F. Buckley devoted several articles in his *National Review* to a discussion of the defendants' misbehavior and its threat to our judicial structure, which "does not have at its disposal means sufficient to counter their kind of Maoist assault."[68] Buckley observed, "Revolutionary crusaders have in the past used the courtroom for extra-judicial purposes—to transform the courtroom, as the old-line Communists put it, into a forum from which to speak to the masses."[69] Buckley's commentary was actually more liberal than the *Tribune*'s: Rather than labeling the Chicago Seven "longhaired hominoids" or "frenzied aberrants," he subtly acknowledged that there may have been reasons to question the constitutionality of the federal antiriot statute and to disapprove of Judge Hoffman's conduct of the trial: " . . . one hopes to see a division between those who—for whatever reasons—disapprove the 1968 Act under which the defendants were being tried, and those who disapprove the conduct of the case by Judge Hoffman: between them, and those whose single concern is to side politically with the defendants. It is up to the former to tell us what ought to have been done, and how a judge is supposed to maintain order in such a situation. They must do so even at the risk of being called pigs, fascists and racists."[70] Buckley admitted that by meting out such harsh contempt sentences, Judge Hoffman had "made martyrs" of the Chicago Seven—"but there is nothing more passé than last year's martyr. And the long sentences were surely proper."[71] The *Chicago Tribune* echoed Buckley's analysis, dismissing the defendants as "a bunch of hasbeens, transitory symbols of a fleeting era which most Americans, including the campus dissenters whom the seven pretended to represent, would just as soon forget."[72]

In his *Commentary* article, Alexander Bickel seemed to agree with Buckley and the *Tribune* on this point; he added that the Chicago Seven would "unmask themselves" because "The faith embodied in the First Amendment is not only that in a free society few will want to make a revolution, but that where the revolutionary idea may be freely ventilated, it will defeat itself."[73]

The Moderate Press

The "moderate" media considered here are *Time, Newsweek, New York Times* articles as well as *New York Times* reporter Anthony Lukas's book on the trial and some academic accounts of the trial.[74] These moderate media seemed to be so concerned about giving equal space to both the conservative and liberal angles that they leave one thinking of the old maxim, "Moderation in all things, including moderation." In other words, they were perhaps too moderate.

Some observations would have appealed to conservatives: for example, *Time*'s assertion that "By choosing to disrupt their trial through guerrilla tactics, the Chicago defendants and lawyers not only forfeited the sympathy of the majority of the public, but the moral authority they might have brought into the courtroom."[75] A *New York Times* editorial suggested complete disgust with both defendants and Judge Hoffman: "[The jury] was given precious little help from a judge who often acted as though in alliance with the prosecution and from defendants who, more interested in discrediting the courts than in looking to the legal process for vindication, richly deserved contempt sentences—though not of the severity they received."[76] Like their conservative counterparts, all of the moderate media bemoaned the defendants' "brutal test of the American judicial system,"[77] insisting that the judicial process *must* be respected by both the judge and the judged. But *Time* also acknowledged that the trial had contributed to polarization: "The defendants' antics have outraged many Americans who now deplore dissension more than ever. At the same time, the trial has tragically convinced many young people that the U.S. judicial system is a tool for 'repressing' dissent. Hostility toward the courts has already reached New York and Washington, where Black Panthers and antiwar clergymen have tried to turn their trials—for more palpable offenses than those committed by the Chicago defendants—into similar arenas."[78]

On the other hand, *Time* compared Judge Hoffman unfavorably with County Judge Charles Larson who quietly and patiently lectured the "Milwaukee 14" draft resisters on their behavior and overlooked minor outbursts.[79] *Newsweek* objected to the courtroom being used either for a political trial *or* a propaganda demonstration, concluding that the Chicago Seven case "was both—and its consequences would reverberate in American law for years to come."[80] The question most frequently raised by the moderate media was whether "the trial system itself might have to be modified in order to cope with defendants and lawyers who refuse to observe its fragile rules of decorum. . . . "[81] When it was all over, Ely observed that "it was the very legal system which [the defendants] and their supporters condemned that ultimately saved them from prison."[82]

In addition to questioning the motives of the defendants, some of the moderate media drew negative conclusions about the longterm effects of the trial. Ely observed that "Aside from the vocal protest constituency, much of the public was indifferent or hostile to the defendants."[83] He added, "Due in some measure to the Chicago prosecution, [antiwar protest] began to wane. . . . After the Kent State incident in May 1970, large demonstrations waned. . . . the proceedings [of the trial] unquestionably helped to still militant protest."[84] Like the conservative media, the moderate media thus sounded the death-knell for the antiwar movement. *New York Times* editor Tom Wicker said that there was "a hard new resistance" to the peace movement, for example.[85]

Newsweek suggested that the government might be more wary of starting "quasi-political trials" in the future because their potential for "making martyrs of radical agitators would seem to be great."[86] Whereas Ely asserts that the Chicago Seven trial marked the beginning of the end of large-scale political demonstrations, *Newsweek* seems to suggest that the Nixon administration's first attempt to suppress dissent in the form of this trial may have actually sparked further rebellion: "The Chicago conspiracy case was the first of the Nixon administration's attempts to teach America's noisier domestic dissenters an object lesson—an effort that led on to the Mayday mass arrests, the Berrigan case, the Pentagon Papers inquiry and kindred adventures and misadventures."[87]

In reporting these protests, the media were least sympathetic to violent demonstrations protesting the trial such as that by "The Weathermen," a faction of the sundered Students for a Democratic Society. *Time* described their demonstration, as "a senseless rampage," in which they "stopped cars and beat the bewildered passengers, smashed windows and glass doors and urinated on everything in sight."[88] Finally, when a downpour washed out an attempt to hold a rally in Lincoln Park, the Chicago *Sun-Times* reported: "The revolution was called on account of rain."[89] But *Time* also observed that The Weathermen were not representative of the antiwar movement: " . . . the faltering effort at disruption underscored the fact that premeditated violence is still alien to most of the protest movement."[90] Although the Weathermen's "Days of Rage" soon after the trial began were ostensibly on behalf of the Chicago Seven, several defendants told *New York Times* reporter Anthony Lukas privately that they were unhappy about the rampage: "But at news conferences, they refused to distance themselves from the young street fighters. As one defendant put it: 'When the Movement is embattled, you don't start denouncing your brothers.' "[91]

Because of selective perception on the reader's part, much of what the mainstream media reported could be interpreted according to the reader's own biases. For example, after the jury verdict, which found five of the seven defendants guilty, *Time* reported demonstrations in seven different cities by crowds as large as 25,000 protesting the jury's verdict. In response to such coverage of the demonstrations in cities across the United States to protest the jury's guilty verdict, one can assume that right-of-center readers would be angered, moderate readers would be concerned, and left-of-center readers would be pleased to see that the jury's verdict of "guilty" provoked such a strong reaction across the country. Referring to Ronald Reagan's decision to dispatch a helicopter to gas students at Berkeley, Tom Wicker concluded " . . . wherever the action is, since Chicago, things seem sharper now, more pointed, more dangerous. Mr. Nixon may tell us to lower our voices, but we are raising them instead."[92] *Time* acknowledged, "The trial was not only a symptom of the division in America; it also deepened it."[93] *Newsweek* dealt directly with the question of selective perception: "In the end, the question of which side has been hurt most by the Chicago trial comes down, as do so many of the trial's other features, to a matter of political perspectives. Radicals will see the government put to shame. Most traditionalists will regard the defendants' behavior as reprehensible. But neither side in the trial can claim to have been very much helped by the case. And the chief loser has almost certainly been the American judicial system itself, whose dignity has rarely been so cruelly mocked and whose limitations have rarely been so starkly exposed."[94]

At times the moderate media seem to suggest that the entire trial and maybe even the 1968 Convention violence could have been prevented if communication had been better or if Chicago officials had just taken the yippies less seriously. When the defense called Mayor Daley to testify at the trial, Abbie Hoffman "sauntered up the aisle toward the mayor and in his best Gary Cooper-*High Noon* drawl said, 'Why don't we just settle this right here and now—just you and me? The hell with all these lawyers.' The mayor laughed aloud and settled back in his chair. He had finally learned the correct way to react to a yippie. So much trouble could have been avoided if he had only wised up sooner."[95] Others were to draw the same conclusion: four years later at the 1972 Democratic convention in Miami Beach, Mayor Chuck Hall welcomed Abbie Hoffman and Jerry Rubin, who "roamed about . . . the convention floor wearing press passes labeled *Popular Mechanics* and *Mad Magazine*."[96]

When the U.S. Court of Appeals reversed the defendants' convictions because their trial had been unfair, but ruled that the government could try the case again, the media gave very little coverage to the specific condition set by the Court of Appeals: The government could retry the case only if it were willing to disclose what it heard over its secret bugs and wiretaps which picked up the defendants' conversations. Aside from brief paragraphs by Danelski[97] and *Newsweek*,[98] the moderate media were silent on this point. If the "agenda setting" theory[99] were applied to this puzzle, we would have to conclude that the moderate media simply did not find Attorney General John Mitchell's order to use electronic surveillance against the defendants to be a matter of serious concern. The agenda setting theory suggests that the press "may not be successful much of the time in telling people what to think, but it is stunningly successful in telling its readers what to think *about*."[100] In this case, none of the moderate media "set the agenda" for their readers to be concerned about the disturbing precedent set by John Mitchell for the invasion of privacy of any citizen who might engage in lawful dissent.

The moderate press did set the agenda, however, for their readers to question whether the Chicago Seven received a fair trial or not. *Time* focused on the trial's polarizing effect: "Americans were divided between those who saw Federal Judge Julius Hoffman as upholding the American judicial system and the sanctity of the courts against outrageous and sometimes filthy attacks by the Chicago Seven; and those who thought that, however impossible their behavior, the defendants were being victimized by a bad law and a biased judge."[101] *Time* quoted New York Mayor John Lindsay who said: "All of us, I think, see in that trial a tawdry parody of our judicial system. When a trial becomes fundamentally an examination of political acts and beliefs, then guilt or innocence becomes almost irrelevant."[102] Although noncommittal at first, *Time* finally agreed with Lindsay that the decision to prosecute the Chicago Seven "could be taken as evidence of political contamination of the judicial system."[103] The moderate media also expressed concern about the fact that Judge Hoffman refused to allow expert witnesses to testify for the defense—including former Attorney General Ramsey Clark, who believed that violence had been avoidable in August 1968,[104] and Ralph Abernathy, president of the Southern Christian Leadership Conference.[105]

The moderate press also frequently questioned the constitutionality of the federal anti-riot statute under which five of the seven defendants were convicted. *Time* commented, "In the view of many legal scholars, the law ... is unconstitutional."[106] *Newsweek* was more specific: "A number of constitutional scholars have doubts about this law. Its emphasis on 'intent' ... smacks of punishments for thoughts rather than deeds. Critics also contend that the law's definition of intent and incitement is too vague.... (For example, does 'incitement' cover the actions of one's opponents as well as one's followers? If so, a public speaker's political antagonists would hold the power to incriminate him by their own acts of violence)."[107] When the Court of Appeals finally overturned Judge Hoffman's contempt sentences and reversed the jury's "guilty" verdict, *Time* concluded that "justice, in the end, prevailed."[108]

Left-of-Center Media

Left-of-center media considered here are the *Washington Post*, the *New Yorker*, the *New Republic, Commonweal*, the *Nation*, and *Ramparts*, as well as books published by defendants, witnesses, counsel for the defense and their sympathizers.[109]

A year before the trial began, *Commonweal* predicted that "the government is about to crack down on the New Left by singling Tom Hayden out for arrest. The FBI has been scouring the country for evidence to indict Hayden under the infamous 'Rap Brown' law— crossing state lines to incite to riot. Hayden himself is philosophical about his pending arrest. 'Whoever the media make into a left leader will be put away,' he said recently. ... Hayden's arrest, however, will be significant in that it will point the way for the return of overt repression of those who still challenge the system openly by attempting to utilize 'legitimate' channels of protest and confrontation."[110] One might interpret *Commonweal*'s prediction as reflecting the tendency on the left to perceive the trial as a "police conspiracy."

In addition to expressing anger at the idea of a police conspiracy to arrest antiwar leaders who had tried to use legal channels of protest, the liberal media evinced astonishment at the abysmal lack of humor on the part of the establishment: "Some of the intelligence picked up by the Red Squad of the Chicago police department is exotic. For instance, its files contain a copy of [an article which] summarized suggested Yippie tactics for August. 'Yippies plan to paint their cars like cabs, pick up delegates, and dump them off in Wisconsin,' said one of the suggestions. This supposed plan to disrupt the convention ran through months of straight-faced intelligence summaries until, three weeks before the Democrats arrived, the idea was mentioned as a serious possibility in a memorandum by David Stahl, Deputy Mayor. A lot of information of this quality was given to the jury."[111] Writing for the *Nation,* reporter Ralph Whitehead added that U.S. Attorney Thomas Foran and his staff were bullying unfriendly witnesses to get statements to corroborate with those of the police undercover agents who would testify against the Chicago Seven.[112]

The *Nation* later predicted that the trial would probably have the effect of breathing new life into the antiwar movement "which it was supposed to arrest."[113] Another editorial argued that with political trials such as those of Sacco and Vanzetti and the Chicago Seven, "our jurisprudence is not as far removed from that of the Soviet courts as we would like to believe. . . . Such trials are in themselves a form of violence and provoke counterviolence."[114]

Like the moderate media, the liberal media referred to the defendants as Nixon's "scapegoats" whom his administration would have "picked off one by one."[115] The liberal media reminded readers that the use of indictments "is a powerful tool in the hands of a government eager to suppress dissent. The authorities can tie up in court politically active opponents for long periods. Political trials also serve to intimidate others."[116] Writing for the *Nation,* law professor Jon Waltz described the conspiracy charge against the defendants as a "worn-out piece of tyranny."[117] He observed, "Dissenters in tyrannical states are unceremoniously shot or imprisoned; in democracies they are charged with conspiracy first."[118]

Whereas the moderate media questioned whether the federal antiriot statute were constitutional, the liberal media were certain that it was not: "The effect of the 'anti-riot' act is to subvert the First Amendment guarantee of free assembly by equating organized political protest with organized violence and premeditated incitement."[119] But while the moderate media focused much of their coverage on speculating about the law's constitutionality, the liberal media attempted to keep the original issues of antiwar protest and the Chicago police riot at the forefront of discussion about the trial.

Such attempts at agenda setting could include criticism of the moderate media as when Nachman also accused the *New York Times* of flip-flopping on the issue: During the convention week in 1968, the *New York Times* had published a scathing editorial accusing Mayor Daley and his cohorts of making violence inevitable by enforcing a curfew in a park where large numbers of young people had peacefully congregated. But a year later, the *New York Times* concluded that "much of the evidence indicated that [the defendants] were guilty of inciting to riot."[120] Writing for the *Nation*, Larry Nachman made these observations:

> Far from engineering a test case of a new law, the defendants were innocent of the charge, even if the law were constitutional. And this fact the *New York Times* once knew well. . . . The discrepancy in the editorials points to the way a trial functions and the effects it has even on people who are intelligent, informed and liberal. . . . Once the trial began, one could retain one's original view of the Chicago violence only at the cost of raising some deep and ugly questions about the nature of the United States Government that was prosecuting the case and of the federal court that did not immediately dismiss it. The trial itself, independent of its results, gave legitimacy to the suppression of dissent in Chicago.[121]

The liberal media emphasized other questions regarding police power as well. In contrast to the moderate media's silence about the government's extensive electronic surveillance of the defendants, *Ramparts* warned that the establishment was "already totalitarian in scope," as witnessed by the Executive Branch's assertion of a right to wiretap without legislative or judicial review."[122]

Although the moderate media touched on Ramsey Clark's interest in prosecuting Chicago police for brutality,[123] the left-of-center media gave this fact greater emphasis. *Ramparts* observed that when Attorney General Ramsey Clark has "sent Justice Department lawyers to Chicago to initiate proceedings against police for committing acts of brutality, he could get no cooperation from either the local police or the FBI and was able to indict only eight policemen (on the basis of photographs taken by newsmen). The five policemen who have thus far come to trial—prosecuted by the same Tom Foran who is prosecuting the [Chicago Seven]—have all been acquitted."[124] The *Washington Post* also reminded readers that "excessive use of force by the Chicago police department had been the principal cause of the riots."[125] The *New Yorker* commented on the irony that "among the lessons that an organizer of a demonstration might learn is that even if he behaves himself at a demonstration he may end up being tried and imprisoned if the police don't behave themselves. It is interesting to reflect that there almost surely would not have been a trial in Chicago if the police had not rioted."[126] When the U.S. Court of Appeals decision reversed the trial court's antiriot act conviction, the *Washington Post* cheered its decision, adding, "The government now has the option to retry the case. It is ardently to be hoped that it will not."[127]

Finally, whereas the moderate media tore their hair over the defendants' "guerrilla-tactics" in court, the liberal media defended their courtroom behavior: "If the defendant is convinced that he is being railroaded, that the verdict will be not the result of the evidence adduced but of predetermined arrangement, he has nothing to lose by turning the proceedings into pandemonium."[128]

Production Constraints: Judicial Control of Speech; Media Emphasis of Deviance and Visual Imagery

To the extent that courtroom "decorum" renders deviant all behavior such as guerrilla theater or any visual display, the popular trial can be the perfect scene for the media because "deviant" translates as "newsworthy." In their attempts to gain media coverage of their opposition to the war, however, the defendants faced the formidable hurdle of Judge Hoffman's consistent denials of the relevance of their statements on Vietnam.

Judicial Control of Defendants' Speech

The defendants tried hard to redirect attention to the larger issue of the Vietnam War. For example, a few weeks into the trial, on 15 October, they wore black armbands and draped Viet Cong and American flags over the defense tables in observance of the national War Moratorium. David Dellinger attempted to read the names of both Americans and Viet Cong who had died, and asked for a moment of silence, which Judge Hoffman of course denied.[129] The *New York Times* did report this on page 18 as part of its extensive coverage of the Moratorium, but referred to the defendants as having "the most extreme positions on the war."[130]

Or consider the following colloquy, which begins with a reference to Mayor Daley's order for police to shoot to kill all arsonists and to maim all looters in the black community on 15 April 1968, when Martin Luther King was assassinated.[131]

LEONARD WEINGLASS, a defense attorney: Mr. Schaller, is it an obscenity for the mayor . . . to advise his police to shoot to kill all arsonists and shoot to maim all looters?

RICHARD SCHULTZ, a government attorney: Objection.

THE COURT: I sustain the objection.

MR. WEINGLASS: Do you consider it an obscenity for the United States Government to use napalm in the bombing of civilians in North Vietnam?

MR. SCHULTZ: Mr. Weinglass can't be serious in contending that these questions are proper on this re-cross-examination.

MR. WEINGLASS: That is perhaps my most serious question in this trial.[132]

Thus, when defense attorney Len Weinglass tried to emphasize the abomination of napalm used on civilians in North Vietnam, Judge Hoffman cut him off, and except for Lukas, most of the media found it more entertaining to report the antics of Abbie Hoffman and Jerry Rubin than to consider the atrocities the United States was committing in Indochina.

When Rennie Davis testified, he held up part of an antipersonnel bomb dropped by an American fighter jet, an F-105, over Nam Ding, a city in North Vietnam:

. . . when this bomb exploded over Nam Ding, about 640 of these round steel balls were spewed into the sky. When this ball strikes a building or the ground or slows up in any way, these hammers are released, and an explosion occurs which sends out about 300 steel pellets. . . . with 640 of these bombs going off, you can throw steel pellets over an area about a thousand yards long, and about 250 yards wide. Every living thing exposed in that 1000 yard area, 90% of every living thing in that area will die, whether it's a water buffalo or a water buffalo boy. . . . This bomb would not destroy . . . the walls, the ceiling, the floor. If it is dropped on a city, it takes life but leaves the institutions. It is the ideal weapon, you see, for the mentality who reasons that life is less precious than property. . . . in 1967 . . . one out of every two bombs dropped on North Vietnam was this weapon. One out of every two. And in 1967 the American government told the American public that in North Vietnam it was only bombing steel and concrete. . . . I went to Vietnam . . . as an American citizen who was deeply perturbed that we lived in a country where our own government was lying to American people about this war. The American government claimed to be hitting only military targets. Yet what I saw was pagodas that had been gutted, schoolhouses that had been razed, population centers that had been leveled. . . . [133]

Judge Hoffman's response to Davis's testimony was predictable: "The [bomb] is wholly irrelevant and immaterial. If an exhibit like this were to be permitted, you could fill this room with bullets. I am not trying the Vietnamese war here. . . . There is no such charge in the indictment."[134] Rennie Davis gave this testimony on 23 January 1970. No immediate reports of this testimony were found in any of the news media; for example, the *New York Times* did not carry any stories on the trial at all till a week or so later. Remembering the trial in 1976, Jerry Rubin wrote, "If it were God and not Julius Hoffman, I would have liked to stand up and say, 'A country that is bombing Vietnam should have a riot in its center so that it can look at itself and make necessary changes, not ignore the reality that we are dropping bombs on people in Vietnam. The city officials are crazy enough that instead of figuring out how to co-opt us, they will do the same to us that they did to the Vietnamese, and use force.' But Julius said, 'This is not a political trial and your views of Vietnam are irrelevant here'—so my defense would not have been allowed. [Hoffman and Daley] . . . were part of the violent system of Vietnam."[135]

Status-Conferral: Media-Made Celebrities

Although Judge Hoffman exercised significant constraints on the speech of Jerry Rubin and the other defendants, all of them had the advantage of being in the media spotlight, but at the expense of deliberative debate on the Vietnam War. Mere recognition by the media of some person or group singles them out and bestows prestige and authority on them in what Lazarsfeld and Merton described as the mass media's "status-conferral function." They explained that the audiences of the mass media "apparently subscribe to the circular belief: 'If you really matter, you will be at the focus of mass attention and, if you *are* at the focus of mass attention, then surely you must really matter.' "[136]

Media certify leaders and officially noteworthy "personalities"; indeed, "they are able to convert leadership into *celebrity,* something quite different. . . . For what defines a movement as 'good copy' is often flamboyance, often the presence of a media-certified celebrity-leader."[137] The media thus promoted the leaders of the antiwar movement *selectively.* The leaders who became celebrities were flamboyant and knew what rhetoric the media would amplify. No one understood this better than Abbie Hoffman and Jerry Rubin: When Jerry Rubin was subpoenaed by the House Un-American Activities Committee (HUAC) in 1966, he wore an American Revolutionary costume because, as Todd Gitlin wrote in *The Whole World is Watching,* he realized that the press "*might not report what he had to say, but they would take a picture of him. It was unlikely* that the press would have listened to his statement."[138] Jerry Rubin and Abbie Hoffman, the two most famous celebrities, were the least attached to any grassroots organization; rather, they used the media to invent the Yippies.

The tendency of the mainstream press to focus on the flamboyant rather than the substantive was evident throughout its coverage of the Chicago Seven trial. For example, Stanhope Gould, the field producer who supervised much of CBS's coverage of the trial, chose to accompany Jerry Rubin and Abbie Hoffman rather than Rennie Davis, Tom Hayden, or Dave Dellinger because they were more colorful. Gould had earlier produced a six-minute takeout on Rennie Davis dealing with the question of how Rennie Davis, son of one of President Truman's Council of Economic Advisors, had become a radical leader, but CBS refused to air it. Thus, according to Gitlin, the CBS standard "that ruled out a respectful investigation of Rennie Davis' political evolution permitted coverage of more 'colorful and symbolic'—and more easily dismissible—movement celebrities. Yippie avantgarde defiance was permissible as entertainment; sympathetic treatment of a would-be organizer of communities was not."[139]

Furthermore, as Gitlin has argued, the media's conferral of celebrity influenced the selection of the antiwar movement's leadership. Rubin apparently "didn't really believe in" the antiwar or yippie movement but "moved toward it for opportunistic reasons."[140] Of course, Rubin could only thrive as a celebrity if the media reported him. Although he flaunted the antiwar movement's genuine attempts to influence government leaders to end the war, Rubin was colorful, which made him a success as a celebrity. Gitlin emphasizes, *"It was precisely the isolated leader-celebrities, attached indirectly to unorganized constituencies reached only through mass media, unaccountable to rooted working groups, who were drawn toward extravagant, 'incidental,' expressive actions—actions which made 'good copy' because they generated sensational pictures rich in symbolism."*[141] Because of the temptation of achieving a celebrity status like that of Abbie Hoffman and Jerry Rubin, it was difficult for leaders like Tom Hayden, Rennie Davis, and David Dellinger to maintain a plain, consistent, utilitarian approach to the media, to use the spotlight without getting burned up.

Thus, those who oppose the status quo "can achieve media standing only as deviants; they become 'good copy' as they become susceptible to derogatory framing devices; and past a certain point, precisely what made them 'good copy' may make them dangerous to the State and subject, directly or indirectly, to blackout."[142] When the defendants presented a birthday cake to Bobby Seale, which was confiscated by a marshal with Rennie Davis yelling "They have arrested your cake, Bobby,"[143] the media reported this because it was "good copy," but when Dave Dellinger attempted to read the list of names of Americans and Viet Cong killed in Vietnam, this was "blacked out" in the sense that it was not reported in the daily or weekly press. If the media label radical groups as deviant, and portray demonstrators as "performers within a spectacle," how long can radical groups continue to act "without internalizing and acting out their ascribed role as 'deviants' and outsiders and hence reinforcing the very processes they are seeking to challenge?"[144]

If the defendants' goal for the trial was that it should be a forum for debate on whether the federal antiriot statute was constitutional, or whether they received a fair trial, they succeeded. If, however, their goal was for the trial to serve as a forum for public debate on U.S. involvement in Vietnam, they were less successful. Of all the articles cited above, only two, from *Newsweek* and the *Nation*, even acknowledged the problem that the trial was actually diverting people's attention from the larger issue of the Vietnam War. *Newsweek* considered the possibility that tying up the radicals in court may have served the government's interests: " . . . the trial in Chicago has been successful in forcing radicals to divert their energies from the political arena. For nearly half a year . . . the country's top radical leaders have been spending virtually all their time either at the trial or raising money for their defense. And even if they win this case, they seem likely to face contempt citations that could place them behind bars as soon as the trial is over."[145] Berating the *New York Times* for paying too much attention to the antiriot statute's constitutionality, Nachman commented in the *Nation:* "This deflection from one issue to another was a major victory for the government."[146]

Of course, the media cannot afford to ignore ideological changes or major social conflict. "*Through the everyday workings of journalism, largescale social conflict is imported into the news institution and reproduced there: reproduced, however, in terms derived from the dominant ideology.*"[147] Discrepant statements about reality are acknowledged, but muffled:

The news routines are skewed toward representing demands, individuals, and frames which do not fundamentally contradict *the dominant hegemonic principles . . . the legitimacy of the national security State; . . . the right and ability of authorized agencies to manage conflict and make the necessary reforms. . . .* Political news is treated as if it were crime news—what went wrong today, not what goes wrong every day. A demonstration is treated as a potential or actual disruption of legitimate order, not as a statement about the world. These assumptions automatically divert coverage away from critical treatment of the institutional, systemic, and everyday workings of property and the State.[148]

For these reasons it was far less threatening for the media to focus on the Chicago Seven defendants' behavior during the trial ("what went wrong today") rather than their underlying, far more important effort to draw attention to U.S. involvement in Vietnam.

There are numerous examples of the media's simultaneous willingness to cover stories of demonstrations and refusal to explain the underlying motivations for the demonstration in any depth. At a mass demonstration against the Vietnam War in London in 1968, the media "focused almost entirely on incidents of violence and on the personalities involved, and by-passed completely any consideration of the demonstrators' political perspective."[149] When 1,414 members of the Clamshell Alliance were arrested for protesting against the Seabrook nuclear reactor in 1977, the *New York Times* and other newspapers published respectful articles on the demonstrators' conduct. But the Clamshells' case against the reactor was limited to one line about ocean water used in the reactor's cooling system being returned to the ocean 38 degrees hotter, thus endangering marine life[150] without a word about other risks of nuclear power.[151]

Thus, if the "establishment" is challenged by a social movement, the mass media are literally mediators, providing a neutral ground for the elites to deal with the challenge by resisting or adapting to it. News organizations are thus constantly "balancing here, absorbing there, framing and excluding and disparaging, working in complicated ways to manage and contain cultural resistance . . . to tame and isolate intractable movements and ideas."[152] The right-of-center and mainstream media thus framed the Chicago Seven trial in terms of debates over the defendants' courtroom behavior and whether the anti-riot statute was constitutional but downplayed the defendants' efforts to stress the obscenity of dropping napalm on North Vietnamese civilians. The left-of-center media also became caught up in showing that the defendants had been unjustly arrested and tried.

The Chicago Seven defendants could claim certain successes, however: They created a cohesive story, attracted and held national attention, supplied good narrative material for the left-of-center press, and produced some critique of our cultural constraints. They also succeeded in making their trial a public forum, but failed to make this forum work well for their desired purpose of debating the Vietnam War.

The defendants' strategy of using the trial to protest the war was deflected by (1) the normative constraints imposed by the prosecution's narrative which emphasized the defendants' motives, (2) the political constraints demonstrated by the selective coverage of the mass media, and (3) the production constraints governing both Judge Hoffman's admission of testimony within the courtroom and the portrayal of the trial by the media. Thus it appears that the defendants in a political trial such as that of the Chicago Seven face formidable gatekeepers in the persons of the judge, lawyers, reporters, editors, publishers, and broadcasters; and each of these agents can affect the message and aid or obstruct the intention to make the trial a successful forum for public debate. As public persuaders, defendants in political trials face the difficult, delicate task of casting their message in a manner that can satisfy the court while gaining the attention of the media, that can be disseminated by the press yet resist the inevitable agenda setting in press coverage, and that can stimulate public debate yet avoid being categorized as deviant. These are not easy conditions for persuasive success; when such conditions are met, however, the potential for influence is considerable. If the Chicago Seven are to be evaluated as persuaders, perhaps we should begin by asking how well they succeeded on these terms.

Power, Knowledge, and Insanity
The Trial of John W. Hinckley, Jr.

William F. Lewis

He intended to assassinate the chief executive but shot the secretary instead. There was no doubt that he had attempted the crime, and his near success seemed to indicate both planning and self-control. Nonetheless, he was brought to trial and pled not guilty by reason of insanity. As Daniel N. Robinson writes in *Psychology and Law*, "Experts were summoned on both sides and testimony was taken from many persons who knew and had dealings with the defendant. The entire nation watched as the insanity plea worked its way through the days of testimony and argument. Then, when the court acquitted [him] all hell broke loose."[1] The case had become a symbol. According to Jacques M. Quen, "The anxiety over lawless violence found a target in the . . . verdict. It focused attention on the violent criminally insane and on the protection the law offered society. The effectiveness of that protection probably was perceived as being directly proportional to the stringency of the law."[2] As a result, courts were put on the defensive and the laws were changed in an attempt to limit the use of the insanity plea.[3]

This case was one of the biggest stories of 1843, when Daniel McNaughtan attempted to kill the Prime Minister, Sir Robert Peel, but mistakenly shot Peel's private secretary, Edmond Drummond instead.[4] The case is famous because it resulted in the McNaughtan Rule which is still used widely as a standard of insanity in criminal cases. Today, of course, the description recalls John Hinckley's attempt to assassinate Ronald Reagan and the continuing furor over his subsequent acquittal. The parallels between these two classic cases of criminal insanity suggest that trials invoking the insanity defense can touch close to the heart of a society's forms of power and understanding,[5] and that these forms will be displayed especially clearly in cases involving attacks on the political leaders.

This essay examines the public discourse surrounding the trial of John W. Hinckley, Jr., in order to identify the structures of knowledge that were assumed in that discourse and to discuss the corresponding patterns of power and privilege. I will argue that this popular trial functioned as a stage for playing out dramas in the social order embodied in Hinckley's actions and focused on points of ambiguity or contradiction in American ideological structures. More specifically, both the reporting of the Hinckley trial and the accompanying debate over the insanity plea were an active interplay of institutional "texts." The major texts were Law, Family, and Medicine, with Psychiatry playing the role of intermediary (thereby becoming more powerful, more dangerous, more questionable[6]). The result of this inter-textual drama was to reinforce the legitimacy of Law and the Family at the expense of Psychiatry, and to reinforce prevailing patterns of understanding and morality. Despite the familiar conservative objection that the insanity plea subverts the legal order, I conclude that the discourse on the use of the insanity defense in the Hinckley trial embodied powerfully a political and social form of understanding that reinforced conventional patterns of legal authority, family structure, and medical treatment.

One might object that an inquiry into power relations cannot be objective and is therefore likely to tell us more about the ideological coloration of the analyst than about the substance of the trial itself. Such an objection, however, assumes that other sorts of analyses of trials do not have political consequences and that political grounding necessarily sacrifices claims to knowledge. Such assumptions are themselves political. "Perhaps," as Michel Foucault wrote in *Discipline and Punish*, "we should abandon the belief that power makes mad and that, by the same token, the renunciation of power is one of the conditions of knowledge."[7] Following Foucault's lead, this paper will examine the relationships between power and knowledge—and madness—not as a corruption of scientific knowledge or of dialectical reasoning, but as the reconstitution and negotiation of the structures of reality that comprise public life and that legitimate (or de-legitimate) patterns of social relationships and the exercise of political authority and economic privilege. The reason that the dispute over the insanity plea in the Hinckley trial followed such clearly defined lines was that the range of positions in the dispute was grounded in a set of commonly held but normally implicit assumptions about the nature of the world, about the nature of appropriate action, and about the nature of social relationships.

The Trial

After attempting to assassinate President Andrew Jackson in 1835, Richard Lawrence proclaimed that he was king of England, the United States, and Rome. It took his jury just five minutes to return a verdict of not guilty by reason of insanity.[8] John Hinckley's eight-week trial was quite different. In fact, Hinckley differed from all of the apparent models drawn from previous assassination attempts because, unlike Richard Lawrence, Hinckley suffered from no obvious political delusions and because, unlike Lee Harvey Oswald or Sirhan Sirhan or Squeaky Fromme, there was no discernable political motive for Hinckley's act. The public demand for making sense out of important events therefore focused attention on the central question of the trial: Why did he do it? A fragmented story emerged as the trial progressed.[9] John Hinckley was a loner, estranged from a wealthy family who lived in suburban Denver. He had seen the movie *Taxi Driver* about fifteen times and became infatuated with its young actress, Jodie Foster, to the extent of writing her letters and poems, and attempting to contact her at Yale where she was a student. He had apparently stalked both Carter and Reagan before. Finally, on 30 March 1981, Hinckley wrote a farewell letter to Jodie Foster, loaded his pistol with Devastator bullets, and went to the Washington, D.C., Hilton Hotel where he shot six times at Ronald Reagan as the President walked to his limousine.

The trial featured the dramatic and tearful testimony of Hinckley's family members, an appearance by Jodie Foster (during which Hinckley first averted his eyes and finally walked out), and an array of psychiatric experts attempting to interpret his motives and his mental state. There was little dispute about the circumstances of Hinckley's life that led up to the attempted assassination and there was general agreement that Hinckley was suffering from some degree of psychological disturbance, but there was a difference regarding the degree of disturbance that led to differing interpretations of the meaning of Hinckley's prior life and differing accounts of his motives and mental state on the day of the crime. The prosecution attempted to focus attention on the act of the shooting, arguing that Hinckley's actions on the day of the crime were planned and that his evident self-control indicated that he was sufficiently sane to appreciate the wrongfulness of his actions and to conform them to the dictates of the law. They portrayed John Hinckley as lazy and manipulative, looking for an easy way to achieve fame.[10] The defense focused attention on Hinckley's character, his relationship with his parents, and his attachment to Jodie Foster, arguing that his loneliness and solitary lifestyle had pushed him into an inner world of "false premises, false assumptions, false ideas."[11] They portrayed Hinckley as being so deluded that he believed that the shooting might be a way (quoting from Hinckley's own letter) "to accomplish his ideal union with Jodie Foster, whether it be in this world or the next."[12]

A report in the *New York Times* described the trial as "a classic battle between opposing teams of expert witnesses [in which] contradictory psychiatric diagnoses and arrays of multisyllabic medical labels dominated 24 of the 32 days of testimony."[13] Following the trial, the jury deliberated for three-and-a-half days before declaring John Hinckley not guilty by reason of insanity on all thirteen counts of his indictment. The extensive press reports portrayed an American public who were "stunned" by a verdict that "struck many as an affront to common sense."[14] Russell Baker called the verdict "an exercise in legal absurdity" and argued that "a shot President is just as shot, regardless of whether his attacker is insane or not."[15] The theme of being stunned or outraged was pervasive. Nearly all parties, including the judge, the courtroom audience, the defense lawyers, the nation, the Congress, the Reagan Administration, and Hinckley himself were portrayed as being shocked by the verdict. "Even the judge was stunned" began *Newsweek*'s report on the verdict.[16] *Time* wrote, "If John Hinckley's bullets seemed to hit dangerously close to the heart of a nation, his acquittal struck explosively at its sense of moral righteousness."[17] Political response was immediate. Both houses of Congress and twenty-six states considered proposals to reform the law on criminal insanity, the jurors were interviewed, Reagan submitted his own ideas for change, and all of the action was covered extensively by the press.[18]

The problem was that the trial had struck upon a contradiction in the inevitably inconsistent common sense understanding of aberrant behavior. The day after the Hinckley verdict was announced, an ABC News poll found that three-quarters of the respondents felt that "justice had not been done" and that 70 percent favored the elimination of the insanity plea.[19] In a poll in Delaware conducted a week later, 87 percent of the respondents agreed that "the insanity defense is a loophole," 73 percent said that they would have found Hinckley guilty, and 66 percent felt that Hinckley was not legally insane. On the other hand, when asked what should happen to Hinckley, 14 percent said treatment, 26 percent said punishment, but almost 60 percent wanted both treatment and punishment.[20] Similarly, when a writer for the *New Republic* conducted "an informal poll" in the line outside the Hinckley trial he found that "everyone in line agreed on two points: first, that Hinckley was absolutely loony, and second, that he should be convicted so that he'd be off the streets."[21]

Despite the expressed opposition to the verdict and the emphasis on controversy, one of the most striking impressions that results from examining the reports and commentary about the Hinckley trial in the popular press is the degree of consistency with which the issues were defined and debated. The distinctions that one would expect to find in a case that generated so much controversy were muted by an underlying consensus about the nature of the case and of the issues that it raised. There was a widespread feeling that Hinckley should be imprisoned, but there was no question that criminal acts could be the result of mental illness or insanity and little question that Hinckley was insane. There was widespread skepticism about the expertise of psychiatric testimony, but widespread support for the idea that the mentally ill should be treated and no question of relying on other than medical or psychiatric authority. There was never any doubt that the legal system was the appropriate arena in which to deal with Hinckley, nor was there any question that justice was the appropriate goal. The problem is that out of these underlying assumptions arise mutually contradictory desires: We want punishment for those who transgress against the basic moral code at the same time that we want treatment for those who are too sick to control their actions; we want safety from those whom we perceive as threatening at the same time that we recognize the need to be caring and fair; we want to be true to our "natural," "common sense" revulsion to heinous crimes at the same time that we want to be "civilized" and "humane"; we want both punishment and treatment, both justice and compassion.

The reason that the Hinckley trial generated such intense and enduring concern is that confronting these contradictory social desires precipitated a conflict among basic principles of social understanding and institutional power.

Structure of the Texts

LAW/FAMILY/MEDICINE. The Hinckley trial brought together, in a highly charged dramatic setting, the three principles of social order expressed symbolically as *Law, Family,* and *Medicine.* Each of these structures of discourse represents a connection between belief systems and patterns of social authority—*Law* is the entitlement of a primary institution of the public moral order, *Family* is the entitlement of the primary institution of the private moral order, and *Medi-*

cine is the entitlement of a primary institution whose moral force depends upon the creation and application of scientific knowledge. All three are institutions of social morality, but because they differ in the beliefs that are accepted, the relationships that are assumed, and the power that is legitimated, their intersection provoked a moment of social crisis. Such moments challenge implicit conceptions of the social order and thereby create a need to confront, by either revision of reaffirmation, the prevailing and normally implicit definition of prominent social ideas and relationships. Hinckley's act provided the focus, his trial provided the forum for such an examination. Although there was substantial dispute about the relationship among these three systems of understanding, the news media's descriptions and explanations were grounded in a broad consensus about their fundamental nature.

The basic character of the three symbolic structures is laid out schematically in Table 1. In this section I will consider the basis for these structures and their interaction in the news media texts regarding the Hinckley trial.

The Law: The legal system uses reason
to punish criminals in jails to achieve justice.

The central focus in the Hinckley trial was the law. The specific point at issue was the law on the insanity plea; more generally, the case raised questions regarding the legitimacy of the exercise of legal authority over the mind and the adequacy of the protection that the law could assure. Its presumed primacy provided the perspective for the interplay of the major symbolic structures in the trial. The central conception of the nature of criminal law as it emerged from the discourse on the Hinckley trial is summarized in the brief sentence above. Although other elements may be emphasized that would also

TABLE 1

	Law		Medicine		Family
	lawyers	psychia-trists	doctors	psychia-trists	parents
use	reason	science	science + art	art	love
to	punish	understand	treat	treat	raise
	criminals	the mind	patients	patients	children
in a	jail	laboratory	hospital	hospital	home
to achieve	justice	knowledge	health	mental health	morality

be sensible and significant, the important thing to note about the propositions that are implicit in this sentence is that they are un-challenged. "Law" is itself the major actor embodied in "the legal system" consisting of judges, lawyers, and juries. Reason is the basic principle of action in law. Punishment is the expected outcome, but only for criminals; that is, ideally, all criminals are punished and only criminals are punished. Jail is the expected locus of punishment for this type of criminal and justice is the goal.

The description here is neither exceptional nor exceptionable, and it was used extensively (if implicitly) as a standard against which to judge the particular trial. Hence arguments arose during the Hinck-ley trial as to what constitutes the legal system and whether the process was reasonable. Following the verdict, there was discomfort because John Hinckley, whom millions had watched as he shot at the president, would not be sent to jail. News stories frequently discussed the conditions in St. Elizabeths Hospital and nearly always mentioned the possibility of release. And, since the events did not provide a smooth fit for this expected story line, there was a question about the achievement of the ultimate goal—justice.

The immediate question raised by the discussion of the Hinckley verdict was how could such a thing have happened?[22] The answer that pervaded the reporting and commentary on the trial was that the Law enables us (the implicit audience, the persona of the Public) to transcend our natural desire for revenge by imposing the require-ments of Reason which are the basis of civilized society.

Consider the jury. The trial's ultimate decision of guilt or inno-cence was made by the jury in the case, but the jury was portrayed as a passive agent acted upon by the force of the law. The jury was described in condescending, sometimes racist terms. *Time* maga-zine's report on the verdict described the first foreman of the Hinck-ley jury as "a retired janitor," the second as "a burly hotel banquet assistant" who "dug heartily into [his] barbequed ribs" just before the final decision was made.[23] *New York Times* reporter Stuart Tay-lor, Jr., began his later commentary about the trial by quoting "Wood-row Johnson, parking lot attendant, one of the Hinckley jurors" as saying, "I do not think nobody knows what was within his head that day."[24] The verdict was described as the outcome of applying the law. The jurors were interviewed extensively and their doubts were reported widely: "I was tired," explained one juror. "Nobody seemed to think there was any other way. We felt locked in by the law."[25] Some admired the jury's willingness to risk public censure by ac-quitting Hinckley; the more common response was to use the jury's verdict as a means to attack the law that had (by assumption) re-quired it. "I don't blame the Hinckley jury," said Sen. Orrin Hatch, "They applied the law as it is. I blame the law."[26]

The implicit syllogism went something like this: "The Hinckley verdict was a result of the law. The Hinckley verdict was a bad verdict. Therefore, the law was a bad law." Thus, the logical response, which was also the almost universal progression in articles about the trial and the eventual progression of political action, was to reform the law on the use of insanity as a defense in criminal trials. In addition to explaining the legislative response, the implicit syllogism also reveals some of the assumptions underlying the understanding of the trial. First, the major premise was never questioned. The Law was assumed to be the major determinant of the result by both supporters and opponents of the verdict. Second, there was no doubt that the Law could be reformed if reform were found to be necessary. Third, despite the generalized objection to the result of the trial, pleas to eliminate the insanity defense were considered extreme and the actual action taken by the Congress provided for only moderate reforms of the existing plea.

Law was portrayed repeatedly as a force which lifts humanity above its natural state. It is presumably "natural" to desire revenge against a lawbreaker, but it is also presumed that reason must prevail in a civilized society. Since the law is portrayed as the active force of reason in society, the force and legitimacy of law are reinforced. We distinguish ourselves from the insane by our ability to control our will and our emotion by our reason. The application of this faculty psychology was summarized when Judge Irving Kaufman of the U.S. Court of Appeals quoted Francis Bacon in the course of his analysis of the Hinckley verdict: "revenge . . . is a kind of wild justice which, the more man's nature runs to, the more ought law to weed it out."[27] In more mundane terms, *Time* quoted "a Detroit psychologist" as saying that "we need the insanity defense so that we can say we are a civilized society and we don't execute sick people."[28] In the end, we were shown the triumph of reason over emotion, of civilized humanity over natural instinct.

Such a conception of the law as a higher power can effectively encompass public disapproval of the results in individual cases. Disapproval is neutralized as being the expected ("natural") reaction, the opposition is placed on a lower moral plane, and the assumed moral superiority of the law is reinforced.

The Family: Parents use love to raise their children in a home to achieve morality.

If the Law was offered as the primary model for interpreting the public meaning of John Hinckley's actions, the Family was the primary alternative emphasizing their private significance. John Hinckley was characterized repeatedly as "a drifter" who had separated from his family and who, either despite their love and support or because of its inappropriate character (were he a "spoiled child"), was led into tragedy. The opening sentence of a *Newsweek* article examining the trial provides a cogent summary of the themes that would be repeated in the coming months: "John W. Hinckley is every family's nightmare come to life. He is the child who drifts off into private hells of depression, despair and finally irrevocable disaster, leaving his parents only the bitterness of 'perhaps,' the futility of 'if only.' "[29] Hinckley is the picture of a family life gone wrong. His "irrevocable disaster" was the result of drifting away from the family into "private" despair. "If only" he had stayed within the family structure, the picture implies, the disaster would never have happened.

The family was a repeated theme in reports about Hinckley and about the trial. From the first reports, the importance of his family relationships was in evidence. An editorial in *U.S. News and World Report* speculated that Hinckley's motives might be analogous to those of John Wilkes Booth, who was said to have assassinated Lincoln in order to prove himself to his father,[30] and other reports questioned the influence of family relationships on Hinckley's actions.[31] Reports on the trial depicted twenty-six-year-old Hinckley as a child, frequently referring to his "child-like" appearance and to how small he looked. He was described as looking like a child, acting like a child, and being treated like a child. A *New York Times* report on the verdict illustrates the character of the depiction: "The jury saw frequently erratic courtroom behavior by the boyish-looking defendant, who walked out of his trial without seeking permission once, was excused on four other occasions, and drew a warning from Judge Parker on 4 June that 'you had better get this clearly implanted in your mind, that you don't get up and leave when you want to.' "[32] The identification of Hinckley as a child was reinforced by the testimony of a defense psychologist who "liken[ed] the defendant's self-image to that of 'a little boy with a gun' who has done a naughty thing."[33]

The fit of Hinckley's experience with the conventional picture of the family as the foundation of social morality was reinforced by reports of the parents' testimony. The mother, Jo Ann Hinckley, who was referred to as "the week's most memorable witness," described the family's attempt to remove their son from their home on the advice of Hinckley's psychologist, Dr. John Hopper. "It seemed like the harder we were trying to push him from us, the more he wanted to stay," she was quoted as saying.[34] Reports on the father's testimony further strengthened the connection between home and tragedy: "Hinckley's father, weeping openly, tried to explain how a national tragedy had sprung, in his view, from a family that turned its back on a troubled son."[35]

The message was clear: Social morality depends upon parents providing a home for their children. The story and its attachment to a conservative Christian morality were played out in the press over the coming months implicitly in the standard news media and explicitly in media aimed at "family-oriented" audiences. *Newsweek* and *Time*, for instance, accepted the picture of Hinckley as a "drifter" and reported on the suit against his psychologist filed by the victims of Hinckley's attack.[36] *Reader's Digest, Redbook,* and *Christianity Today,* on the other hand, published extensive reports on and by Hinckley's parents including excerpts from their book and descriptions of their campaign to help families cope with mental illness.[37] The themes depicted in the articles on Hinckley's parents were reassuring. The Hinckleys begin their story by noting that, though they were having trouble with their son John, "it helped to know that many of our friends were going through something similar." The excerpt concluded by offering direction: "There are so many anxious parents across the nation—yet relatively few, perhaps, who are aware of the nature of mental illness and how it may be affecting their child."[38] What could have been seen as a message about the failure of the American family or about the mistakes of a particular family was portrayed instead as a message of reassurance and reform: Many families are having trouble; parents are doing the best that they can, but sometimes mental health is the real problem. There is no sense in these discussions that mental health could be related to interactions among family members or that the family structure itself might contribute.[39] The problem is that an individual is sick. The solution is to educate parents to help them deal with their sick members.

The portrayal of the Hinckley family in reports about the Hinckley trial also positioned the institution of the family with respect to the law and to psychiatry. The portrayal suggests that these are essentially private problems, that the insanity plea is appropriate, and that psychiatry can help by assisting the family in dealing with the problems of mental illness. Thus, the integrity of the law was upheld and psychiatry's proper role was defined in terms of treatment rather than judgment or expertise, all of which reinforced the role of the family as the foundation of the social order.

The picture of John Hinckley and his role in the family has potentially significant implications for other power relationships as well. Portraying twenty-six-year-old John Hinckley as a child reproduces a common description of the mentally ill: They are just children, they are irresponsible, they need guidance. The picture suggests that the mentally ill need to be controlled and that the control should come from the family (parents), from the law (deciding about disposition following socially disruptive behavior), and from medicine (providing treatment and confinement in hospitals). It is a picture of the family that grants absolute authority to parents, to courts, and to doctors along with the presumed obligation to use it lovingly. In this way patterns of both knowledge and control are re-legitimated through the report of the Hinckley trial.

One reason the story of Hinckley's family created relatively little difficulty in its social portrayal and interpretation was that the story was easily integrated with the dominant legal perspective: The Family retains central control up to a point, but it relinquishes control to the law when the potentially tragic consequences of separation are realized. Medicine, however, and particularly psychiatry, were more problematic.

Medicine: Doctors use both the science and art of medicine to treat patients in hospitals to achieve health.

There was neither challenge nor discussion about the *nature* of medicine in the discourse on the Hinckley trial. There was, however, a great deal of discussion about the *relationship* between Law and Medicine and between Medicine and the Family.[40] The focus of the discussion in and about the trial was the nature of psychiatry. The two major issues were concern about the reliability of using psychiatric testimony in the trial and fear about the results of bringing psychiatric considerations to bear on criminal actions.

The first question challenged the appropriateness of using psychiatric testimony in making legal determinations. It was presumed that "science" could properly be a part of the law since experts could provide objective knowledge that could be used to reason about legal disputes. It was also presumed that "art" should not be a part of the law since matters of taste or opinion are merely personal views that fall outside the range of acceptable legal evidence.

One challenge to the legitimacy of psychiatric testimony was based on the claims that the object of psychiatric study is the mind and that the mind is not subject to objective scrutiny. *Newsweek* emphasized a commonly expressed distinction in describing the task for Hinckley's lawyers: "They face heavy odds, for they must lead the jury of five men and seven women to suppress the evidence they can see and accept the evidence of Hinckley's invisible psyche."[41] The *National Review*'s position that "since mental defenses are meaningless, they can only work arbitrarily"[42] was extreme, but it represented a frequently voiced concern about applying conclusions about the mysterious mind to bring the reasoned process of legal decision making. Even the one attempt to the technological apparatus of objectivity to bear on Hinckley's mental state was not well received. When the defense introduced CAT scan evidence on the width of the fissures in Hinckley's brain, it was dismissed as being both indeterminate and of questionable validity.[43] The effort demonstrated the demand for scientific proof, but its reception demonstrated the dominant skepticism about psychiatry's ability to provide this kind of objectivity.

The major question raised in the portrayal of the Hinckley trial concerned the role of psychiatric testimony in the trial. The most frequently voiced concern was that conflicts between psychiatrists testifying for the defense and those testifying for the prosecution turned the trial into a "spectacle." Alan Stone's statement that the conflicting testimony was like "clowns performing in a three-ring circus" was cited frequently.[44] The circus is an inversion of social values—the opposite of the function served by the court. To suggest that psychiatry turned law into a circus is to suggest that it held up the institution to ridicule, that its role was actively harmful to the process of legal judgment. A *Wall Street Journal* editorial stated that "the spectacle of prosecution and defense psychiatrists drawing diametrically opposite conclusions from the same evidence deflated the claims of psychiatry to any scientific pretensions."[45] A related attack on the expert status of psychiatrists suggested that the conclusions of the psychiatrists were based as much on the payment of their fees (a subjective basis) as on the evidence of their investigations (an objective basis). *Newsweek* wrote that "juries tend to forget that psychiatry is as much an art as a science. 'Psychiatric testimony is so unreliable and open for sale to the highest bidder that it's a national scandal,' says Stanford University Law Prof. John Kaplan."[46] The St. Louis *Globe-Democrat* expressed the common view that "laymen understandably are cynical about the credibility and possible venality of the so-called 'expert' witnesses, particularly psychiatrists who mouth conflicting opinions—for a fee—on the state of mind of a defendant."[47] The combination of using "so-called" and placing "expert" in quotes was a deadly commentary on the popular opinion of psychiatry that emerged from the Hinckley trial.

It was also suggested that law and psychiatry are separated by a difference in perspective: Illness is the province of medicine; morality is the province of the law. On the one hand, it was argued that psychiatry has no place in the legal judgment. An editorial in the *Indianapolis News* was typical: "The Hinckley trial is merely showing the whole nation what has been going on in a few trials for several years. Psychiatrists have been asked to testify about matters well beyond their expertise, drawn into matters of philosophy of criminal justice and ethics that cannot be resolved on a medical or scientific basis."[48] On the other hand, it was also argued that law has no place in psychiatric assessment. A later analysis in the *New Republic* made a similar distinction with a different emphasis: "The problem for both critics and defenders of the insanity defense is that mental illness is probably best thought of as a spectrum of irrational behavior, not as an either-or condition. . . . Such complexity could probably never be reflected in the terms—'guilty' or 'not guilty,' 'sane' or 'insane'—which the law must use."[49]

A second set of themes regarding the relationship between psychiatry and the law was expressed in concerns about public safety. Insanity, it was asserted, allowed criminals to get away with their crimes.[50] The insanity plea was criticized as being unfair and dangerous—unfair because criminals would not be punished, and dangerous because it might encourage future criminals to think that they could escape punishment. Some commentators worried about Hinckley going free following a verdict of not guilty by reason of insanity. *Time,* for example, reported that: "If they [the jurors] accept the contention of Hinckley's lawyers that he was legally insane, the would-be assassin will be confined to a mental hospital until a judge concludes that he is no longer a threat to himself or fellow citizens. Then he may go scot free."[51] Another version of this concern emphasized the limitations of psychiatric hospitals in determining the dangerousness ot their patients or of guaranteeing the continuing effect of treatment after release. So, on the same day that it reported John Hinckley's acquittal, the *New York Times* ran an article about an Alaska man who had been acquitted on the grounds of insanity and was later accused of murdering four teenagers while on a pass from the Alaska Psychiatric Institute. The parallel was drawn explicitly in a subhead which announced: "Similarity to Hinckley Case."[52] The overwhelming feeling that Hinckley should not be released was expressed as a contrast between law and psychiatry when the emphasis was placed on the ability of the law to keep its prisoners behind bars in contrast to the lack of guarantee of keeping mental patients in hospitals. The objection that the rights of the prisoners might be protected better than the rights of the mental patients was mentioned occasionally in the public discourse, but never stressed. An exchange which expressed many of these concerns occurred in an interview with President Reagan by Julius Hunter of KMOX-TV in St. Louis shortly after the Hinckley verdict was announced:

MR. HUNTER. Does it mean to you that a President is open game for anyone who can prove that he or she is insane?

THE PRESIDENT. Well, you don't have to limit it to a President. This defense is being used more and more in murder trials. And we've seen, I think, something long before this trial that led to the study of this question, with the incidence of people found innocent by reason of insanity put in a mental hospital and turned loose, you might say, virtually by the members of the same profession that had gone into court and proved they were insane, then a few months later telling them they were cured. And we've had the double tragedy of they go right out in the street and commit the same crime over again.[53]

The primary significance of these distinctions between law and psychiatry is that in all but one case they relied upon a conception of the law that denigrated psychiatry by contrast. The law was presumed to have both more fairness and greater certainty than psychiatry. Where the trial was seen as a reasoned process, psychiatry turned it into unreasonable spectacle. Where the focus of the law was on tangible acts, the focus of psychiatry was on the intangible mind. Where monetary influence was seen as a correctable fault in the legal system, it was portrayed as an essential weakness of psychiatric testimony. Where law could guarantee that its prisoners would remain in jail, psychiatry provided no guarantee that its patients would remain in the hospital. The only exception to this effect was the distinction based upon the goal of the process. When treatment was the primary concern, psychiatry became the superior discourse; when justice or safety was the primary concern, law became the superior discourse. One of the clearest conclusions to be drawn from examining the portrayal of the Hinckley trial is that the legal framework of crime-responsibility-punishment dominated the medical framework of sickness-treatment-recovery. The effect of such domination was to reinforce the status of the law at the expense of psychiatry.

Conclusion

Hinckley's acquittal caused nearly as great a furor as his crime. As this study demonstrates, however, the portrayal of the trial and the controversy that it engendered served to strengthen and to reinforce the assumptions behind primary institutions of social morality. The trial's dramatic display made Hinckley's seemingly senseless acts intelligible in a variety of socially sanctioned ways, and it allowed troublesome ambiguities in such fundamental, socially defined categories as morality, science, illness, and punishment to be aired publicly. The trial is significant both for our understanding of the discourses involved in the trial—particularly in the relationship between law and psychiatry—and for our understanding of the nature of popular trials.

LAW AND PSYCHIATRY.   Popular trials have consequences for the relative status of the discourses involved.[54] Since trials are conducted in the language of the law, the action is likely to be interpreted within the frame of legal understanding, and alternative or competing perspectives are likely to appear to be limited (like the Family) when there is no apparent conflict with the authority of the law, or to appear to be inept, inappropriate, or dangerous (like Psychiatry) when the clash of understanding and authority is manifest.

Psychiatry's claim to exercise power legitimately in cases involving accusations of criminal conduct rests on its claim to scientific knowledge. The potential status of psychiatry as a science, however, was disrupted by the form of the trial. The trial's adversarial structure made fundamental disagreements between the psychiatrists on the two sides of the case inevitable. These conflicts, in turn, brought psychiatry's claims to knowledge into question because, in the conventional wisdom, science is not science when there is no ground for the resolution of disputes. Law, on the other hand, was certified as capable of handling questions about the mind of the individual. It was not Hinckley's actions that were presented as being on trial in this case, but his mind. Although the legitimacy of legal consideration of such questions was challenged, the issue was resolved in favor of the legal standard of reason. In cases involving the mind, legal reasoning was declared superior to science, and, since the form of knowledge was thereby legitimized, so was the accompanying form of authority. It is significant that, while a variety of reforms of the insanity plea were considered, those that succeeded—shifting the burden of proof and altering the legal definition of insanity[55]— were tied directly to legal procedure. Reforms that would have diminished the scope of legal decision making (by, for example, restricting consideration of the mental state of the defendant only to his or her ability to form the requisite intent) were not enacted.

The effect of the Hinckley case on the relative distribution of power in cases involving socially disruptive behavior has been recognized by both law and psychiatry. Psychiatrists have argued that the form of the criminal trial—the sensationalism, the competition, the emphasis on winning—can distort psychiatric judgment and degrade the image of psychiatry. Several reports during the trial presented defenses from psychiatrists who realized that their profession was under attack.[56] Within a few months of the verdict, the American Psychiatric Association responded by adopting a proposal to restrict the insanity defense that would remove the volitional prong of the insanity test because, they stated, "many psychiatrists . . . believe that psychiatric information relevant to determining whether a defendant understood the nature of his act, and whether he appreciated its wrongfulness, is more reliable and *has a stronger scientific basis* than, for example, does psychiatric information relevant to whether a defendant was able to control his behavior" (emphasis added).[57] The National Commission on the Insanity Defense, commissioned by the National Mental Health Association, was led by similar considerations to recommend that psychiatrists not testify to "ultimate legal questions of criminal responsibility."[58] The belief that the trial process was responsible for the denigration of the status of psychiatry is expressed vividly in the analysis of the Hinckley trial by Alan Stone, a psychiatrist and professor at Harvard Law School: "If there is something flawed about the psychiatric testimony, it is the sense one gets of the psychiatrists getting caught up in and succumbing to the adversarial process. There is a kind of overstatement in their testimony as though they had taken on the responsibility of convincing the jury and outwitting the opposition. Clinical working hypotheses became scientific truths. Clinical possibilities became certainties. And as these truths and certainties from one side meet contradictory truths and certainties from the other side, one has the feeling that psychiatry's credibility hangs in the balance."[59] For most observers, the courtroom, not the clinic, was the focus of attention. So, in the dominant popular discourse, law was presented as being distorted by psychiatry. Within the profession, however, psychiatry was presented as being distorted by law.

Within the legal community, the diminution in the status of psychiatry has become evident in the apparent assumption that the influence of psychiatry needed to be further limited by the law. The reach of this assumption is reflected clearly in the Supreme Court case *Jones* v. *U.S.* (1983), in which the Court affirmed that a defendant found not guilty of shoplifting by reason of insanity could be confined to a mental hospital indefinitely on the grounds of his initial commitment. The court's reasoning depended in part on a generalized social judgment about the nature of insanity: "Nor can we say that it was unreasonable of Congress to determine that the insanity acquittal supports an inference of continuing mental illness. It comports with common sense to conclude that someone whose mental illness was sufficient to lead him to commit a criminal act is likely to remain ill and in need of treatment."[60] The decision has been the basis for much dissatisfaction. One commentator concluded that "the Court's statement that one can assess the validity of a presumption by simply applying common sense is contrary to both legal and medical learning," and that "it is not merely inaccurate, but disdainful of the psychiatric profession to presume, as the court implicitly did, that they still suffer from the mental illness [following treatment]."[61] What this critique fails to notice is that the basis of the presumed "common sense" is legal understanding. While the Court used the language of sickness and health, it also legitimated the assumption that psychiatry distorts legal judgment and that it is proper to treat legal decisions as the superior discourse.

The relative status of law and psychiatry also remains clear in the Hinckley case. Courts have repeatedly denied Hinckley's requests for leave from St. Elizabeth's Hospital despite the conclusion of his doctors that he constituted no danger and that it would be in his best interests to be able to make some visits to his family.[62]

Not all power over decisions about the mind was reserved for the law, of course. The attempt to impose a plea of "guilty but mentally ill" would have had even greater consequences for the distribution of power in favor of the law. In that case, the disposition of the defendant would have remained within the range of legal power even after the determination of insanity. This apparently appealing solution was rejected in all but a few jurisdictions because the ability to "treat" mental patients was seen as being both outside of the expertise of the law and beyond its legitimate power. The assumed limits on the law's legitimate expertise are evident in the widely used argument that defendants found guilty but mentally ill do not receive treatment for their mental illness.[63] The assumed limits of the law's legitimate power are evident in the argument that it would be inappropriate for the law to punish someone for his or her mental illness.[64]

POPULAR TRIALS, IDEOLOGY, AND CRITICISM.   One model for understanding popular trials has been the Chicago Seven trial, in which flamboyant defendants combine with a repressive judge over a divisive national issue to produce a challenge to the social order in general and to the legitimacy of the law in particular. This analysis of the Hinckley trial, however, suggests that the status of the law is likely to be reinforced by the forms of criticism and analysis active in most popular trials because trials are likely to produce discourses that reproduce the assumptions on which the legitimacy of the law is based. First, the pattern of beliefs that support the institution of Law will appear to be natural.[65] The form of presentation, after all, is not neutral. If the conflict among various sources or definitions of social power is presented through the trial, then the implicit assumptions of the trial's form—argument as the essence of reason, reason as the essence of legal procedure, responsibility as the focus for judgment, judgment as the focus for action—will be reinforced and the legitimacy of its assumptions will be presumed. It is only when the form itself is brought into the frame of understanding—which is what distinguishes trials like the Chicago Seven trial from trials like the Hinckley trial—that legal assumptions are held up to challenge directly in the discourse about the trial. If not, such assumptions become the context for interpretation, with potentially significant consequences for the relative distribution of power.

The trial of John Hinckley, Jr., illustrates vividly the ability of an accepted ideology to encompass criticism within such a context of interpretation. The objections to applying the insanity plea in this trial appeared as an attack on the institution of the law, but they emerged as a reinforcement of the legitimacy of legal knowledge and of the power of legal institutions. The presumption of the reasonableness of the law was sufficient to make the public's rejection of Hinckley's verdict appear unworthy of its ideals. The reforms that were initiated accepted the view that the law raises our society above our (otherwise natural) status as brutes intent on revenge. As long as the assumption prevailed, criticism served only to reinforce the status of the system being criticized and to diminish the status of those voicing the criticisms.[66] These considerations suggest that change can come, and perhaps can only come, when the agents of change are conscious of the barriers imposed by assumptions of knowledge and power and design their strategies accordingly.

Rhetorical analysis provides one means for discovering these unstated, implicit relationships. Such an inquiry requires adjusting some conventional assumptions about rhetorical discourse, however. We are accustomed to thinking about rhetoric in terms of the relationship between speakers and audiences. We look either at the strategies that speakers design to influence audiences or at the uses that audiences make of messages sent by speakers. And we are accustomed to thinking about trials in much the same way. It is evident that both participants and observers of popular trials have highly articulated sets of intentions. We look at the strategies that participants design to influence decision makers, or at the ways in which messages are used to make decisions or at the ways in which the trials are reported (or distorted) by other media to other audiences. This essay has shown how a trial's discourses flowed through a structure of meanings that was independent of intentions, independent, in fact, of instantiation in any particular expression or incident or action. It is certainly true that the Hinckley trial was about guilt or innocence and that it was about the insanity plea. In an important sense, however, the Hinckley trial was really about the way in which society understands action, the way in which knowledge is determined and legitimated, and the way in which comprehensive power relations are challenged and defended.

The focus on the subject that is fundamental to much of legal and rhetorical analysis can hide other sources of influence. Because they display discourses in action and motivate public involvement, popular trials provide an especially revealing focus for examining implicit struggles over power and knowledge. Trials make dramas of our social texts.

6

The Claus von Bulow Retrial
Lights, Camera, Genre?

Susan J. Drucker and Janice Platt Hunold

She was the beautiful, rather shy young heiress whose marriage to an Austrian prince resulted in two beautiful children and a divorce; she was Martha (Sunny) Crawford von Auersperg. He was Claus Cecil Borberg, the Danish son of a father who was a playwright and drama critic and of a mother who was a member of the Bulow family related to the distinguished German von Bulows; he officially changed his name to von Bulow.

He graduated from Cambridge with a law degree at the age of nineteen—the first person ever to have done so. He had to wait two years until he could enter the bar. He was tall, handsome, intelligent, well mannered and a success at drawing room parties in England. He gained the reputation of being a bachelor without much money who maneuvered himself into the highest social echelons.

When she was ready to return to her life in America, Claus von Bulow was the right person to fit into Fifth Avenue and Newport society. Twelve years later, in December of 1979, Sunny von Bulow slipped into a coma but was revived. One year after that she again collapsed into a now irreversible coma. She is curled in the fetal position, her once blonde hair completely gray; there is a tube implanted in her throat and a feeding tube in her mouth. Claus von Bulow has been tried twice for the attempted murder of his wife.[1]

For most Americans, there is little distinction between a trial and its portrayal in the media. Public knowledge of the law comes through the media in general, and now increasingly through television as cameras are being admitted to an ever increasing number of courtrooms throughout the country. As television is the medium providing much of our information about the legal system and the societal conflicts it seeks to adjudicate, we should ask this: Does televising affect the information itself and the public's understanding of that information? This exploratory essay examines the conventions of production, the entertainment environment enveloping televised trials, and the way in which they are processed by the television audience. We will consider how television may have molded understanding and misunderstanding of the von Bulow retrial itself, and in turn, how the coverage of this particular trial may have shaped the public's comprehension of the legal system and society in general. Although our analyses of both the methods of production and the possibilities for audience interpretation are admittedly preliminary, we hope to outline an approach to the study of televised popular trials that can raise and generally answer key questions regarding their meaning and effect.

Genre analysis provides the critical tools for this examination of the ways in which television can shape popular understanding of judicial events. Our aim when dealing with televised trials is to isolate the dominant influence upon audience apprehension of the televised trial. Do the conventions of the televised trial come more from "the trial" itself or from its production as a television program? Is the televised trial, by the sheer power of the television medium, being forced into popular daytime programming genres, or is the televised trial developing its own generic characteristics? Will a genre of televised trials affect public knowledge about the law and public interest in the trial system?

The retrial of Claus von Bulow provides an appropriate arena for the examination of the relationship between the media and popularized trials. We will analyze this trial as a mediated communicative event, identify its generic composition, and discuss its implications for perceptions of the legal system and constitutionally guaranteed rights to a fair trial.

The Popular Significance of the von Bulow Retrial

This case has everything, declared the prosecutor. It has money, sex, drugs; it has Newport, New York and Europe; it has nobility; it has maids, butlers, a gardener. Clarendon Court [the mansion where the critical events took place] has a big gate. Most people can't see inside. This case is where the little man has a chance to glimpse inside and see how the rich live.[2]

Public knowledge of trials such as von Bulow's cannot be analyzed fully without considering the amount of media coverage those trials receive. From the occurrence of the coma that occasioned the charges through the second verdict and well beyond, this was a story which captured media attention and the public imagination. Harvard Law Professor Alan Dershowitz, one of von Bulow's attorneys, said, "the American trial has always been an entertainment,"[3] and the von Bulow retrial was no exception. The headlines screamed "Puccio: The Guilt Rests with Sunny,"[4] "Stepchildren Dare Claus to Take Stand"[5] and "Hottest Ticket in Town."[6] The cover of *People Magazine* called it "A Shattered Family";[7] *Vanity Fair* featured Claus von Bulow's "Fatal Charm."[8] There was continuing comprehensive coverage in *Newsweek* and *Time*. Daily coverage on national network and local news reflected the presence of more than two hundred media people.[9] Cable News Network (CNN) broadcast the proceedings. There were nationally televised interviews. The stepchildren, Alex and Ala, appeared on *60 Minutes* to label von Bulow a liar.[10] The defendant himself told Barbara Walters on ABC's *20/20* that he loved his wife.[11] A heated debate on ABC's *Nightline* addressed the contention that "money available on both sides may have distorted justice."[12] The books followed: *The von Bulow Affair* by William Wright resulted in a stinging rebuttal in Alan Dershowitz's *Reversal of Fortune*.[13]

Distinct and recurring themes developed in the trial and media coverage; these themes differed slightly to fit the situation. One of the major themes was money. There were tales of riches and the power of money. In the courtroom the spotlight was on Sunny's excesses, from money to medication, but the media coverage accentuated the notion that a rich person on trial is very different from an ordinary person on trial. "The powerful defense team assembled by von Bulow . . . so outshone the prosecution that the trial often seemed like a football game between the New York Jets and Providence High." Von Bulow even hired his own court stenographer finding that the court-appointed one couldn't produce quickly enough.[14] The net worth of all involved was reported repeatedly; Sunny weighed in at $100 million,[15] while von Bulow, living off the interest on a trust established by his wife, would receive $14 million, the Newport mansion, and the Fifth Avenue apartment upon his wife's death. The cost of the defense generated much conjecture. There was speculation that the second defense cost von Bulow between $700,000 and $1 million.[16] Not to be overlooked is the fact that money may have been responsible for the case having been investigated and pursued in the first place. The stepchildren hired an attorney and private investigator who conducted all of the preliminary investigations which were handed over to the police. It was only after this private expenditure of $100,000 that the Rhode Island police began to look into this case.[17]

Did the state or the power of money investigate and prosecute this criminal defendant? Did the defendant or the power of money establish his innocence? This trial could not only give the "little man" a glimpse at the rich, but also verify that he had the power of judgment over the rich. Equality under the law would mean that an aristocrat would be judged by people he would rarely encounter in his stratified world.[18] The popular significance of the von Bulow case is, in part, from the public's perception that the verdict could be the result of either justice or money.

Other stories involved themes of loyalty and betrayal. Loyal children continued a crusade to seek justice and speak for their mother who could no longer speak for herself. A loyal daughter sacrificed a fortune—a $25-million inheritance revoked by her maternal grandmother—and the love of her half brother and sister for her unjustly accused father. A loyal German maid who devoted her existence to "her lady," a loyal lover who masterminded the defense were all dramatis personae of the trial. Loyalty was balanced by the betrayal of Sunny by Claus, of Claus by his mistress, Alexandra Isles, who testified against him, of Alexandra by Claus, and of Claus by his stepchildren.

Whatever the story being told, however, their cumulative effect was to make von Bulow a celebrity. Daniel Boorstin argues that the media celebrity has replaced traditional American heroes, much to the detriment of societal values.[19] The heroes of a culture are a function of cultural priorities and values.[20] The celebrity is a person who is known for being well known. The celebrity does not have to be a great person or even very good, but he or she must be seen, heard, or referred to regularly. The socially prominent characters in the von Bulow case did not become well known until the media coverage of the trial and retrial.[21] Once in the light, however, von Bulow played his part supremely: "All von Bulow has to do is walk past the line of trial watchers and the hallway crackles with excitement. He is tall as a lodgepole pine and just as stately. . . . With such style, no wonder von Bulow has cultivated a coterie that is absolutely convinced of his innocence."[22] We have asserted elsewhere that the shift from hero to celebrity is related to the form of information made available through the dominant medium of communication.[23] Since it is primarily the filmic/electronic media that creates and maintains the celebrity hero of today, this essay focuses on that coverage and particularly on the gavel-to-gavel coverage by Cable News Network.[24]

The Trial as Mediated Communicative Event

Human behavior may be viewed as a rhetorical act when the act creates a message designed to influence an audience on a given issue to achieve a particular end.[25] As behavior is patterned rhetorically it articulates social values which can link speakers to audiences. The von Bulow trial contained three distinct messages concerning values. The first value, "justice," was embodied in the judicial procedures of the courtroom. In a trial the adversarial forum is used to adjudicate and resolve competing interests; however, the rules and procedures and the proscribed or litigable issues may be said to have been designed not solely for purposes of judicial resolution. They also function as a means of informing the populace that the trial system provides a fair and orderly mechanism which seeks the truth and promotes the opportunity for fair and just resolution of conflicts. For example, the jury and audience always are guaranteed two stories of what happened. The defense argued that von Bulow may have cheated on his wife, but "monstrous" charges of attempted murder were drummed up by a hostile stepson and servant and fueled by a scorned mistress.[26] The prosecution maintained that a cold-blooded, premeditated act was committed to rid himself of his wife without ridding himself of her fortune. Whatever the outcome, the public sees a balanced proceeding.

"Justice is as much a process as a result."[27] The value of justice was underscored by the fact that this was a retrial of Claus von Bulow. Media coverage during the second trial was not merely coverage identical to that given the initial trial phase of this or other cases. Media reports gave blow-by-blow comparisons of testimony, evidence and stars of the first and second trials. The media drew inferences from these comparisons. Both maid Maria Schrallhamer's edited version of events in the second trial and her delivery of her testimony were subjects of debate in the press.[28] The absence of the banker's testimony providing financial motive and witnesses lost due to death in the intervening years, were also carefully noted.[29] Evidence suppressed at the first trial and admitted at the second was commented on by legal experts.[30] Perhaps the most pervasive and consistent reminder that this was a retrial was provided by the cable coverage. CNN—with its ever present graphic superimposed on the screen: "The Claus von Bulow Retrial"—[31] freely injected videotaped excerpts from the first trial into their coverage. In sum, the retrial legitimated the appeals process. Although some decried the reversal of the original conviction as based on a mere technicality, others applauded the inherent merit of a system that contained the mechanism for resolving doubt in favor of the accused after a verdict had been rendered.[32] This message obviously legitimates the legal system even as it might also be rationalizing the interests of the defense.

We can recognize that social values are expressed by procedures and that "like certain specific substantive institutions, procedural institutions are not just means to an end. They are the concrete expressions of significant moral relations, and as such they have a value which is not adequately understood by analyzing them simply in terms of their consequences."[33] The elements that marked this institutionalized opportunity for justice were present regardless of the verdict rendered. The von Bulow trial, appeal, and retrial—all carrying high-intensity media coverage—were concrete expressions of the significance of justice in relation to the institution of the law.

The selection of cases for trial and for media coverage also indicates a second class of values: the "golden rules" for personal conduct. Actions that violate the rules for interaction deemed significant by a society garner legislative and judicial attention. The media by their choice and treatment of subjects select, reflect, or reinforce such values. The von Bulow case, having been selected for scrutiny twice by both the legal system and popular press, became a study in these values. Fidelity in marriage and outside of marriage, loyalty and betrayal within a family and beyond family boundaries, the lengths one might go for love or love of the "good life," and the manner in which wealth corrupts to destroy families were all examined within the von Bulow retrial. Generally, the courts deal with these acts in order to determine if societal norms formalized in law have been violated. The media magnify these acts in order to criticize and reaffirm values. Claus von Bulow was a man charged with both criminalized behavior and conduct that offended the common morality. The legal system found von Bulow was not guilty of criminal acts; a large segment of public opinion found him guilty of moral transgressions.[34]

The third, and most transparent value is inherent in the media: entertainment. A trial is inherently dramatic; it is filled with the tension produced when adversaries meet. When a trial is televised it no longer operates within the restraints imposed by the technology of the law alone. When a trial is televised, the restraints imposed by the technology of the electronic medium shape the broadcast and impose the values of entertainment upon the audience. "Audiences have come to expect [that] the media technology will produce entertainment, and every type of medium has done exactly that."[35] The norms of entertainment control the electronic media in particular. Even a trial such as the von Bulow retrial, which received gavel-to-gavel coverage, combines information with entertainment.

As our focus is on the power of television to affect public perception and use of information about the legal system, it is the gavel-to-gavel televised trial coverage we wish to examine more fully. Although television may appear to be a neutral medium, in actuality it is not. The "realistic illusion," the idea that the camera simply records reality, is reinforced by the sense of immediacy which television adds, the sense of coverage of news events as they happen.[36] After all, Cable News Network presented the trial daily, as if it were a realistic portrayal of a legal landmark in the making. The coverage appeared to be a presentation of news about a newsworthy event. CNN's stated intent is to provide for the public's right to know, provide for public education, and continue to look for "newsworthy" trials they believe to be of "public interest."[37] But why was the von Bulow retrial newsworthy? It was the final stage of a case that already had been popularized by vast media coverage. We believe the intensive coverage of this final stage was motivated by the need for closure of the popularized story rather than interest in the judicial resolution.

Television Grammar and Genre

Rhetorical forms that establish genres are stylistic and substantive responses to perceived (situational) demands.[38] These forms provide the means through which we may come to understand how a rhetorical act works to achieve its end. A genre analysis involves isolating typical recurring elements and identifying a constellation of these that may appear in more than one genre. It is the recognizable characteristic groupings of these typical forms that produce a unique genre.[39]

Genres found in television include situation comedy, nightly news programs, daytime soap operas, dramatic prime-time programs, game shows, and talk shows. Daytime programming is dominated by talk shows, soap operas, and game shows. All of these genres are recognizably distinct in structure and content, but are not exclusively confined to their own characteristics. For example, the extreme close up, previously seen chiefly in soap operas, has "crossed over" to news programs. Factual events, such as Oliver North's testimony before Congress about his involvement in the Iran-Contra affair, will appear in fictional dramas such as *Cagney & Lacey*.[40] Docudramas, a popular genre, further blur the conventional distinctions among factual and fictional forms. All genres share televisual techniques but each composes its own distinct blend of visual, auditory, and substantive or content characteristics by which the audience recognizes it.

By using genre as a basis for comparison, we sought to determine whether the television coverage emanating from the von Bulow courtroom showed characteristics of one or all of the major daytime genres: talk show, soap opera, game show. We have shown previously that nonfictional programs or programs labeled as "news" assume structural and aesthetic features of genres other than "news."[41] Other studies have contended that television structure may influence perceived content of these programs.[42] These studies explain that while the content of "news" programs remains nonfictional, the televised images assume "fictional" structures. Structure is capable of dominating content. The comparison between *The Von Bulow Retrial* (carried on the Cable News Network) and these major genres might also reveal a similar transformation away from news to popular daytime programming structure.

Studies by Althiede and Snow[43] and Tannenbaum[44] have shown that the sheer appearance of a program on the television screen forces the content to be perceived as "entertainment," regardless of structure. If a presidential debate or a newscast may be regarded as entertainment, then what happens to the trial? If the trial is overpowered by the form and function of television, perception of trials may be affected by the messages provided by diverse genres.

To compare televised trial coverage of the von Bulow retrial with established genres, we must first explore the recurring elements of the competing programming, which was comprised of the three major daytime genres.[45]

TALK SHOW: The major substantive features were found to include themes that ranged from sex to the political system, generally presented as attempts to reveal information and truth. The ever present host appears worldly and well informed and capable of controlling guests and the direction of the proceedings. Talk shows rely on "celebrities" who appear to plug their next project or promote themselves.

Talk shows, or talk show-like segments, appear at all times during the broadcast day. "Informational" talk shows appear in early weekday mornings, Sunday mornings, or late afternoons, such as morning network "news" programs, *Meet the Press*, or affiliates' late afternoon news shows. "Entertaining" talk shows appear during the broadcast day (*The Oprah Winfrey Show*) and late at night (*The Tonight Show*). One cost-cutting feature for all talk shows is the location, which is within the confines of a television studio. Expensive location shots are not used beyond openings or closings.

The major structural features include a variety of shot sizes, with particular use of two-shots and chest shots. There is limited shot variety. Cuts are the predominant shot transitional device and camera movement is characteristically composed of limited slow zooms. The pacing is moderate, and the tension is low, as the camera angle is straight on.

DAYTIME SOAP OPERA: The substantive features of daytime soap operas are themes that deal with unresolved conflicts over sex, romance, money, drugs, diseases, homicides, and familial relationships. There are core characters who sustain the moral tone of the program and archetypal female heroines who are benevolent mothers, and women faced with rivals. Frequently males are portrayed as villains or anti-heroes.[46] Storylines are dominated by well-groomed, high-fashion, socially prominent characters. Soap operas are composed of an indefinitely expandable middle with no end.[47] Continuous stories are primarily advanced by dialogue dealing with several simultaneous plots within the context of a sometimes clandestine portrayal of interpersonal relationships.[48] The tone is serious and somber; the time frame is slow moving.

When we come to the major structural features of the daytime soap opera we find that shot size is marked by the characteristic extreme close-up and large-shot variety. Shot transitions are generally cuts, and limited quick zooms are the major camera movement. Pacing is moderate and, as with the talk show, tension is low.

Daytime soap operas have been defined by the hour and frequency of broadcast, low production costs, and the predominantly adult female audience it attracts.[49] Porter notes that soap opera time is fantasy time in an active day. The experience of watching involves a combination of sympathy and distance.[50] Soap operas typically air during the afternoon hours, traditionally 12 noon to 4 P.M., Eastern Standard Time. The settings required are traditionally not as sophisticated or involved as prime-time dramas, thus lowering the cost of production. In addition, like the talk show, the locations are interiors, with infrequent expensive location settings.

The similarities between the Talk Show and the Daytime Soap Opera are based on the reliance on "conversation" or dialogue as their "action." While other genres, such as the prime-time detective story or the situation comedy, may include more physical actions with little or no dialogue, the Talk Show and Soap Opera contain very infrequent use of such scenes. Therefore, the use of dialogue as the main action of a program dictates the structural and aesthetic grammar of these genres. The use of multi-camera techniques, the location of shooting (usually inside on a sound stage), and the action of scripted or non-scripted dialogue all determine the type of structure enforced by the directors.

GAME SHOW: The substantive elements of the game show are characterized by the animation of the studio audience and the enthusiasm of the contestants. The gracious host provides information concerning ritualized rules and time constraints. There may or may not be celebrity panelists, but there are always winners and losers and always friendly opposition.

The unique structural features of this genre include long and medium shot sizes with great shot variety. Special-effects wipes and cuts serve as transitional devices, while frequent snap zooms add to the quick pace of these shows.

The action of this genre, based on the rules and procedures of the game that is afoot, dictate the director's decisions. While the game is unfolded through verbal instructions or clues, the contestants and panelists may also be involved in more physical actions, such as spinning wheels or pounding on a buzzer. The more complex "action" requires a more complex mixture of structural and aesthetic features. Game shows are aired in the morning, afternoon, and prime access or fringe time. They are low budget productions since contestant winnings do not exceed prizes furnished by sponsors. Permanent studio sets also cut costs.

In all of these genres, there are no startling changes in format, structure, or content. The use of graphics, music, plot changes, and use of characters, both fictional and factual, are combined to satisfy the audience. This continuity in production elements provides a sense of comfort on the part of the audience, which has come to expect certain forms and contexts on television for each genre.

The method used to study the television coverage of the von Bulow retrial involved observation of the "video transcript" of the trial from the CNN satellite coverage for the week of 13 May 1985. The major substantive features emphasized the contest or adversarial format of the proceedings and the outcomes of victory and the discovery of truth and justice. The plot or storyline of the trial included the elements of romance, adultery, money, drugs, sex, disease, and familial relationships. The set included recurring symbols of the courtroom: flags, defense and prosecution tables facing the elevated judge's bench, uniformed officers of the court, the select occupants of the jury box set off from the rest of the courtroom personnel, the witness stand upon which the spotlight was trained. All participants were in uniform, ranging from the actual uniform of the bailiff to the judge's robe to the conservative attire of the attorneys, court stenographers, and witnesses.

The image of the judge was that of an authority figure reigning and in control, able to keep events flowing smoothly and capable of making many quick decisions. Attorneys appeared knowledgeable, calm, unflappable, and in control of witnesses and proceedings. The image of witnesses was that of individuals with particular expertise and worthy of respect even while they were put on the spot. The camera was often trained on the defendant, eloquent in his silence.

The tone of the proceedings was somber, formal, ritualized, and took place in a time frame that was "real time" rather than "television time." In this case, real time was very slow moving although the atmosphere of the set was peopled, hectic, and busy. There were always several activities going on at once and court personnel in constant motion.

We also sought to establish major structural features of this television production. We found that shot sizes ranged from extreme close ups to medium long shots. Shot transitions were made through camera zooms that were limited in number and quick. The trial coverage was characterized by slow pacing and low tension. As with other popular daytime genres, the axis movement of "characters" across the screen was predominantly from side-to-side, creating low depth or visual interest.

In many instances, the coverage of the retrial differed dramatically from popular genres. This is due in large part to restraints on the production technology allowed into the courtroom. While the content and locations of daytime genres are designed for televising, the courtroom does not provide the same freedom or aesthetic quality as does the sound stage. The use of a single camera per feed inhibits the camera operator's choices for shot sizes. Natural lighting, natural sound (with voiceover play-by-play and updates periodically), and lack of transitional devices dictated the structure.

Although the structure was influenced by the accessibility to technology, the resulting video transcript did reveal that this television programming contained some structural elements similar to those found in popular daytime genres. For example, the Soap Opera's extreme close ups and quick zooms appeared. As with any Talk Show guest, when the witness's speech became too lengthy, the courtroom camera operator would zoom in on a jury member or courtroom audience member for a reaction shot.

Within the larger schema of televising, the trial was interrupted periodically for breaks, consisting of commercials and news updates from the CNN desk, or for recesses called by Judge Grande. Therefore, both in detail (shot size) and in program flow (commercial breaks) the retrial resembled other daytime programming. Yet, the technological provisions for coverage resulted in footage with a rather amateurish appearance. It resembled a home movie more than a professional television program.

Substantive elements resembled selected aspects of all three genres we have chosen for comparison. Like the Talk Show and the Game Show, there was the host, the judge who was in control of the proceedings. Like the Talk Show, there were attempts to reveal information and truth through the medium of guest witnesses. Like the Game Show, there were ritualized rules, winners and losers. The themes may be seen as most similar to those found in Daytime Soap Opera. The characters included Sunny as the archetypal female heroine, Alexandra Isles as the rival. Claus himself was either villain or victim depending upon which attorney wrote the script. The omnipresent defendant was unparalleled in other genres.

In general, the trial appeared to contain a cross section of genre characteristics. The structure and cutting format resembled that of the Talk Show, with its reliance on showing the speaker and of following the dialogue. The content, in this trial particularly, seemed to resemble a Soap Opera. However, it must be stressed that although the televised von Bulow trial contained some genre attributes, the trial formed its own genre due to the technological restraints imposed by the legal system. Therefore, it would appear that in both content and form the televised trial program cannot be completely placed into any of the existing genres examined. Trials seem to have a generic resilience; they occupy a distinct genre. Typical elements found within diverse extant genres are brought together to form a new and unique grouping of recurring elements—a new genre. Apparently, this new genre is restrained chiefly by technological rather than aesthetic or structural considerations.

Implications for Knowledge about Trials

Televised trials adapt to the conventions of the television medium and its organizations. The institutional position of stations carrying trials is that they seek to produce "good television." The production staff and crew may work on news, sporting events, soap operas, and game shows. Staffing decisions are based on availability of crew members rather than on a philosophical view of the event being televised. From this perspective it may be seen that the information being disseminated about the law and the trial system may be shaped by the requirements of television production.

Since audiences see television primarily as a form of entertainment, they process reports of the real world as entertainment. It is now generally agreed that even the presentation of reality on television has taken on certain properties of television's entertainment format and style.[51] Television creates its own reality for all of the programs it presents to the viewing audience. The television audience has come to expect entertainment and the substantive and structural features of extant genres help fulfill that expectation. We suggest that the increasing coverage of trials emanating from cameras placed in courtrooms has been forced by the sheer power of television to become another type of television program—that of the newly emerging televised trial genre. A popular interest can be accounted for easily by both the informational and the entertainment elements of the productions. The selection of cases to be covered, the themes, stock characters, and dramatic confrontational nature of the substantive features of the genre attract viewers while focusing attention on certain aspects of the trial process. The use of structural features such as the extreme close up and camera zooms heighten drama and action. These generic elements provide increased exposure to information about the trial system and might affect the processing of that information. Our current research is attempting to document the effect of structural generic features on perceptions of guilt or innocence, and perceptions of credibility.[52]

Conclusion

In form, in substance, and by audience perception, the televising of actual trials might be affecting not only the amount of information being disseminated about a particular trial and the legal system, but the way in which that information is being processed and used. The televising of the Claus von Bulow retrial may have shaped public understanding of this trial in a number of ways.

The extensive television coverage brought Claus rather than "the defendant" into homes each day. Television personalizes whenever it can by attaching concepts to individuals. According to John Langer, " 'Good television' is television that embodies and articulates a world of 'personalities' who thoroughly penetrate and organize its viewing agendas, or enter television by being on those agendas."[53] Von Bulow appeared on screen every day; he became the central persona of the program. As with other television shows, the title of the program took its name from its leading character. "Television appears to have benefited Von Bulow in [a] . . . subtle way. It is much easier to impute heinous crimes to anonymous names in the newspapers than to people known personally. To an extent, someone seen regularly on television becomes 'known.' This would be particularly true of one seen—not glowering for a mug shot or dashing into court with a coat over his head—but turning up calmly in court each day, reserved, well dressed."[54]

Sunny von Bulow would normally be characterized as the victim, the anticipated recipient of public sympathy. Her children characterize her as a non-person because she is lying in a deep coma,[55] but Sunny von Bulow became a non-person for the viewing audience when she did not appear on screen "live from Providence on the Claus von Bulow Retrial." Claus, familiar through his constant presence on the small screen, garners sympathy. We all saw "his eyes darting again and again to the door from which the jury would emerge . . . tears . . . real emotion."[56] The form of the programming promotes the illusion of intimacy. Television suggests a reduction of distance between itself and the viewer, television personalities and viewers share a common universe and experience.[57] The television representation may have strengthened the appeal of the defense strategy, which followed the old principle of trying the victim.

This emphasis upon character and the illusion of intimacy both are reinforced by the ritualized regularity of television. Like the world, television never stops, it is more or less continuous.[58] As the trial wore on day after day, viewers would become impressed by the palpable constancy of von Bulow's character. Like the ever-present talk show host, his role never changed. Witnesses could come and go, attorneys and the judge would move in and out of the spotlight, but Claus's role, his presence, was unchanged. While critics called for the defendant to take the stand,[59] and his attorneys reminded all that he need not present his account to the jury, von Bulow's televised performance in the courtroom did address the popular audience.

Moreover, von Bulow "groupies" emerged,[60] suggesting the trial constructed what might be a new cultural relationship, that of the celebrity and fan.[61] This represents a new "media relationship" linked by the dominant electronic mode of communication. This relationship is distinguished from that of hero/worshiper, which has been denuded by the entire context of scientific and economic information on all levels of mass mediated perception. By contrast, although von Bulow's deed is not heroic, his "well-knownness" fosters a new celebrity/fan relationship with viewers. Once celebrity is conferred, the defendant's deeds need not be consistent with virtuous aspirations.

Television coverage of the von Bulow retrial may have shaped public understanding of significant institutions and ideals well beyond the case at hand. The audience sees the familiar soap opera themes of the power of money and the destruction of a family. A member of the victorious defense team informed the viewing audience that "the tragedy of American justice today is that there are thousands of innocent people languishing in prison for failure to launch an adequate defense. It costs a lot of money to get the experts."[62] Whereas the conviction of the first trial might well have left the viewing audience with the impression that the meek may inherit the justice system, in the retrial, we see the mighty winning on appeal. The audience could be left with the nagging doubt that while the innocent languish in their cells, the guilty luxuriate in their freedom.

Gerbner argued that televised trials that emphasize the lurid and sensational may strengthen the existing negative impressions about crime and justice shaped by television entertainment programming.[63] This may be particularly true when these trials are viewed as another entertainment genre within the continuous daily television schedule. Even before the television coverage of the trial, the von Bulow story simultaneously went through a legal process and a process of popularization. Both the multi-media process of popularization and its subordinate process of televising the retrial affected viewer perception of the case and the people and issues within it. The power of television and television genre as we enter an era of "mediated law" may prove to be more powerful than historically rooted due process guarantees of the Fifth and Fourteenth Amendments to the Federal Constitution. We must investigate the power of the television medium to alter traditional notions of guilt or innocence.

This essay has examined the televised coverage of the retrial of Claus von Bulow to consider both the societal implications of trials as newly televised events and the implications for the rights of individuals within the trial process. We have focused on genre as it helps determine audience expectations. We have established that specific substantive and structural elements have already recurred in televised trials so as to have established a distinct genre, which was found to be a compilation of its own unique characteristics and of characteristics from existing genres such as the Talk Show, Game Show, and Soap Opera. Once a genre is established, that genre imposes constraints upon future televised events within the genre. Audience expectations have been established, and any televised trial that deviates from the established expectations might become less appealing. Only additional research will allow us to understand the manner and extent of this process.

The Saga of Roger Hedgecock
A Case Study in Trial by Local Media

Larry A. Williamson

If you were home this afternoon and watched live coverage of Judge Todd's courtroom, you know there was very little doubt as to what you were seeing. It was not Divorce Court and not the People's Court, it was very, very real! Make no mistake about it, T.V. can at times blur the lines which should so clearly separate the two. This was not one of those days. Watching Roger Hedgecock today was like watching the Watergate hearings nearly a decade ago. We cannot take our eyes from it because we are seeing the trappings of power so completely stripped away.[1]—Loren Nancarrow, Evening Anchor, Ch. 8 News, CBS, San Diego

I argue that the organizational, practical, and other mundane features of newswork promote a way of looking at events which fundamentally distorts them.—David Altheide, *Creating Reality*

For "two years, six months, and seventeen days," Roger Hedgecock was mayor of "America's finest city."[2] Half of Hedgecock's tenure was spent fighting the most widely publicized, long-lived, and in many ways convoluted legal battle in San Diego history. The actual litigation was made up of the original trial, a drawn-out retrial, and a subsequent appeal for mistrial, all of which received near-obsessive media attention. Indeed, the legal saga of Roger Hedgecock possessed all the requisite ingredients for a media drama: a compelling cast of local power brokers, political graft, suspense, big money, and intrigue. As one local television anchor put it, the Hedgecock trials were a "classic story for a reporter, trouble at city hall with the mayor in the heart of it all."[3]

Hedgecock's drawn-out legal battle acts as the backdrop for this case study of trial-by-media. And though his trials are legally, politically, and for some San Diegans, even culturally significant, I will examine them as examples of the role that the media can play in shaping public perceptions of legality. We shall see how the local media's coverage of the trials painted a misrepresentative mosaic of scenes, images, and characterizations which, for most San Diegans, constituted the *real* trials.

I will argue that the media's version of the Hedgecock trials was the product of an identifiable set of recurrent dramatic conventions— institutional conventions of production molded more by commercial necessity than ideological or political bias. Identification of these conventions of production serves as the basis for my argument that the media's coverage of the trials was shaped more by drama than their own espoused standards of balance and objectivity. To help support this argument I will also examine the local media's attempts to rationalize their role in affecting public perceptions of the trials—a peculiarly self-conscious attempt to critique themselves that offers a different kind of insight into their production biases.

Although one could argue that media coverage of trials is shaped by the same conventions of production that pervade all news reporting, in the case of trial coverage two dimensions of this production bias make it uniquely significant: (1) For most Americans, media representations of litigation are the only referents they have for constructing their understanding of the legal process. And, since every citizen is a potential juror, media portrayals of the legal system can have either immediate or latent effects on juror objectivity. (2) Legal communication is rule-governed. Unlike other "newsworthy" events, it is a highly structured form of rhetorical activity that does not lend itself to the media's dramatic reduction. Such reduction is particularly problematic when one considers that courtroom protocols, unlike other types of discourse, are uniquely contextual— they are constituted by forms and rules of legal argument that defy acontextual recreation on the front page or in a lead story on the evening news. It is for these reasons that mediated litigation is at least worthy of close critical attention and ethical scrutiny.

Background

Hedgecock is a young, intelligent, sometimes abrasive yuppie. He surfs, plays in a rock band, supports ecology, and publicly derides any plans that would tend to "Los Angelize" San Diego. He was/is one of the most popular, high-profile figures in the local political arena. Pending appeal on his current indictment, he holds a position as political analyst for a local television station and hosts a daily radio talk show where he adamantly pursues any and all local controversies. He has established a reputation as an opinionated, hard-hitting opponent.

On 19 September 1984 Mayor Hedgecock was indicted on fourteen counts of perjury and one count of conspiracy. The key co-defendant in the indictment was J. David Dominelli—a prominent local financier, whose own legal problems included charges that he employed an elaborate ponzi scheme to bilk local investors of some $51,000,000. Also named in the indictment was Nancy Hoover—ex-mayor of Del Mar, an exclusive beach community, whose relationship with Dominelli was stylized to the point that the local media reduced her to descriptors like "live-in lover, girlfriend," etc.[4] The third co-defendant was Tom Sheppard—head of a supposedly "false front" political consulting firm. The indictment alleged that the mayor conspired with the co-defendants in establishing Sheppard's firm, a move that the prosecution claimed made it possible for Dominelli and Hoover to "funnel" some $350,000 into Hedgecock's campaign coffers.[5] This practice violated a $250 ceiling imposed on corporate contributions to candidates.[6] In addition to this criminal indictment, the California Fair Political Practices Commission filed suit against all the defendants for $1.2 million, to date the largest such political suit in California history.

Beyond the indictments were the widely publicized charges and countercharges issued by Hedgecock and his opponents. First, and perhaps most relevant, was the "vendetta" theme. According to Hedgecock, the indictments were the end product of an eight-year-old feud between himself and the district attorney, Edwin Miller. He claimed that Miller had been trying to ruin him since the beginning of Hedgecock's tenure as county supervisor in 1976.[7] By 1984 Hedgecock had repeatedly offered his vendetta argument in public. Only by this time the "opposition" included a past political foe, Maureen O'Connor (his successor after his resignation from the mayor's office), and Copley Press, the publisher of the two most prominent newspapers in town. The vendetta theme reached its zenith when Hedgecock filed a libel suit against Copley for, allegedly, carrying on a "blatant political campaign against him." The suit claimed that the paper "lied" and "twisted" everything about his involvement with Dominelli and Hoover.[8] Hedgecock's anger over the story is captured in this quotation which, ironically, ran in the same paper he was suing: "I think the San Diego Union every day for the last year has convicted me in their news pages as well as editorial pages, they have created a climate of conviction through the use of the big lie technique to defeat me at the polls, which was unsuccessful, and to produce a conviction in this case."[9] The suit stemmed from a 20 April 1984 story linking him to some "$400,000 in unexplained funds controlled by Hedgecock, which allegedly came from J. David & Co. through the mayor's friend Nancy Hoover."[10] Late in July 1984 the *Union* printed a front page retraction of the story.

In the face of some undeniably bad press, Hedgecock still managed to defeat the opposition by a 16 percent margin in the 1984 mayoral campaign—a feat that many thought was impossible in the wake of the indictment. Through December and into January the trial continued to dominate the local media. On 13 February 1985 a hung jury resulted in the declaration of a mistrial. As the *Union* put it, "one lone holdout juror," Leon Crowder—"a city sanitation worker"—was solely responsible. The district attorney's office immediately scheduled a retrial, which began 31 July 1985. At this juncture one would expect the mayor to request a change of venue since by the summer of 1985 San Diego was saturated with coverage of the trial. Yet Hedgecock was still mayor and he still had his political credibility to worry about, in spite of the fact that he was facing criminal indictment. Thus, a request for change of venue could have been perceived by his constituents as a de facto lack of faith in their judgment. And since Hedgecock wanted desperately to remain in office, he decided not to request the change. We can only conclude that this decision to lay it all on the line was grounded in the belief that his continued political popularity would somehow compensate for his legal dilemma.

On 29 September the prosecution rested its second case against Mayor Hedgecock. They had called sixty-two witnesses and added new evidence to the reams of detailed documents already filed in the first case. The defense, on the other hand, surprised the entire city by resting its case without calling a single witness of its own—a ploy that was questioned by many. On 9 October the jury found Hedgecock guilty of thirteen counts of perjury. Two days later the mayor announced his decision to resign as of 18 October.

The long awaited verdict brought the closure necessary for the local media to begin to write Hedgecock's political epitaph. But it was an epitaph that proved to be premature. On 15 October 1985— three days before the resignation was to take effect, the district attorney's office as well as the local newspapers simultaneously received letters from one of the jurors of the second trial—letters which detailed allegations of jury tampering on the part of one of the court's marshals. After further investigation a second juror confirmed the allegations. It seemed as though Hedgecock wasn't through yet. On 18 October he withdrew his resignation and vowed to see that justice was served. William Todd, the presiding judge, saw things differently, however, and refused to grant a mistrial. Thus, after unsuccessful appeals to the State Supreme Court and Attorney General's office, Hedgecock's conviction went forward. He was sentenced to 365 days in jail and three years probation. On 19 December 1985, over a year after the original indictments were made public, Mayor Roger Hedgecock became a private citizen once again.

Since his appeal of the court's present decision is still pending, Hedgecock has yet to serve any of his sentence. Add to this his presence on a daily FM talk show, a weekly television news program, numerous public appearances, and a giant freeway billboard bearing a disturbingly large and leering characterization of him—an advertisement for his radio talkshow—and one gets the distinct impression that Roger Hedgecock is still an active feature of San Diego's public consciousness. There is some irony in the fact that the popular ex-mayor, whose chances of receiving a fair trial were certainly complicated and perhaps perverted by an overzealous local media, has now become a media personality himself, and makes no qualms about using his radio talkshow as a forum for his own, often derisive, views about local government.

Several issues intersect in this story: First, in what ways did the local media dramatize the trials? How could such dramatic reduction act to bias coverage? How does this type of production bias differ from other forms of political or ideological bias? And finally, as a case study, what can we learn about the broader genre of news messages referred to as trial-by-media?

Theoretical Perspective

The constrained role behaviors and protocols, lengthy testimonies, and general tedium that comprises most courtroom activity are inherently unsuited for popular media, and especially commercial television. I argue here that media coverage of trials shapes and is shaped by conventions of news production that conforms more to dramatic form than espoused standards of "objectivity."[11] In 1968 Robert MacNeil (of MacNeil-Lehrer) observed that entertainment values, which obviously guide all television programming, also shape the news.[12] Altheide supported this view when he concluded that a unique set of production biases act to mold the news into a narrative form, an arbitrary form that reduces events to fit into finite beginnings, middles, and ends, and often links unrelated people and events together in an attempt to foster continuity between stories. Such narrative license amounts to what Altheide sees as the main source of distortion in news coverage, or "the news perspective."[13] Similarly, Paul Weaver noted that television news creates psuedo-contexts for events. The narrative context of the news, or storyline, possesses a set-up, climax, and often an epilogue—structural elements that are amplified through such technical devices as sound and the juxtaposition of pictures and images.[14]

In short, news professionals rely on dramatic form in the creation of news messages. News stories have become stylized accounts of reality whose dramatic conventions prefigure events significantly. They have evolved into "real fictions" that bias representations of empirical experience.[15] Such fictions are part of the repertoire of dramatic conventions that news professionals employ, a tendency that lends new meaning to the expression "story line." As Mark Fishman observed, editors and reporters tend to "organize an otherwise confusing array of events into packages or groups of interrelated news events."[16] Or according to Bennett and Feldman, the "grammatical, temporal, and causal regularities in story form set up obvious connections among pairs or clusters of symbols in a story."[17] Storylines are apriori psychologies of form. Unlike intentional political or ideological forms of bias, the dramatic conventions of news production are a well established part of the trade, a form of institutional bias that goes with the journalistic turf.

In order to survive, therefore, news personnel must compete in a marketplace where the status quo requires the dramatic reduction of all newsworthy events and persons. As is the case with other forms of programming, the tried and true forms, the ones that work, are those that gain mimetic status. Thus, the repertoire of dramatic forms is relatively small. For example, the list of likely labels used to characterize a complex event could include terms like strike, riot, crisis, hostage situation, summit, emergency meeting, and so on. Such recurrent labels, like the broader class of conventional forms and frames of reference to which they are related, are manifest in all news storylines.

It follows that these conventions of expression contribute to the overall grammar of news reporting, or as Fishman found in his study of the assembly of crime waves, news personnel employ conventional themes in an attempt to package events in acceptable and pleasing ways.[18] For example, the dramatis personae, episodic nature, and closure expectations peculiar to sitcoms and soap operas bleed over into news programs.

Moreover, the same kind of production bias is operative in newspapers—the bastions of "free" and "objective" reporting. As Condit and Selzer point out in their analysis of newspaper coverage of the Koerner murder trial, the "rhetoric of objectivity" alone biased accounts of the trials significantly.[19] An integral part of the journalistic credo, this *espousal* of objectivity, plays a key role in biasing news expression. Like Altheide's notion of the news perspective, this bias is rooted more in the prevailing conventions of newspaper production than the political or ideological biases of news personnel. Like their television counterparts, newspaper personnel rely on those methods proven effective within their medium and market for getting out the story.

Thus we can begin to illuminate the character of mediated litigation by identifying the media's recurrent conventions of production. A synopsis of all the conventions evident in news coverage of mediated trials is beyond the scope of this discussion. Rather, I will argue that both newspapers and television coverage of the Hedgecock trials exhibited two central production tendencies that acted to bias the coverage significantly. These tendencies, present in the coverage of the Hedgecock trials, will be referred to as *media histories* and *stylized characterizations.*

The news media have a penchant for creating their own historic frames of reference. When attempting to offer parallels or contrasts for the purposes of contextual reconstruction, reporters and editors rely more on popularized histories than legal ones. As Drechsel revealed in his study of the habits of trial reporters, very few of those surveyed ever buried themselves in law libraries when attempting to background a story.[20] Rather than concern themselves with elaborate legal precedents, a process that obviously would limit a reporter's output, they rely instinctively on prior media accounts or histories. As one reporter assigned to the Hedgecock trial put it, "I rely on my extensive file" when fleshing out a story, a file that was made up of news clippings and the opinions of other reporters.[21]

This reliance on media-generated histories is particularly important when attempting to characterize coverage: High profile or highly publicized trials more frequently serve as the substance of historic frames. Dramatic high-profile cases can raise the interest value of "lesser" trials and, it will be argued, act to popularize a trial. (As will be shown later, the local media drew almost capriciously on previous conspiracy trials or other notorious cases of any kind in their attempts to draw historic parallels.) By relying on media histories, then, reporters and editors perpetuate a kind of parochial exposition: they turn to their own stylized histories rather than to other histories that may challenge what they perceive to be the expectations of their audience. Thus they make rhetorical choices in an attempt to identify with their audience(s). These choices are usually embedded in the grammar of popular media expression, and not, as one might hope, in legal precedents.

This tendency is most evident in the detailed and often irrelevant character backgrounds that are offered. One can only wonder why knowing about a defendant's playground habits in elementary school will help clarify our understanding of his/her involvement in a conspiracy some thirty years later. Yet this type of minutiae abounds in trial coverage and seems to be a mainstay of historic frame construction. Beyond the journalistic axiom that knowledge of lesser facts implies knowledge of greater facts, use of such minutiae adheres to a relatively predictable formula: elaborately detailed accounts of a key litigant's life history are offered with special attention given to that sequence of events that supposedly contributed to his/her current criminal dilemma.[22] In the Hedgecock case, for example, the *Union* ran a half-page story which painstakingly chronicled Hedgecock's "political ambitions" by tracing machiavellian tendencies exhibited as early as elementary school through to the present.[23]

Like historic frames, stylized characterizations seem to originate in the collective memory bank of the media itself. So much so that the role models offered in mediated trials are seemingly plucked from a repertoire of "interesting" stereotypes which originate in one of two places: entertainment programming and/or highly publicized trials. As I will show below, the heroes and villians in this trial coverage echoed popular culture characterizations and scenarios. The rest of this analysis will attempt to demonstrate how these two interrelated conventions were at work in the media's coverage of the Hedgecock trials, and how they can figure in rhetorical analysis of popular trials.

Key Players

In his *Morphology of a Folktale,* Vladimir Propp described seven archetypal dramatis personae which he contended are present, in varying degrees, in most folk and fairy tales.[24] There are heroes, villians, princesses, and helpers, acting in conventionally determined ways toward predictable ends regardless of the specifics of the tale. Nimmo and Combs adopted a similar position in their analysis of crisis coverage by television news agencies. Under the heading of "actor," within Kenneth Burke's pentadic approach, they looked for several specific traits. They ask: (1) What role types emerge—heroes, villains, fools, objects of desire, incorruptible people or something else? (2) Are there role reversals? (3) Does an abstraction personified as a character play a role—"The People," "The Experts," or other synecdochic usages?[25] Several of these traits were present in the local media's characterizations of the key players in the Hedgecock saga.

As the central player, characterizations of Hedgecock were abundant. The day after the first grand jury indictment was handed down, the *Tribune*'s headline story described the mayor as having "his rising star halted by seven months of controversy." The report went on to note that Hedgecock would now have to "salvage a political career that has never known defeat."[26] After the indictment was issued Hedgecock was consistently portrayed as an ambitious, overly aggressive politico. An *L.A. Times-San Diego Edition* story titled, "Hedgecock Always Wanted to be in Charge," chronicled his life from high school to the present with dogged focus on two central themes: blind ambition and machiavellianism. The kindest descriptors employed depicted him as a "born leader and hustler" who "thrived on a biting, intimidating style best reflected by how he once advised a friend to run a political campaign: 'attack, attack, attack!' " Relying on an abstraction personified as character, the article cites "prosecutors" who said "Hedgecock was a man so unscrupulous and consumed with 'raw ambition' that he ultimately lied, cheated and connived to steal an election." This same story highlighted such minutiae as Hedgecock's complexion problem, his role as a Gestapo captain in a school play—in which he was "most convincing"—and his tendency to try to dominate his schoolmates. Indeed, his "lust" for power was expressed through adjectives like "honed power," "power base," and "consolidated power." Perhaps most revealing was the inset in bold type that read, "Roger reminds me a lot of the Nixon Syndrome. Either you are my friend or you're my enemy."[27]

Nixon and Watergate analogies were perpetuated and extended on the air as well.[28] One television editorial referred to the "same flaw" that "has been villain time and time again" in the corruption of American politicians. That "flaw," we are told is "blind ambition,"[29] a shibboleth of the Watergate epoch. Whether through osmosis, likemindedness, or lack of imagination, the media's comparison of Hedgecock to Nixon caught on rapidly.

With relatively few exceptions, the local media offered characterizations of Hedgecock as political villain. Though some accounts described him in agonistic terms—"the mayor's woes," his "struggles," or "battles"—most descriptions were perjorative. Hedgecock's association with the lead co-conspirator, J. David Dominelli, helped to round out his villification.

It was Dominelli's indictment that put the district attorney's office on to Hedgecock's trial in the first place. J. David "Jerry" Dominelli was depicted as the arch-swindler extraordinaire. Dominelli's 1984 conviction for bankruptcy fraud, perjury, and running a ponzi scheme opened a watershed of media speculations over the degree of complicity on the part of the mayor's office. Hedgecock's associations with the "high-flying investment firm" were suddenly headline news.

Some $350,000 was allegedly "channeled" through a "dummy" consulting firm (run by Tom Sheppard) into Hedgecock's 1984 campaign coffers—a fact we were repeatedly reminded of through both trials. As swindlers go, Dominelli provided the media with all the right ingredients: There was the estimated $51 million in bilked assets—most of which belonged to San Diegans; then he made a temporary escape to a Caribbean Island—a move that not only smacked of mafioso modus operandi, but that evoked a painful deja vu for San Diegans whose recollections of a previous large-scale swindler, C. Arnold Smith, included much the same scenario[30]; finally, there was Dominelli's attractive, politically enlightened "girlfriend," Nancy Hoover—ex-mayor of a hip coastal suburb and long-standing friend of Hedgecock.

Oscar Goodman, Hedgecock's attorney in the retrial, was depicted as the archetypal, ruthless, big-city lawyer. He possessed all the glitz and tough-guy demeanor that one would expect to find in a "Las Vegas" attorney who specialized in defending "the big guys." In a front page story we were told, "To Goodman, Mobsters are Citizens Too," since among his past clients there existed "organized crime figures"—several of whom were then dutifully listed.[31] Revealingly, Goodman's Las Vegas residence was used synecdochically in most accounts of his character, so that images of sun tans, gambling, mobsters, and brashness were built into the frequent references to "Sin Town." In contrast to this image of Goodman, the prosecutors emerged as the local good guys.

As assistant district attorney assigned to the first trial, Richard Huffman was described as an "aggressive prosecutor, used to the big cases."[32] The D. A. was offered as the government's David facing the popular and ruthless Goliaths—Hedgecock and Goodman. Indeed, both prosecutors, (Charles Wickersham replaced Huffman in the retrial) were described with adjectives like "tenacious, diligent, and well-prepared," modifiers rarely spent on the defense. (In fact, "tenacity" and "diligency" took on a "ruthlessness" when exhibited by the defense.)[33]

As the new David, Wickersham's low-key, thorough-going style was contrasted sharply to that of Goodman. His lack of "theatrics" and "loudness" were juxtaposed with Goodman's "flamboyance."[34] Televised images of the prosecution, usually taped outside of the courtroom at a break in the trial, helped amplify this contrast. Whenever Hedgecock and Goodman emerged from the courtroom a throng of reporters, well-wishers, and courthouse urchins would immediately engulf them, a scene that was always captured on camera. More than once, local audiences saw Goodman and/or Hedgecock shoving and pushing their way through reporters while oftentimes aggressive questions were being thrown in their path. On one occasion a cameraman, who was attempting to maintain a full-front shot while running backwards in front of Hedgecock and Goodman, stumbled over his own cords and fell. The evening news included the rolling footage, taped during the fall, in its report. The resultant image was one of frenzy, met by indifference on the part of Hedgecock, especially since the audio picked up the camera crew's plea to Hedgecock to " . . . slow down for chrissake!!" and the Mayor's well-amplified reply to this plea: "I'd rather not."[35]

By contrast, televised images of the prosecution were much more serene. No throngs attended Wickersham when he emerged from the courtroom. There were no harried onlookers. On one occasion he even stood patiently by while reporters and others pursued Hedgecock into the elevator, after which he conducted a calm one-on-one interview with a local television anchorman.[36] The resultant image was one of clear contrast between the prosecution and the defense: The prosecutors appeared peaceful and orderly on camera, while the defense appeared chaotic and unruly.

Of all of the players in the Hedgecock drama, Leon Crowder—dubbed "the Lone Holdout Juror" after creating a hung jury in the first trial—was the one whose actions seemed to test the elasticity of the media's stereotypes. Crowder's status as a city sanitation worker became the mainstay of the media's attempts to neatly package his persona. *Every* print and electronic news story dealing with him made clear, usually through innuendo, his potential "indebtedness" and sense of duty to his "boss."[37] In addition to his civil service loyalty, *every* newspaper story on Crowder referred to his "past criminal record" (possession of marijuana), and his "new found" religiosity. One story began with a scenic lead which described the "rainbow hued decal" on the living room window which read "I love Jesus."[38] Televised images included footage of trash trucks on the job, his wife and children, and an interview with a fellow juror—a very WASPish woman whose bitterness over the hung decision was obvious.

In short, the local media relied on an amalgam of suggestive typifications which cast him as myopic, religiously dogmatic, and possessed by a disproportionate sense of duty to his "boss." In their apparent quest for a dramatic angle, they painted Crowder as a misguided zealot, whose strange sense of loyalty to Hedgecock had clouded his judgment. Crowder was, in Proppian terms, a "helper" who momentarily played a key role, but who could only forestall the inevitable conclusion to the media's drama: a guilty verdict. Thus, stylized characterizations helped mold public perceptions of Hedgecock's guilt and, when juxtaposed with the use of historic frames, a clear impression of the overall production bias emerges.

History in the Making

One day after the original indictment was issued the *Union* ran a story headlined, "Politics: Mayor will fight, but indictment can be the kiss of death."[39] As support for this portent of doom, the article "recalled" a similar indictment some fourteen years earlier involving "then-Mayor Frank Curran." That evening the *Tribune,* sister paper to the *Union,* ran a similar story entitled, "Hedgecock's not the first indicted San Diego Mayor."[40] As was so often the case in the local media's coverage of the trials, these two Copley stories were echoed by the major television affiliates.

What these mini-histories in San Diego political graft represented were Mayoral indictments revisited: Two of the stories began by reminding us that "for the second time in 14 years, San Diego's political scene has been rocked by grand jury indictments of its mayor." The "rocked" metaphor recurred several times in these accounts. With varying degrees of detail, each story "recalls" how the Curran indictments, which involved alleged bribes and illegal contributions for political favors by Yellow Cab, "marked the beginning of the end for Mayor Frank Curran's political career."[41] On the same day the *Union* ran a lengthy "analysis" of the Hedgecock indictment, entitled "indictment seen as the 'end of the beginning,' " a title whose obvious jingle value was intended to enhance reader perceptions of historic parallels between Curran's and Hedgecock's cases. These enticing comparisons were featured in spite of the fact that the case against Curran ultimately ended in a complete acquittal.

In spite of Curran's acquittal, we were reminded that it had "swept [him] out of office" in 1971, the year of the mayoral election. At the time this story was run, Hedgecock was also facing reelection. To help reinforce this historic parallel, the *Union* showed a picture of a downtrodden Curran gazing off into his "ruined" political future. Alongside of this picture was the reminder that "the Curran indictment alleged a traditional bribe-for-favors scenario . . . and that in both cases popular mayors seemingly on their way to reelection were hit by charges of unholy alliances with financial figures."[42]

Again, the evening news broadcasts constructed this same historic frame, drawing nearly identical conclusions. In one particular story, the comparison to the Curran indictment received "special focus" by the anchorwoman. During this "special focus segment" we were reminded of the "Yellow Cab scandal" that helped topple Curran, a reminder that drew several explicit parallels between the 1971 trial and Hedgecock's 1984 indictments.

The Curran parallels alone offer support for the argument that the San Diego news media relied heavily on its own sense of history in the construction of frames of reference. Considering the notoriety of both cases, such parallels did add pizzazz to the otherwise tedious conspiracy proceedings. But it was a pizzazz that over-represented similarities that, from a legal perspective, simply didn't hold up. The two indictments actually had very little in common outside of the office of the defendants.

Perhaps it was for want of a new kind of historic precedent that the *Tribune*, during the later stages of the retrial, evoked a more notorious parallel. In a headline entitled, "Hedgecock's Silence: A Dramatic Gamble," Goodman's decision to rest the Mayor's second case without calling a single defense witness was likened to similar legal maneuvers by the attorneys for Claus von Bulow and John DeLorean. We were dutifully reminded of the specifics of those cases in the course of the story: " . . . in the celebrated trials of John DeLorean, charged with buying cocaine to save his automobile empire, and socialite Claus von Bulow, charged with attempting to kill his wife, . . . " both defendants' attorneys employed similar tactics.[43] Thus, through association Hedgecock becomes a member of a notorious club, whose membership—though charged with crimes of a completely different nature and in contexts that defy any credible legal analogy—all share one important characteristic: They gained enough media attention to attain the status of historic stereotype. They have become part of the media's repertoire of historic frames which are molded more out of an interest in dramatic appeal than objectivity or legal accountability.

Thus the media's historic frames of reference function as rhetorical topoi to the extent that they become commonplaces or precedents for media-generated arguments. For the public, these frames of reference supplant the actual and obviously more accountable legal precedents. The Curran parallels offer an excellent example of this: Curran was not convicted, thus no *legal* precedent exists. Yet the media used this case to construct a rhetorical precedent for embellishing the Hedgecock case. The results of such a practice are obvious. By evoking the historic frame of Curran and Yellow Cab, and defining Hedgecock's case in terms of it as a "clear historic parallel," the media reframed public perceptions of the Hedgecock case along this particular bias.

Media-on-Media

Self-reflective commentaries on their own practices offer an after-the-fact attempt by news professionals to balance coverage. At one point, a local television station addressed its commentary specifically at the role the local media played in shaping public perceptions of the trials. Aired during the aftermath of the second trial, while the motion for mistrial was being heard, this self-conscious rationalization of the local media's role in the trials says much about both their own sense of accountability and about news production bias in general. Further, it offers an intensive variation on my argument that production bias played a significant role in the media's representations of the trials.

One commentary began with an admission of guilt, then moved on to a short litany of self-effacing examples of media abuses and excesses, and ended with a less than credible call for viewer skepticism. The following are excerpts taken from this media-on-media editorial:

> . . . at times the story has forced the news media to become part of the story they are covering . . . and whether true or not, has also given the perception that some news organizations are either anti-Hedgecock or pro-Hedgecock. The *Union* and the *Tribune* are perceived as being mostly anti-Hedgecock, maybe the *Transcript* is the most fair paper, and the *L.A. Times* is the most pro-Hedgecock. . . . Perhaps some editors are anti-Hedgecock, and certainly don't like him, but I think they go out of their way to make sure that that opinion is not reflected in their newspapers. . . . I think everyone has done a rather commendable job covering the story fairly. . . . One example of how the Roger Hedgecock case has become a media event was today at the community concourse, [at] a rally held in support of Roger Hedgecock. When you looked around though, you saw as many media people as Hedgecock supporters. Each reporter wants to make sure his story contains something extra—something the competition doesn't have. . . . If there is a lesson to be learned from all of this it is perhaps that the public must open its eyes, as well as relying on the media to bring them the news.[44]

Like its national network prototypes, this rationalization was offered more as an attempt to assuage criticism than account for the media's role in the legal process. There are several features of this attempt at apologia that highlight the self-serving character so evident in the strange abdication of accountability that comes at the end. First, note how the media were "forced" by the "story," no less, to become part of the news coverage: Their decisions to become involved are hidden by the editorial use of the passive voice and reified agent. Then we learn that this blameless involvement has created the *perception* that the media are biased. This "perception" is apparently the worst aspect of media involvement in newsmaking, and qualifiers, such as "perhaps" and "maybe," add a tone of skepticism about the validity of the "perception." Furthermore, the writer then settles the matter by deciding that everyone has covered the story fairly—a rather surprising assertion of authority, given the context. The confessional gesture of humility that follows nicely completes this begging of the question, and so brings us to the (patronizing) lesson. In the final analysis it is "the public that must open its eyes" to find the truth either hidden in the media's coverage or somehow accessible outside of that coverage (the recommendation is not clear). Thus, while awkwardly praising the media's objectivity and "fairness," the burden of deciphering the truth of the trials rests with the public—who needn't worry too much, since they live in a marketplace of "commendable" news coverage. In short, we should respect the media while excusing their excesses; above all, we should continue to rely on them for our information about public life.

At no point in this commentary, or others like it, did the reporters offer criticism that was truly insightful. They adhered to a news perspective, not a legal perspective, not a socially or politically sensitive perspective. They saw the need to address their role in the Hedgecock story more as a newsworthy item than as a deleterious influence on the legal process. Thus, even in this attempt to police its own influence on the legal process, the local news media did little more than qualify its excesses and reinforce its aura of objectivity. (In many ways "objectivity" is expressed through carefully staged plurality: entertain several viewpoints on the way to buffering your own!) Besides, self-effacement is one of the best means of assuaging criticism and feigning humility.

This instance of media self-criticism reveals much about the nature of production bias. Rather than offer any judgment regarding their own, admitted commitment to competition as their highest priority, they simply reported its presence. Rather than probe the potentially confounding implications of a libel suit against the most powerful newspaper in town, a suit which resulted in a front-page retraction, they simply report its occurrence. And rather than address the absurdity of a "rally held in support of Hedgecock" that was populated mostly by "media people," they were content to flash an image on the screen that offers verification of their interpretation. In short, this "critique" relied on the very conventions of news exposition that called forth critical scrutiny in the first place. A more genuine critique of their professional actions would not be so beholden to their conventions of production. The "rhetoric of objectivity," to name one constraint, blinds them from treating motives, purposes, and other "non-objective" qualitative dimensions of mediated litigation in favor of the verifiable (video-tapeable) events that take place somewhere "out there." Thus, production biases acted to screen out a more useful analysis of their motives and actions.

Conclusion

From Drechsel's study, which found that 90 percent of trial reporters surveyed lacked any form of legal education,[45] to Parenti's neo-Marxist litany of complaints against the structure of the entire system of news dissemination in the United States,[46] the critics have made one thing clear: Mediated litigation, at its best, offers a fragmented, stylized image of the American legal system. This essay has attempted to strengthen this criticism.

Through reliance on rhetorical devices like stylized characterizations and historic frames, the local news media painted an image of Hedgecock that was anything but "fair" or "balanced." I have suggested that the conventions employed result more from production techniques and priorities than intentional bias. This fact makes the subsequent misrepresentation no less real, simply more embedded in the business of news reporting.

This analysis is offered as a partial demystification of the rhetoric of trial-by-media, aimed at the conventions and habits of persuasive expression peculiar to trial coverage. The case study examination of the Hedgecock trials represents one critical foray into the perplexing rhetorical context created by mediated litigation. Without media attention, legal discourse, with its myriad rules for argument and implicit protocols, is difficult for an outsider to comprehend. Add media attention and its rhetorical character becomes more complex. A news perspective is a form of dramatic reduction touted as balanced and fair journalistic coverage. This essay has sought to demonstrate how the journalistic commitment to objectivity can remain a very distant ideal.

Crime as Rhetoric

The Trial of the Catonsville Nine

J. Justin Gustainis

The trial of the group whose members called themselves the Catonsville Nine did not lack moments of irony. One of the most interesting of these occurred early in the proceedings when Judge Roszel C. Thomsen felt obliged to warn one of the defendants, Rev. Daniel Berrigan, that the courtroom was not to be used as a "propaganda forum."[1] That was irony, indeed, for, as has been observed, "Propaganda was precisely what the trial was all about."[2]

The trial was about propaganda—and more. It has been called "the peace movement's biggest success,"[3] as well as "the most dramatic courtroom encounter between civil disobedient [sic] and the law up to that time."[4] Nancy Zaroulis and Gerald Sullivan, in their study of protest against the Vietnam War, concluded that "the style of the presiding judge, the nature of the crime in question, and, above all, the unanimity of the defendants, combined to give focus, clarity, and impact to the Catonsville trial."[5]

The trial might also be considered a failure, however. Certainly the legal tactics employed by the defense failed to win acquittal—although whether the defendants held reasonable expectations of acquittal is problematic. The Catonsville Nine admitted their guilt in court, did not offer a traditional legal defense, and prompted their attorneys to employ tactics which lacked a firm grounding in accepted legal principles. The rhetorical tactics (aimed principally at audiences outside the courtroom) also had limited success.

This essay discusses four aspects of the trial of the Catonsville

Nine: First, the criminal action which led to the trial—the entry into a draft board office and the removal and subsequent destruction of hundreds of draft files; second, the trial itself, with particular focus on the legal tactics of the defense lawyers (including an attempt to apply the so-called "doctrine of nullification" to the case) and the rhetorical appeals of the defendants; next, the weeklong "festival of support" which surrounded the trial and brought hundreds of anti-war protestors to Baltimore for a series of rallies and demonstrations; and, finally, the use of trials as vehicles for protest.

The "Action" at Catonsville

In the afternoon of 17 May 1968, a group of nine people, two of them wearing clerical garb, entered Local Selective Service Board #33, located in Catonsville, Maryland. After using minimal force to restrain the two female clerks, the intruders removed several file drawers marked "1–A," emptied their contents into wire baskets, and adjourned to a nearby parking lot. There, they poured homemade napalm on the files and set them alight. They then stood around the blaze, praying aloud and waiting to be arrested.

From the start, the action was intended by the group to be a media event. Local television stations and newspapers had been notified anonymously that something newsworthy would take place in that parking lot at a particular time. The burning of the draft files was recorded by the videotape of television news crews and the notebooks of print reporters. The group also handed out a press release which read, in part, "We believe some property has no right to exist. Hitler's gas ovens, Stalin's concentration camps, atomic-bacteriological-chemical weaponry, files of conscription, and slum properties are examples having no right to existence."[6]

The group, which was soon to become known as "the Catonsville Nine," consisted of Rev. Daniel Berrigan, Jesuit priest and award-winning poet; Rev. Philip Berrigan, Daniel's brother, a Josephite priest; David Darst, a Christian Brother; John Hogan, a former Mary-knoll Brother; Thomas Lewis, an artist; Marjorie Bradford Melville, a former nun and missionary in Guatemala; Thomas Melville, Marjorie's husband, a former Maryknoll priest and also a former missionary in Guatemala; George Mische, who had worked throughout Latin America for the Alliance for Progress; and Mary Moylan, a nurse. All were Catholic, and, as noted above, several were either members or former members of the clergy.

The nine were arrested and then arraigned on both federal and state charges. Six of them were then released on bail pending trial.

Philip Berrigan and Thomas Lewis, however, were held in custody because they had taken part in the Catonsville protest while out on bail pending appeal of an earlier conviction: Some months earlier, in the first of the "draft board raids," Berrigan and Lewis had joined two other protestors in pouring blood over draft files in Baltimore.

It should be clear that the actions of the Catonsville Nine involved more than mere criminal activity. Rather, they constituted an act of calculated civil disobedience, intended to draw attention toward a particular viewpoint on the war.[7] The raid on the Catonsville draft board falls under the heading of "indirect civil disobedience." The usual forms of civil disobedience that had been directed against the Vietnam War were not open to the members of the Catonsville Nine. For example, unlike many young men who had burned their draft cards publicly as a protest against the war (thus engaging in "direct civil disobedience"),[8] the Berrigans and their colleagues were not subject to the draft. The Selective Service system did not draft clergy, or women, or married men, or men over a certain age. By issuing a draft card to a man, the government was saying, in effect, "We reserve the right to send you to war." By burning his draft card in public the protestor was saying, in effect, "I deny the government's right to make me fight in this war." The members of the Catonsville Nine, not subject to the draft, could not defy it. They could, and did, destroy the draft files of others.

Given the unusual nature of the crime committed, it might be reasonably expected that the trial to follow would not be typical of criminal proceedings. As the next section will show, such an expectation would be justified. The action of the Catonsville Nine was, in many ways, a rhetorical event. Due to the defendants, their attorneys, and their supporters, the trial of the Catonsville Nine was also a rhetorical event.

The Trial

This discussion of the Catonsville Nine trial proceedings will focus on two areas: the legal tactics employed by the defendants and their attorneys, and the rhetorical tactics used by the defendants and their supporters. Although the distinction between these two forms of tactics is sometimes difficult to make, it is important to do so if the Catonsville Nine trial is to be understood. The distinction was well made by Charles Wilkinson, who noted that "[The trial] was a forum in which the status quo addressed itself to what was *done* rather than to what was *said* or *meant*. This more than any other factor isolates the basic difficulty of Catonsville's rhetoric as addressed to the status quo—its clash, its confusion, its contradiction between symbol and act."[9]

Perhaps the most interesting aspect of the defense at this trial was that there was really no defense at all, in the usual meaning of the term. The attitude of the defendants was well summarized by Daniel Berrigan at a meeting of the Catonsville Nine Defense Committee: "Well, this is the defense: we did it, we're glad, and here's why."[10] The defense team, led by attorney William Kunstler (who had gained some measure of fame as the lawyer for the Chicago Seven), never disputed the facts of the case as they were presented by the prosecution. Nor did the defense lawyers quibble over jury selection—the first twelve jurors proposed were accepted without challenge. These actions had a rhetorical purpose. As Zaroulis and Sullivan observed, "The uneasy dispatch with which the technical, prosecutorial aspects of the case were handled served to heighten anticipation in the courtroom for the presentation of the defense."[11]

To the extent that legal maneuvering did take place in the trial, it revolved around two issues. One of these was the so-called doctrine of nullification. As Kunstler told the jury in his opening statement, "We have what the defendants consider a historic moment, a moment when a jury may, as the law empowers it, decide the case, not on the facts at all, but decide the case on the principle issues involved."[12]

The doctrine of nullification says, in effect, that a jury may refuse to convict defendants in a criminal trial, even if its members believe those defendants did commit the acts with which they are charged. The jury has the right to say that the law violated by the defendants was an unjust law, and the jury may "nullify" that law, at least with respect to that particular case. However, Judge Thomsen refused to let Kunstler develop this idea in his speech to the jury. Instead he interjected, "The Court will instruct the jury, Mr. Kunstler, to decide the case on the facts as they appear from the evidence and upon the law as it may be given to them by the Court."[13]

Apparently, conflicting legal principles were involved here. On the one hand, the doctrine of nullification does exist in the law. Andrew Hamilton employed it in 1735 to defend John Peter Zenger against a charge of seditious libel. The jury found Zenger guilty on the facts of the case, but was persuaded by Hamilton to set aside the law in this instance and free the defendant. The principle became part of American legal doctrine after the revolution. On the other hand, however, there exists a principle of criminal law which states, "Juries should not be told that they may disregard law and decide according to their prejudices and consciences."[14] What this means in terms of actual courtroom practice is that the jury may have the right to nullify a law as it applies to a particular defendant, but it may not be *told* it has that right; the decision must be arrived at independently during jury deliberations. Thus, Kunstler was silenced by the judge, who also pointed out that the *Zenger* case took place before the adoption of the U.S. Constitution.

Of course, if the jury had in fact nullified the law under which the Catonsville Nine were charged, the implications (legal, social, political, rhetorical, and otherwise) would have been tremendous. Future protestors might, through appeal to precedent, be granted nullification when brought to trial on charges of breaking and entering and destruction of government property (which were the charges levied against the Catonsville Nine). The legality of the Vietnam War might itself have been called into question. This is precisely the kind of outcome the defendants hoped for, although they did not reasonably expect it. But it was not to be. The trial record gives no indication that the jury ever considered the question of setting aside the law in this case.

The other major legal tactic employed by the defense at this trial involved the claim that the Constitutional guarantee of free speech covered the defendants' actions at the Catonsville draft board. Kunstler suggested that his clients were in a position similar to that occupied by those Germans who had opposed the Nazi regime in the 1930s. "They were trying," he told the jury, "to make an outcry, an anguished outcry to reach the American community before it was too late. . . . I think this is an element of free speech to try—when all else fails—to reach the community."[15]

But this approach was neither legally sound nor rhetorically astute. The legal ground was shaky in light of a Supreme Court decision, handed down five months previously, which held that the burning of one's draft card did not qualify as "symbolic speech" under the First Amendment. If the burning of individual draft cards were not protected free speech, then the burning of the government's draft files would not be, either.[16] The rhetorical error was in suggesting to an average group of Americans that their government was akin to that of Nazi Germany, and that, by extension, they were all "good Germans," who had been standing by, allowing inhumane acts to go on. Few Americans would be willing to see their government, or themselves, in such a light, and none of them were part of the jury trying the Catonsville Nine.

Further, the Manichean worldview expressed by the defendants, which held that the only possible reaction to the war was either unqualified support or civil disobedience, was unrealistic and rhetorically insensitive. Public opinion had begun to turn against Lyndon Johnson months before the action at Catonsville. Antiwar politicians, such as Eugene McCarthy and Robert Kennedy, had received widespread support in their quests for the Presidency. Other "doves" were active in both houses of Congress. The members of the jury could thus be expected to reject the claim that the only viable protest against the war involved napalm and draft files.

Although this unusual defense was not likely to prevail, it did allow the defendants to use the trial for the pursuit of more expressly public objectives. The first rhetorical tactic masqueraded as a legal tactic. It is common trial practice for defense attorneys to call their clients to testify on their own behalf. This Kunstler and his colleagues did; each member of the Catonsville Nine had his or her chance on the witness stand. But the purpose was not, as is usually the case, to allow the defendants to deny their guilt. Rather, each defendant admitted his or her guilt, and then proceeded to explain the motivations that brought him or her to Catonsville. Each defendant's testimony followed a pattern. In response to questions asked by members of the defense team, the defendants discussed their backgrounds, their religious training (where applicable), their experience with war and with the Third World, their views of the symbolism of the Catonsville action, and their explicit motivations in burning the draft files. Daniel Berrigan was recognized by Kunstler and the others as the most eloquent of the defendants, and so his testimony was given last, to heighten its impact. The following is illustrative of the form and tone of his testimony:

So I am trying to suggest that my decision to go to Catonsville was not taken in a vacuum. It was taken as a result of this enormous moral push that was on me, because of what I had seen in Hanoi, because of what my brother had done previously in the pouring of blood, and because I was realizing also at Cornell that one simply could not announce the gospel from his passbook, and not be allowed, let's say, to speak or act as a Christian, when he was not down there sharing the risks and the burdens and the anguish of his students, whose own lives were placed in the breech by us, by this generation that I and others belong to.[17]

The use of this testimony is referred to here as rhetorical tactic because it is not designed to address legal issues raised in the trial. Instead, its purposes were to move the jury (on human, rather than legal, grounds), to influence spectators in the courtroom (about whom more will be said presently) and to be reported in the media with a view toward influencing others outside the courtroom. That this tactic was allowed use at all in a courtroom is noteworthy. Questions of intent are not always considered germane in legal proceedings and in this case it quickly became evident that intent was irrelevant from a legal standpoint. Indeed, in his charge to the members of the jury, Judge Thomsen reminded them that, "The law does not recognize political, religious moral convictions, or some higher law, as justification for the commission of a crime, no matter how good the motive may be."[18]

That conventional legal viewpoint notwithstanding, the judge had allowed the defendants and their lawyers what has been called "unparalleled leeway" in their testimony regarding intent.[19] Thomsen could simply have stifled the defendants with a ruling that their testimony on this issue was irrelevant and immaterial. But, for whatever reason, he did not.

A second rhetorical tactic, related to the first, was the defense's use of what classical theorists called *ethos*—persuasion based on the personal credibility of the speaker. During his opening statement, Kunstler introduced each defendant, briefly mentioning such aspects as education, academic accomplishments, religious training and status, and service in the Third World. For example, he described Daniel Berrigan as "an extremely well known American poet. He is 47 years old. He is a priest, a member of the Society of Jesus. He, as the evidence will indicate to you, was instrumental in returning three American pilots from Hanoi to the United States, captured American pilots, as a result of which he wrote a book, which he will describe to you when he is on the stand, called *Night Flight to Hanoi*, which, coincidentally, will be published this week, and which covers this particular episode."[20]

As noted earlier, when each defendant took the stand to testify, defense lawyers asked questions designed to flesh out these biographical sketches. Each defendant described in detail his or her background and accomplishments. It seems clear that the defense was attempting to portray the Catonsville Nine as men and women possessing qualities worthy of admiration. They were priests, Christian Brothers, poets, authors, artists, teachers, and nurses. They were, the defense was implying, the kind of people usually described as "pillars of the community." They were not wild-eyed bomb throwers or Communist subversives. Instead, they were portrayed as prisoners of conscience who were taking a moral stand against an immoral war.

Thomsen also allowed another episode to occur, one which had rhetorical significance even if it lacked legal impact (since the jury was not present in the courtroom when it occurred). After the jury had left to begin its deliberations, the defendants asked for, and received, permission to address the court. Each of them, in turn, engaged the judge in a dialogue concerning the action at Catonsville and the law's failure to recognize moral intent as exculpatory. As might be expected, neither side succeeded in convincing the other. Thomsen was obligated by his role to argue that the rule of law must be paramount, or anarchy would result. The members of the Catonsville Nine had long since ceased to place much faith in the law, which they perceived as being administered by the same government which caused napalm to be dropped on children in Vietnam. And so judge and defendants were at an impasse, but one gesture of reconciliation was made. At the conclusion of this series of dialogues, the defendants asked if they might be allowed to pray the Lord's Prayer. After a quick consultation with the chief prosecutor—(who replied, "The government has no objections, your honor. In fact, it rather welcomes the idea.")—permission was given, and the defendants prayed aloud; they were joined by many of the spectators in the courtroom.[21] It was a rare moment of community. For a few minutes the belief in God, the basis for the defendants' actions which had been repeatedly deemed irrelevant by prosecution and judge, was allowed to prevail in the courtroom.

Coverage by the news media was central to the development of these rhetorical strategies. Indeed, the entire Catonsville Nine affair meets the criteria developed by Daniel Boorstin to describe a "pseudo-event," that is, something which takes place only because it will be reported in the media.[22] The Catonsville Nine had invited the media to the burning of draft files; they also knew the media would cover the trial. News coverage was important to the Berrigans and their colleagues, because it would allow them to reach a mass audience with their message of resistance to the war. As noted earlier, there were three audiences for the rhetorical tactics used in the courtroom: the jury members (although the Catonsville Nine never realistically expected to be acquitted), the spectators in the courtroom, and the American public.

Outside the Courtroom

It has been suggested that the Catonsville Nine incident is best understood when perceived not as a legal, political, or moral issue, but as drama.[23] If so, then the actors in this play were the Nine themselves, and the role of Greek chorus was performed by the two thousand or so people who took part in the week-long "festival of support" for the defendants during the course of the trial.

The activities of the festival of support included daytime rallies and evening marches, both featuring such familiar protest activities as singing, chanting, speechmaking, and the burning of draft cards. The nighttime activities were often attended by one or more of the defendants (who, with the exception of Philip Berrigan and Thomas Lewis, were free on bail).

The first reported act of the festival of support, however, involved neither a march nor a rally. A group of about seventy-five protestors formed a protective ring around Thomas Melville and George Mische as police tried to arrest them on the evening of October 6th. Although Melville and Mische were planning to appear in the court the next morning with the rest of the Nine to begin the trial on Federal charges, they had yet to be arraigned on State of Maryland charges stemming from the Catonsville action. They had promised to surrender to state authorities the previous Friday, but had not done so. When police attempted to serve arrest warrants on Melville and Mische Sunday night, the small crowd of supporters interposed their bodies between the officers and their quarry, long enough for the two fugitives to get into a car and flee (the victory was short-lived; police followed the car from a distance and arrested the two later).[24]

The other activities of the festival of support followed along more traditional lines of protest. Most of these activities were organized and orchestrated by the Catonsville Nine Defense Committee, an organization which had been operating out of New York City, but which had moved its base to Baltimore in time for the trial. The group had raised money to help pay legal expenses, and had coordinated the movement to Baltimore of groups of antiwar protestors from several cities.[25] It is estimated that at least 800 supporters of the Catonsville Nine had journeyed to Baltimore for the trial.[26] They were joined by others from the local area. Members of the Defense Committee also acted as press agents for the Nine, providing reporters with photographs of the Catonsville action and biographical information on the defendants.

Monday, 7 October, was the first day of the trial. It was also the date of the largest protest demonstration in support of the Catonsville Nine. A group of protestors estimated to be as large as two thousand marched for three miles through Baltimore, held a rally at the War Memorial Plaza, and then formed a picket line around the courthouse where the trial was taking place. The marchers were peaceful and orderly. This may have been due in part to the pacifist leaning espoused by many of them; it was also partly the result of instructions from the march's organizers. The demonstrators were advised especially to avoid confrontations with police; they were advised that, if they felt the need to yell something at the police, the cry should be, "More pay for cops!"[27] The marchers were heckled by supporters of the war effort, including a group from the National States Rights Party. But, apart from a few isolated scuffles, no violence or arrests were reported. The marchers included groups of clergy, members of the Students for a Democratic Society, students from Cornell University (where Daniel Berrigan had been a chaplain), and a delegation from the Baltimore Welfare Workers' Union.

That evening, over eight hundred of the demonstrators attended a rally held at St. Ignatius Church in the city. A number of well-known opponents of the war spoke, including Noam Chomsky of MIT, Rev. James Pike, former Episcopal Bishop of California, Dorothy Day, one of the founders of the newspaper *The Catholic Worker,* and Harvey Cox of the Harvard Divinity School, a respected theologian.

A smaller demonstration occurred the next day at noon, as a group of about 250 protestors marched through Baltimore to the city's Custom House, where the draft board was located. The marchers carried a facsimile of a coffin, which, they said, represented both the slow death brought on by poverty in America and the quicker, more violent deaths occurring each day in the Vietnam war.[28] The demonstrators were received politely at the Customs House, where officials accepted delivery of the coffin and even provided a receipt. Less polite was a group of counter-demonstrators across the street from the Customs House, whose members booed and shouted such slogans as "We want war" and "Gas the nine!"[29]

The next day, Wednesday, 9 October, was the last day of the trial. The jury's verdict: guilty on all counts (the members of the Catonsville Nine were later given prison sentences ranging from two to six years). With the exception of Thomas Lewis and Philip Berrigan, who were ordered to begin serving the six-year sentences imposed for pouring blood on draft files in Baltimore the previous year, the defendants were released on bail pending appeal. Outside the prison, they participated in a prayer vigil by candlelight which was already in progress. Then the defendants and their supporters marched quietly away. There was no longer any reason to remain: The trial, which had been the focus of the Nine's efforts and the demonstrators' activities, was over.

Conclusion

Did the Catonsville Nine succeed in achieving their goals? The answer to that depends on how one defines what their goals were. Some of their goals were undeniably personal and spiritual. Their achievement can only be determined by the Nine themselves. But they had other goals which were clearly public: the goals of communication and persuasion. As one student of the Catholic Left, Gordon Zahn, has written: " . . . the very symbols employed [such as] the use of homemade napalm at Catonsville . . . testify to an overriding intent to make a point, to get a message across as effectively as possible. This, I submit is communication and to that extent it can be judged as communication."[30]

Although Zahn concludes that Catonsville, viewed as communication was "astonishingly successful,"[31] he does so in a very narrow sense, since he is referring to the fact that some of those who attended the festival of support in Baltimore were moved to imitate the actions of the Catonsville Nine. As former Catholic radical Charles Meconis put it, " . . . the environment created around and within the [Catonsville] trial had quickly borne fruit."[32]

The exact nature of the fruit quickly became apparent. A series of draft board raids, mostly undertaken by groups of Catholics, followed the Catonsville Nine trial. The first group became known as the Milwaukee Fourteen, and it was followed by the D.C. Nine, the Chicago Fifteen, and others. All together, over two hundred people, many of them Catholics, were arrested for taking part in civil disobedience against the Selective Service system.[33] For these men and women, the message of Catonsville was clear, and if one considers them alone, then Zahn's conclusion seems correct.

For many active and potential war protestors, the Catonsville Nine, and the Berrigan brothers in particular, became a potent symbol of resistance.[34] Not only were others persuaded to act against the war effort, they were moved to act in the same way as the Catonsville Nine. For a time, the draft board raids taking place across the country were virtually Catonsville clones. A daylight attack was made on a Selective Service office; files were destroyed; the raiders distributed to the media (whom they had summoned) a manifesto explaining the reasons for their actions; the protestors waited at the site to be arrested; at the trial, the accused admitted their guilt but defended the illegal action on moral grounds.[35] Indeed, the "manifestos" issued at the time of the raids often had many elements in common with that written by Daniel Berrigan and delivered to the media in Catonsville.[36]

But the Catonsville Nine had a wider audience in mind. Their message was aimed at all American Catholics. As Sarah Fahy concluded, "Insofar as there was an appeal to a special group within society, the Catonsville Nine appealed to Christians and especially to their own Church."[37] Among this group, with the exception of the two hundred active imitators discussed above (who, along with their supporters, became known collectively as the Catholic Left), the message of Catonsville fell on deaf ears. This can be seen by considering both the Church hierarchy and the lay members.

The American Catholic Church hierarchy (the bishops and cardinals who actively run the Church) was mostly either hostile or indifferent to the Catonsville Nine. The Archbishop of Baltimore, Cardinal Shehan, issued a statement proclaiming that the Catholic Church had nothing to do with the actions of the Nine and did not support them. In a possibly unfortunate turn of phrase, the archbishop announced (as had Pontius Pilate) that he had "washed his hands" of the matter.[38] The Jesuit Province of New York, which had jurisdiction over Daniel Berrigan, refused to make any public comment concerning his actions at Catonsville. The rest of the American Church hierarchy was equally silent.

American Catholics who were not members of the clergy also failed to heed the message communicated by the Catonsville action and trial. This is not really surprising. As a group, American Catholics have historically been among the most patriotic of this country's citizens. They have traditionally given strong support to any armed conflict in which the United States might be engaged.[39] One explanation which has been advanced for this phenomenon centers upon the claim that the Protestant majority in this country has long viewed Catholics with suspicion, believing that a Catholic's first allegiance was to Rome, not Washington, D.C. In response to this, and in order to be considered "good citizens," Catholic Americans have tended to support this nation's foreign policies, whatever they were. Certainly, in all the history of this country's wars, declared or otherwise, there was no substantial opposition by Catholics until Vietnam—and, as has been shown, that opposition involved a small number.

By making no attempt to conceal their identities during the Catonsville raid or to flee the scene afterward, the Nine had practically guaranteed their arrest and subsequent trial. This was done deliberately, and it allowed the protestors to place themselves squarely within the ancient Catholic tradition of martyrdom. During the first two centuries A.D., many early Christians had defied the state, refused to worship Roman gods, and paid for their intransigence with their lives. The Berrigans and their cohorts might thus have been seen as following in the footsteps of a long line of their church's saints. But they were not so perceived. The Catholic Church has not crowned martyrs for at least a century, and modern Catholics are accustomed to think of such people as dim figures out of the distant past, not living, breathing contemporaries. It is also true that martyrs tend to be extremists who are unpopular in their own time—which is often how they came to be martyrs in the first place.

Another possible explanation for the failure of the Catonsville Nine to move many of their fellow Catholics into opposition against the war involves expectations of appropriate role behavior. In any society, individuals are supposed to behave in certain ways because of who and what they are. Behavior which fails to conform to these role expectations can produce shock and confusion in observers. Feminists, for example, have faced this problem because traditional expectations of women's behavior do not usually include such characteristics as assertiveness and self-reliance. Since rhetoric usually calls for both of these qualities, feminist rhetors have faced considerable difficulty with tradition-minded audiences.[40] A similar dynamic existed between the Catonsville Nine and their intended audience. Four members of the Nine were members of the clergy—the Berrigans and John Hogan were priests, and David Darst was a Christian Brother. In addition, Thomas Melville was a former priest and his wife, Marjorie, was a former nun. For most American Catholics, the concepts of "priest" and "law-breaker" are mutually exclusive; the prospect of any priest committing a felony, regardless of the motivation, is simply scandalous. For example, when a 1971 Gallup Poll asked a sample of American Catholics "Do you think Catholics who raid draft boards to protest the war in Vietnam are acting as responsible Christians?" 67 percent said "no" and 15 percent were undecided.[41]

Another problem grew from the way in which *any* antiwar protest was likely to be perceived by middle-class Americans. The Catonsville action was, as its participants would admit, illegal, but they took great pains to make sure it was also nonviolent. However, there exists in human psychology a phenomenon known as a "contrast effect"—if something is *somewhat* different or apart from you, you are likely to see it as *significantly* different or apart. Given the great amount of violent anti-war protest that had occurred, it was easy for many Americans to lump the draft file burners with the bomb throwers. As Michael Novak points out, "A dramatic, shocking illegal act may seem 'violent' rather than 'nonviolent' to many—and not far different from the nighttime burning of ROTC buildings, churches, or crosses in yards."[42]

The essential problem with the Catonsville Nine's persuasive effort was one of credibility. Experimental research suggests strongly that source credibility is the major determinant of success in persuasion.[43] One of the most important factors in credibility is perceived similarity. We are more likely to be persuaded by people whom we perceive to be like ourselves.[44]

This explains both why the Catonsville Nine successfully persuaded that small group of Catholics who became known as the Catholic Left, and why they were unsuccessful in reaching the majority of their fellow American Catholics. The values expressed by the Nine at Catonsville and in their subsequent trial were appealing to the small number of people who saw the Vietnam War as immoral and who perceived the Catholic Church as giving tacit support to the war effort. But most Catholics in the United States did not share those views, and thus, for them, the Catonsville Nine lacked credibility.

The Catonsville Nine were faced with a paradox, although they may not have realized it. In order to reach a wide audience with their message about the Vietnam War, they had to attract attention. The burning of draft files certainly achieved that objective, as did their rhetorical approach to the trial. But the very actions which were so effective in attracting an audience made it impossible for the Nine to persuade most of the audience members that their crime was justified and that the war was wrong.[45]

If the message of the Catonsville Nine was not well received by its intended audience, the fault had more to do with the message itself than the vehicles through which it was communicated. Press coverage was extensive and, mostly, fair. The electronic media also gave substantial coverage to both the draft board raid and the subsequent trial. But some people did not receive (or, more likely, did not remember) the message, as evidenced by the 62 percent of polled Catholics who did not recognize the names of the Berrigans.[46] Those who did receive the message, as was argued earlier, were inclined to focus more on what was done (the criminal act) than on the symbolism involved or on the rhetoric used to explain and justify the act.

But all of this does not mean that the trial was unimportant. Without the likelihood of a public trial, and its concomitant possibilities for generating opposition to the war, the draft board raid would probably not have taken place. The action at Catonsville may have been more dramatic (and hence more rhetorically significant) than the trial, but it was only undertaken in order to bring the trial about.

Further, the legal strategy of aiming for a nullification verdict in the trial should not be taken lightly. Had the jury delivered a nullification verdict, the impact upon debate about the war, and on American life generally, would have been revolutionary. The war would have been rendered illegitimate at a stroke, and many who had been silent would have come to see the war as an unwarranted threat to the social order. Given the potential impact of a jury decision to nullify the law, the defense's decision to forego voir dire examination of potential jurors seems incredible. Careful screening of the jurors by the defense might have increased the chances of a nullification verdict being rendered, and such a verdict would have lost little significance for being the result of rigorous voir dire challenges.

Finally, the trial augmented the act of burning the draft records by providing a forum and a legitimacy that could not be present in the act itself. The forum allowed the full meaningfulness of the act to be articulated in words; the act itself was essentially gestural, and was articulated only by the necessarily truncated texts of a press release and a prayer. The legitimacy came from placing the act within an explicitly argumentative process, a process which granted each side (prosecution and defense) equal time. The deviant stance of a handful of radicals thus became proportional to the official position of the state, and the arguments of the protestors were presented within a framework which was self-consciously rational. The trial thus gave the Catonsville Nine a legitimacy which the burning of draft files never could.

It may be that defendants in public trials who wish to generate wide support among the populace have only two options. They can deny their guilt and claim they are being victimized (by society, corrupt officials, the legal system, or whatever), or they can commit an illegal act that is popular with the citizenry and admit as much at their trial. Either approach has the potential for inspiring public sympathy and hence can be rhetorically effective. But the Catonsville Nine fit neither of these paradigms. At their trial, they admitted having committed an act that was simultaneously illegal, unpopular, and inconsistent with the role behaviors ascribed to them by their intended audience. As rhetoric, the Catonsville Nine trial earned high marks for its attention-getting qualities, but its persuasive goal was never realized.

9

Mediating the Laws
Popular Trials and the Mass Media

Barry Brummett

A popular trial is an ideological trial. We have seen ideology at work in many ways in the trials examined in this book: frankly political maneuvering in the Hedgecock trial, yippie anarchy and government repression in Chicago, and fundamentalism against liberalism in Tennessee. Ideology is embodied not only in the language and non-verbal symbols of a trial's discourses but in the ways that those symbols are mediated to the public. For a popular trial is also a mediated trial. This chapter explores some connections among the popular trial, its mediation to the public, and the ideological implications of that mediation.

I shall begin by arguing that the effects of media (considered apart from the effects of the discourses conveyed through media) are not fully apparent to the naïve public. This transparency of the media is a condition for ideological force, because ideology must always disguise its role as ideology. I shall focus on today's most powerful medium, television, to study three ideological influences of television on the way trials are presented to the public: serialization, personification, and commodification. This chapter takes the frankly polemical position, perhaps in opposition to some of my fellow contributors, that the mediation of trials through television perpetuates undesirable ways of thinking about the justice system. I shall suggest that contradictions inherent in the way the system of justice is mediated to us may provide sites of intervention for the activist social critic intent on social change.

Although several of the concepts I shall use, such as ideology and contradiction, are central to the Marxist vocabulary, it should not be supposed that my analysis is narrowly or exclusively Marxist. I shall range widely in media and social theory to show the ideological influence of televisual mediation. By *ideology* I mean nothing exotic or obscure, nor anything narrowly doctrinaire: a more or less consistent system of thought, a connected set of intellectual habits and emotional reactions that structure and inform the way we perceive and respond to experience. Such a system privileges some interests and disadvantages others; ideology always entails attempts at domination and the responses of acceptance or rejection.

Ideology has no life of its own; it must be created and maintained rhetorically. Attention to ideology should entail attention to the rhetoric which sustains it. To look for the ideological component of mediation therefore obliges us to examine the rhetorical dimension of mediation. Putting aside specific references to trials for the moment, let us consider the rhetoric of ideology in mediation generally.

I

To paraphrase what L. P. Hartley once said of the past, the media are a foreign country: They do things differently there. My claim, like Hartley's, is a metaphor which we might pursue for a moment to see what insights it holds for us. In twentieth-century America, the media create a world that is ready to be visited with the turn of a switch or the purchase of a newspaper. The programming available through the media and the skills, habits, and techniques required to use the media are not the sort of experiences one has by walking through the woods, digging a garden, or throwing balls to children. The media create their own world with its own laws and customs, and to visit there without getting into trouble we must learn those laws and customs.

We do not habitually think this way about experiencing media; to see the world of media as a foreign country requires an effort of will to make strange that which is familiar. The experience of media seems like our experience of unmediated reality for two reasons. First, because this foreign country is as close as the nearest elevator music. Mediated experiences are instantly available to us most of the time. In a world of personal stereos and of televisions used as electric wallpaper, many people live their lives half in and half out of mediated reality.

Second, and more important, it is the business of media in twentieth-century America to create the illusion that their world is no different from that of unmediated reality. News reports create the illusion that the popular trial is exactly the kind of judicial experience which *I* might someday have, that the justice that I might experience is continuous with the justice doled out to John Hinckley. The public comes to think of media as not only continuous with other types of experiences, but as essentially the same as this world. The dedicated soap opera fanatic perceives television's characters as inhabiting this world and weeps at their deaths, the network news viewer expects to see Ted Bundy on the street, and the late night horror film addict fears what lies under the bed.

M. Piccirillo sees this realism of television as an effect of its availability: "Because of television's regular injection into our daily lives, televisual experience is as 'real' as our everyday interpersonal experience."[1] David Porter notes that television time intersects with, coincides with, and often duplicates "real" time, and John Fiske argues that this confluence of time hides from the audience the fact of mediation, the fact that what media present has been authored rather than simply discovered by an audience.[2] Fiske and John Hartley point to televisual realism as disguising its own nature as artificial, for "the television medium presents us with a continuous stream of images *almost all* of which are deeply familiar in structure and form. It uses codes which are closely related to those by which we perceive reality itself. It appears to be the natural way of seeing the world."[3] Indeed, "the more closely the signifier reproduces our common experience, our culturally determined intersubjectivity, the more realistic it appears to be."[4] Television's occasional reminders to the audience of its strangeness, reminders such as Max Headroom's commentaries on upcoming commercials, or *Moonlighting*'s occasional addresses to the camera, are the rare exceptions that prove the rule.

Television's attempt to hide its nature as mediated, as artificial, as authored is of course the same move described as a defining characteristic of ideology in the Marxist critique. (Note also that Aristotle ascribes the same masking function to rhetorical technique: "a writer must disguise his art and give the impression of speaking naturally and not artificially. Naturalness is persuasive, artificiality is the contrary."[5]) It is the business of ideology to hide its nature as ideology, as the arguable, as the interested or power-implicated, and to present itself as the most natural common sense.[6] The obvious conclusion is that television and its underlying strategy of realism is ideological. Douglas Kellner explicitly argues that television's form of presentation, the way it constructs its images and integrates them with narrative, is a primary locus of the dominant ideology in modern America.[7] Stuart Hall agrees, noting that the media of any age are ideological because of their role in representation: "There is a specificity to those practices whose principal object is to produce ideological representations. They are different from those practices which . . . produce other commodities. Those people who work in the media are producing, reproducing and transforming the field of ideological representation itself."[8] The media present a world that seems natural and continuous with unmediated reality, a mediated world sutured into "the background canvas of meanings and preferred ways of seeing."[9] The ideology of televisual realism not only hides the nature of itself as ideological, by extension it hides the ideological nature of the motives and thought patterns to which television predisposes its audience. It therefore behooves the student of television to identify the ideology which it offers, the trinkets we will be tricked into buying, when we enter the land of TV.

But there is perhaps a more important reason for understanding the ideology of mediation. The strategy that hides the nature of mediated reality as a strange world *also* must occlude our sense of *unmediated* reality as different from the mediated. If unmediated experience is not privileged or primary in the public's perception, nothing prevents the unmediated from being influenced or structured by the mediated. Tourists who travel to a favorite foreign country again and again may become enchanted by the habits and customs they encounter there, and import them into daily life back home. If it seems good to dine at midnight in Spain, then midnight it shall be in Peoria. Now, suppose a particular medium becomes widely used by the public. Suppose the ways of thinking that are required to apprehend that medium's discourse become deeply ingrained in the public mind. And suppose that the ideology of this medium obscures the difference between experience of the medium and other experiences. The inescapable conclusion is that the discourses of the medium will begin to inform the discourses of life outside the medium; the public will come to think about unmediated experience using the tools which enable them to have mediated experience.

Several scholars have argued that everyday, unmediated life is increasingly influenced by today's master medium of television. The argument that a dominant medium will eventually govern ways of thinking is, of course, nothing new. Harold Innis and Walter Ong have both argued that throughout history, ways of thinking engendered by dominant media have structured the ideology of the age.[10] The argument has been made repeatedly for the effects of television in contemporary America by such scholars as Joshua Meyrowitz, who links television's dissolving of separate information systems to many social effects, and Neil Postman, who decries the harmful result of television's featuring of entertainment values.[11] James Chesebro argues that "mental processes can be a function of the configuration of media operative within a particular culture," and that in particular "the central function of television is to provide a general orientation or awareness" which informs cultural life in general.[12] Gary Gumpert and Robert Cathcart similarly claim that "the modern electronic media have affected what we know, who and what we talk about, who talks to us, and who listens" and that as a result, "people develop particular media consciousness because media have different framing conventions and time orientations."[13]

I believe that the best statement of this argument is David Altheide and Robert Snow's explanation of "media logic." They argue that "the present-day dominance of media has been achieved through a process in which the general form and specific formats of media have become adopted throughout society so that cultural content is basically organized and defined in terms of media logic."[14] They summarize some sources of television's media logic: "The significant features of electronic media grammar are: 1) the manner in which time is used, including compacting time, rhythm, and tempo (inflection); 2) the organization and scheduling of content such as the dialogue/action sequences and the scheduling of programs (syntax); and 3) special features of verbal and nonverbal communication, such as reliance on specific kinds of words and nonverbal gestures which represent words."[15] These features of television inhere in "the grammar of the medium and the norms that are used to define content."[16] Altheide's further analysis of the dimensions of television's "media logic" shows how it structures discourse beyond television.[17] Several scholars, in sum, have argued that media exert powerful influences on the forms and structures of a society's ways of thinking and perceiving.

Another way to phrase that contention is to say that perceptions of reality are determined (to varying degrees) by the media. Such a contention would seem to contradict the widely held view that perceptions of reality are *socially* constructed.[18] This latter argument, no stranger to media theorists, generally holds that "what counts as an 'event' is socially determined: events are what we are accustomed to pay attention to."[19] Altheide or Snow, in contrast, would argue that what counts as an event in our society is determined by what "plays well" on television. Does the contention that consciousness is socially induced contradict the argument that consciousness is induced by media logic? I shall argue that it does not, especially if we realize that media logic is not *all* there is to consciousness, and if we place media logic as a specially potent subset of social reality.

To see the social reality thesis and the media logic thesis as compatible, this essay takes a materialist position toward the question of consciousness.[20] Consciousness in sane adults is always shared and social, never totally idiosyncratic. But the "social" must not be idealized; people are not *socialized* into the discourses of a culture by magic, osmosis, or simply being there. Socially induced consciousness, which I take to be a generic term for different kinds of ideologies, "always exists in an apparatus, and its practice or practices. This existence is material."[21] As Dick Hebdige reminds us, "Social relations and processes are then appropriated by individuals only through the forms in which they are represented to those individuals," forms that are material images, discourses, languages, and technologies.[22] "While human behavior is to a remarkable extent diverse and variable, it tends to be 'formed' and given shape by the attraction or the power of available imaginative materials. ... The storehouse of imaginative materials available to each person provides a sort of repertoire."[23] To see social consciousness, ideology, as embodied in imaginative materials, one need not see discourse as the mere superstructural reflection of economic conditions of production.[24] Because imaginative materials, and the technologies through which they are presented to publics, are manipulable materials, they are then also sites of ideological struggle fully as much as are working conditions in factories. Imaginative materials and their technologies influence publics but are also reciprocally influenced by publics. Therefore, to understand ways in which consciousness and its attendant power structures are presently embodied in media and media content, and to *enable* public responsibility by showing possibilities for changing media and content, should be a primary goal of media criticism.

To think in terms of media logic is to think in terms of the *forms* or *patterns* which particular televisual materials embody.[25] Apart from whatever motives and ways of seeing are imparted by the surface content of a *Leave it to Beaver* episode, the general "reading" habits required to make sense of the episode and to use the television machine constitute the logic of the medium. But that abstract media logic is always induced in the public, and then employed by the public, through concrete technology and the actual imaginative materials, the programming, of the medium. In other words, form is "immanently and intrinsically an ideology in its own right."[26] The forms or structures of media, embodied in specific programs and techniques required to use media, are the bearers of ideology.[27]

The relationship between mediated and unmediated experience becomes especially interesting when we consider the special case of *news*. Here we find ideological disguising of mediation especially hard at work. If television drama is presented *as if* it were real, television news is explicitly presented *as* the real, as common sense experience.[28] Some scholars have complained that news distorts reality, a position that implies an undistorted real plane of events somewhere.[29] For our purposes, it is sufficient to note that for most people, the sorts of events "covered" on the news are available to us *only* on the news. There can never be any question, for most of us, of comparing what really happens in Far Beluchistan with what Dan Rather says happens. For most of us, the news is a prime example of media reality being as real as directly experienced reality.[30] Television news coverage is the legitimator and definer of what is real. Therefore, unmediated experiences that are related to what we have seen on the news will be experienced *in terms of* the meanings and conventions of mediated reality. Because so much of the justice system is experienced by way of the news, I will expect *my own* few brushes with the law (traffic tickets, jury duty, witnessing shoplifting arrests) to be just the way it is on the evening news, even if I "know" that it will be a little bit different from the "fictions" portrayed on *L.A. Law* and *Perry Mason*. For that reason, the news is a site where the ideological dimensions of the medium a) are especially hidden, and b) are especially powerful in terms of how we understand or structure our nonmediated reality.[31]

Trials become popular today only when they are mediated to the public. Furthermore, they are more often mediated as news than as fictional drama. A number of essays in this volume have suggested that we learn about our system of justice through popular trials. This essay urges a retrospective rereading, a meditation, upon the claims about the system of justice which have gone before in this book. I shall argue that what popular trials are, and by extension what the justice system is, must be powerfully influenced by television's media logic. There are many dimensions to television's media logic. I shall focus on three important ones: serialization, personification, and commodification.

II

Serialization

Television, like the long and winding road, goes on and on whether you're there or not. It is among the most continuous of media, for it is "on" all day long. But television's technological capacity for infinite continuity is superseded in this country by an economic need for discontinuity or segmentation. Economic forces which lead to segmentation of air time stem from television's reliance on commercials. Television is a medium supported by and in support of the capitalist economy, and its time is sold to advertisers. That time must be broken up into marketable segments: advertising for this half hour is sold to Exxon and Gillette, while Gulf and IBM buy the next half hour. These advertisers not only buy time in segments, they buy an audience likely to stay tuned during that time. Television needs to retain an audience for as many of those segments as possible, yet the television industry cannot possibly produce novel programming continuously. Television needs to reuse the same characters, plots, themes, and formats. It must therefore cast its programs into the form of *serials*, recurring types of programs or progressive episodes of ongoing programs.

Television's reliance on serial programming cast into marketable form decisively constrains its content in specific ways. The need to sell advertising at regular intervals creates a need for relatively short segments of narrative that occur between commercial breaks. The need to retain an audience during those commercial breaks requires programming to create dramatic climaxes and resolutions at regular, short intervals.[32] The need to reuse material creates a reliance on formulaic, repetitive material. So television programming becomes highly patterned, keeping time to the rhythm of its commercial interruption. The cognitive skills that best enable reception of such programming are aesthetic, pattern-recognition skills.[33]

Clearly, as a number of scholars have noted, television is predisposed (and predisposes its audience) to treat experience in terms of drama, to impose dramatic structure on content.[34] But the need for quick dramatic development and resolution creates television narratives of a particular sort. Altheide and Snow argue that the need to create dramatically interesting material and then conclude it quickly means that *news* coverage is first preoccupied with its subject and then drops it abruptly.[35]

Trials are cast into that sort of narrative form. What is narrative about the trial is foregrounded in covering it: Heroes and villains, fools and foils are featured, and story reigns supreme. Mediated legal discourse takes the form of most televised news reporting, which is "gossip" rather than learned disquisition.[36] If trials create and disseminate public knowledge about the political or judicial system, they do so aesthetically, in presentation of plots and fables. Televised trials are concerned less with legal and political issues than they are with entertainment, a prime value of television.[37]

Furthermore, narrative presentation of popular trials follows television's logic of heavy coverage followed by no coverage at all. Mediation of a popular trial is likely to end with a climactic verdict. Later appeals, motions, or reversals rate but brief mention if any.

For television, the trial is usually over with the jury's verdict. The reader may reflect whether he or she knows the status of any popular trials which have "concluded" in the past year. Are they under appeal? If so, on what grounds? In which court? The public will rarely know that much, nor be spectators of the continuing, long, and untelegenic grinding of the law's machinery. The law, which is an ongoing, complicated process of move and countermove for those who experience it unmediated, becomes discrete, intense stories when mediated. Take, for instance, the Bernard Goetz "subway vigilante" trial. For weeks there was daily, intense coverage of arguments in and out of the courtroom. During several days of jury deliberation, which is hard to televise, coverage was cursory or nonexistent. The jury's verdict and Goetz's eventual sentencing brought a brief but intense flurry of news stories. But any legal moves since then might as well have taken place on the dark side of the moon as far as the national public is concerned, for this week's episode is over.

Serialization of television content is not only a requirement for maintaining interest over commercial breaks, but from one installment of a program to another. The *Cosby Show* appears every Thursday evening; the news is at 5:30 and 6:00 every evening. But programmers cannot count on audience viewing of every installment; indeed, they cannot expect that audiences will stay through the whole of any given installment. For that reason, segments of serial programming must be plotted so as not to lose audience members who have missed the last installment.[38] That entails utter simplicity of narrative, so that audiences may be brought "up to date" on any developments in a very few words, and so that audiences need not pull forward from one week to the next a complicated plot. Utter simplicity must also be the form which trial narratives take. Legal subtleties are lost not only to the need to narrate quickly, but the need to narrate serially in installments to an unattentive audience.

Personification

Television is a medium which speaks to us in domestic, personal surroundings.[39] Its small-sized screen is not suited to vast panoramas or complicated action; instead, it is much better suited to showing us people and characters.[40] Television's focus is on the person, and even scenes of car chases, cattle stampedes, or cavalry charges will return again and again to the personal, for instance, in closeups of the characters' faces.[41]

Televisual logic therefore gives the public a focus on the personal at the expense of a focus on issues. Television inserts the private into the public arena.[42] On this evening's news we are as likely to hear what Roger Hedgecock had for breakfast as we are to hear about the legal and political issues at stake. We are told as much about the strain that von Bulow's trial inflicts upon him personally as we are about relations between the law and the influence of the wealthy. The fine points of the insanity defense pale by comparison with the lurid details of John Hinckley's mental illness. In other words, issues are not presented on television unless they can be personified in heroes, villains, and fools. Fiske and Hartley argue that television's extreme realism contributes to a stress on the individual over the collective.[43] That is because the individual viewer's experience is only of one's own experience; history, collective experience, abstract principles of law or politics cannot be directly experienced. To present itself as real, television must therefore present itself to the individual as individual experience. Even the social issues that are addressed, as Gitlin notes, must be solved by individual heroes.[44] A frontier town's struggle with racism will be embodied in the battle between a concrete Native American and a particular cowboy bigot, and that struggle will be resolved not collectively but by intervention from the Lone Ranger and Tonto.

So it is with trials. As Robert Hariman notes in this volume, trials featured the personal long before television. Media logic in this case furthers a tendency already in place; the medium and its subject matter seem made for each other. Principles must be personified. Oppositional readings of the law are not understandable unless they coalesce in William Kunstler. Overweening pride and flouting of the law is concretized into John Delorean. John Hinckley is not just another psycho: He is the archetype of the disturbed. These personifications of principle are then useful in resolving the social conflicts represented in trials. Personification joins forces with narrative especially in coverage of legal trials because the agonistic nature of law, embodied in the personas of competing counsel, judge, defendant, and so on, fits so well with the agonistic and competitive plots popular in contemporary America. The issue in legal reporting becomes primarily who wins, which bad guys get shot down on Main Street, which good guys get to ride off in triumph.

Meyrowitz's extended analysis shows us that to personify justice is also to trivialize it.[45] He shows us that television is a medium well suited to merging front stage and back stage behaviors. Television's ability to reveal private life at odds with public pretense in realistic, visual ways destroys the mask of pomp and circumstance worn by legal decorum. Not only do we see principal figures in the trial stripped morally naked, we see the process of justice itself so disrobed. Meyrowitz's argument is that television shows us the intemperate outbursts outside the courtroom in a more compelling way than newspapers ever can; it shows us the mansions of wealthy defendants and the squalor of the indigent criminal more clearly than does radio. We see what the characters have planned for us to see, but also what they have not. We see Judge Hoffman looking and acting somewhat less than judicial. We see inside the imposing edifices of justice to find people acting just as we do on Monday morning (whereas newspapers lose much by only reporting it).[46]

One result of seeing the "back stage" elements of the justice system is to trivialize that system. Television trivializes because, as Meyrowitz argues,[47] it creates no sense of place: no sense of the courtroom or the procedures that go on there as special and apart from everyday life. Television coverage of a trial will not report the ceremonies and trappings of justice, which are designed to awe the attending spectator. It looks instead at the sordid revelations and unseemly behavior of the participants.

Television also trivializes the justice system because it introduces it into the public's "back stage." Television inserts every place into our domestic places. Television slots justice in between toilet paper commercials. It squeezes stirring principles into a nineteen-inch screen. That which is covered in a thirty-second news spot after the talking dog story and before the weather cannot seem very impressive. Farrell Corcoran goes so far as to argue that television imparts "a tone of indifference toward everything within its scope."[48] Television's insertion of social issues into the living room trivializes the issues, for everyday television viewing is used in homes as a conversation piece, as a means to set schedules.[49] Coverage of the Catonsville Nine engenders not moral discussion so much as an awareness that bedtime is close at hand. Fiske and Hartley's well known claim that television serves a "bardic" role of mythmaking and myth perpetuation in our society does not help us here, for the result must inevitably be a trivializing of myth itself.[50]

Commodification

Television is a highly commodified medium. The television set itself is an owned commodity.[51] More important is the constant presence of commercials on television.[52] These commercials function not merely as reminders of the capitalist ends which the television industry serves. Commercials are integral with other programming as well; they share plots, characters, themes, and concerns.[53] Robert Young stars as Dr. Welby and then shows up in ads to tout aspirins. Fictitious police officers and lawyers appear on advertisements for soap and makeup.

Television predisposes its audience to consider issues in terms of commodities, it makes "us accustomed to thinking of ourselves and behaving as a *market* rather than a *public,* as consumers rather than citizens. Public problems (like air pollution) are propounded as susceptible to private commodity solutions (like eye drops)."[54] This means that trial coverage will gravitate towards (although it will not be exclusively concerned with) explanations grounded in commodities. The Walker and Jonathan Pollard spy trials focused on the principals' avarice at least as much as on lax security or disillusionment with the United States.

A subtler form of commodification is suggested by the fact that the capitalist system requires a shared currency which enables consumers to purchase commodities. Television usually ignores the issue of currency, paradoxically reassuring the public on that very score. Nobody ever has to pay for anything on television: People finish meals in restaurants and they simply leave. Even more unsettling is the fact that no question is ever raised in advertisements of how commodities are to be paid for. Although price is occasionally mentioned, it is for the purpose of saying that it is a price that anyone can afford with ease. No mention is ever made of the overtime at the packing plant that must be worked to pay for that new car. Television assumes everyone has the currency necessary to share in the world of commodities. At a subtler level, television is a highly centralized and homogenizing medium. It must put on a face which all its diverse audiences can recognize.[55] And so its programming must take the form of a sort of intellectual common currency which everyone can acquire.

The commodification of television commodifies mediated trials. First, legal lifestyles of the rich and famous stand a better chance of becoming popularized because they foreground a cultural preoccupation with wealth. Claus von Bulow would be just another bum who may have tried to kill his wife were it not for the millions of dollars involved. John Delorean would be another alleged chiseler but for his playboy means and image. Trials of drug addicts, prostitutes, and shoplifters do not fit with television's preoccupation with commodities, and so the public is more encouraged to think about the troubles of the wealthy than the problems of the poor.

A more important implication of commodification is the commodification of justice itself. Justice is usually portrayed in mediated trials as a commodity within the reach of all. Television makes it seem cheap and easy to go to trial. No mention is ever made of the financial ruin entailed by having to pay the attorney, who seems to be a commodity as attainable as a new car. The idea that justice may be a scarce resource, that a day in court may be prohibitive for most citizens, is hardly ever raised on television. This presumption of easily available participation in the legal system arises because of television's disregard for the realities of *currency,* as argued above. By encouraging the public to desire commodities and discouraging the public from wondering about the means (currency) needed to get those commodities, television creates a sense that justice is one of those fun trips on a cruise ship that evidently anyone at all can enjoy.

III

I have argued that "the media and the audience share a logic that is used to 'make sense' of social phenomena. The audience develops a 'media consciousness'."[56] The role of television as a locus of those materials that embody ideology is important: "The mass media have now assumed the role of the Church, in a more secular age, of interpreting and making sense of the world to the mass public."[57] What can we say in summary about the sort of consciousness created by television's media logic concerning popularized trials?

It may be that the reader has intuited in these pages a certain dissatisfaction with the mediated image of the legal system. The reader would be right. From here on this chapter turns explicitly propagandistic, for I argue that the ideology of televisual realism has a particularly distressing impact when it mediates the process of justice. Here is where the ideological effects of popular trials become especially important, for as the contributors to this volume agree, trials are representative of the legal system itself. What people are led to expect of that system because of what they see on television influences what we ask of our legislators and lawyers. The public therefore needs to be on its toes with regard to what it expects of the justice system, what it regards as possible and desirable in changing that system, and what can actually happen to it when it falls into the toils of the unmediated law. And what can actually happen to people ensnared in unmediated litigation is nothing like what television's media logic would have us think: You *can* be denied justice because you can't afford as many lawyers as the other side, your heartbreaking trial *can* become a Dickensian Jarndyce and Jarndyce instead of a short story, and the law *can* be a faceless abstract system devoid of cowboy heroes or villains. A responsible scholar *cannot* note the perils of this ideology without suggesting strategies for countering it, so I shall.

Marxists argue that contradictions within an ideological system reveal its flaws, delusions, and illusions.[58] Kenneth Burke argues that contradictions are inevitable within any discourse, and that they reveal strategic moments in a language which allow critics, working within the language, to prompt change.[59] Thus far I have called our attention to some important characteristics of television's logic, and have suggested the motives and attitudes concerning the legal system to which that media logic might predispose an audience. But I would not like to leave the impression that oppositional readings are impossible, that resistance to media logic is futile. For if we look more closely at the logic of television as applied to the legal system, and if we consider it in conjunction with certain truisms about the legal system handed down to us in civics classes and during newscasts of trials themselves, we will see a number of important contradictions emerging. Those contradictions are the sites of possible oppositional reading of the legal system as it is mediated to us through television.[60]

One contradiction emerges within the characteristic of commodification. Commodification predisposes television news to covering trials of the wealthy. Yet on the other hand, justice as commodified is described to the public as something that everyone can have. Mediated justice is a story about interesting lives, yet the platitudes of social knowledge tell me that justice is attainable as part of my uninteresting life. The first half of this contradiction can be exploited by critics to reveal the falsity of the second half. And that undermining of the logic of commodification may be assisted by the concept of personification. For if the distant wealthy can be democratized in television, if we can see them in their moral underwear, the basis of their enjoyment of justice in financial advantage may be clarified. These people get to have widely publicized trials not because they are more deserving or interesting, but for no other reason than that they have currency I do not have and can purchase a commodity that I cannot have.

A second contradiction may be made clear for the public by emphasizing that justice is more akin to mere continuity than to serialization; it goes on forever, and we are forever implicated in its workings. The serialization inserted into television's continuity comes and goes; stories of famous trials begin and end. And so we are given a sense of justice as something that begins and ends during the peak periods of popular trials. Serialization of justice is also homologous with its commodification, for a commodity is something that is used from time to time. That which cannot usually be commodified, like air, is present always. Therefore, cultivation of images of justice as continuous rather than serial, as a system always in place and always constraining us, may be a necessary strategy for critics seeking to counter the serialization of justice.

Hirsch notes that the need to sell more commodities to the public all the time strongly favors that which is new, and that the passion for new products, new faces, new formats, new programs on television may be traced to that characteristic.[61] But the law offers a symbolic resource to critics seeking to undermine the effects of media logic, if the law's reliance on tradition and precedent can be emphasized. That (justice) which is presented as something always new can be shown to be something which must always be traditional, a third contradiction.

It may be that by now the reader will be uneasy about the form which the legal system takes when mediated by television. That was my intention. That uneasiness may become acute when we remember that mediation is how most of us confront the legal system most of the time. I have tried to suggest that oppositional understandings of the legal system are possible, indeed, that they may be enabled by contradictions embedded in the logic of television itself. As teachers and critics, enabling such oppositional readings in students and readers is the task that falls to us in helping to bring about or to maintain, as a myth would have it, the best legal system in the world.

Notes

Introduction

1. See Michael Halloran, "Doing Public Business in Public," in Karlyn Kohrs Campbell and Kathleen Hall Jamieson, eds., *Form and Genre: Shaping Rhetorical Action* (Falls Church, Va.: Speech Communication Association, n.d.).

2. The next essay in this volume offers a more detailed discussion of the generic character of the popular trial, and each of the essays contributes to this definition. For additional discussion of rhetorical genres, see Campbell and Jamieson, as well as Herbert W. Simons and Aram A. Aghazarian, eds., *Form, Genre, and the Study of Political Discourse* (Columbia, S.C.: University of South Carolina Press, 1986).

3. Kenneth Burke, "Literature as Equipment for Living," in *The Philosophy of Literary Form: Studies in Symbolic Action*, 3rd ed. (Berkeley: University of California Press, 1973).

4. See the bibliographic essay in *American Political Trials*, ed. Michael R. Belknap (Westport, Conn.: Greenwood Press, 1981); and the unpublished "Bibliography of Popularized Trials" begun by Ingeborg Chaly and expanded by Kurt Ritter; and John M. Ross, *Trials in Collections: An Index to Famous Trials Throughout the World* (Metuchen, N.J.: Scarecrow Press, 1983).

5. John H. Timmis III, *Thine Is the Kingdom: The Trial for Treason of Thomas Wentworth, Earl of Strafford, First Minister to King Charles I, and Last Hope of the English Crown* (University, Ala.: University of Alabama Press, 1974).

6. The titles are indicative of the approach: Brandt Aymer, *A Pictorial History of the World's Great Trials* (New York: Crown, 1967); Richard E.

Rubenstein, *Great Courtroom Battles* (Chicago: Bayboy Press, 1973); Alice Fleming, *Trials That Made Headlines* (London: St. Martins, 1974).

7. Belknap, ed., *American Political Trials;* Theodore L. Becker, ed., *Political Trials* (New York: Bobbs-Merrill, 1971).

8. Ron Christenson, *Political Trials: Gordian Knots in the Law* (New Brunswick, N.J.: Transaction Books, 1986).

9. Alexis de Tocqueville, *Democracy in America* (New York: Vintage, 1945), 290.

10. Karl N. Llewellyn, *Jurisprudence: Realism in Theory and Practice* (Chicago: University of Chicago Press, 1962), 301. Despite all the ferment today ranging from critical legal studies to the hermeneutical turn taken by liberals such as Ronald Dworkin and James Boyd White, the basic point of departure taken by the older legal realists remains secure. Whether radicals are talking about ideology or liberals are talking about intelligibility, legal realism is being re-activated and broadened methodologically more than it is being displaced. "The Critical Legal Studies movement is the direct descendant of Realism and the law-and-society movement," and the comparison applies *a fortiori* to other, more modest, contemporary theories (Mark Tushnet, "Critical Legal Studies and Constitutional Law: An Essay in Deconstruction," *Stanford Law Review* 36 [1984]: 626).

11. James Boyd White stresses this relationship between law and rhetoric. See "Constituting a Culture of Argument" in his *When Words Lose Their Meaning: Constitutions and Reconstitutions of Language, Character, and Community* (Chicago: University of Chicago Press, 1984), and *Heracles' Bow: Essays on the Rhetoric and Poetics of the Law* (Madison: University of Wisconsin Press, 1985). The current debate about the relationship between the general interpretative character of the law and its claim to special authority is illustrated nicely in the exchange between Stanley Fish and Owen Fiss: Owen M. Fiss, "Objectivity and Interpretation," *Stanford Law Review* 34 (1982):739–63; Stanley Fish, "Fish v. Fiss," *Stanford Law Review* 36 (1984): 1325–47.

12. Lloyd Bitzer, "The Rhetorical Situation," *Philosophy and Rhetoric* 1 (1968):1–14.

13. Robert L. Scott, "Rhetoric as Epistemic," *Central States Speech Journal* 18 (1967): 9–17.

14. Thomas Farrell, "Knowledge, Consensus, and Rhetorical Theory," *Quarterly Journal of Speech* 62 (1976): 1–14.

15. W. Lance Bennett and Martha Feldman, *Reconstructing Reality in the Courtroom: Justice and Judgment in American Culture* (New Brunswick, N.J.: Rutgers University Press,1981). Earlier work by W. Lance Bennett includes "Storytelling in Criminal Trials: A Model of Social Judgment," *Quarterly Journal of Speech* 64 (1978): 1–22, and "Rhetorical Transformations of Evidence in Criminal Trials: Creating Grounds for Legal Judgment," *Quarterly Journal of Speech* 65 (1979): 311–23.

16. See, for example, Robert A. Forston, *Legal Communication: A Bibliography* (American Forensic Association, 1975); the special issue on legal communication in *Journal of the American Forensic Association* 12.3 (1976);

Bennett and Feldman, *Reconstructing Reality;* Ronald J. Malton and Richard J. Crawford, eds., *Communication Strategies and the Practice of Lawyering* (Speech Communication Association, 1983). Also see Michael J. Saks and Reid Hastie, *Social Psychology in the Court* (New York: Van Nostrand Reinhold, 1978). The best example of this perspective, particularly in respect to the contribution it can make to the study of popular trials, is Janice Schuetz and Kathryn Holmes Snedaker, *Communication and Litigation: Case Studies of Famous Trials* (Carbondale: Southern Illinois University Press, 1988).

17. As with any classification, these categories at times can be more neat than true. For recent discussions of the relationships between law and communication see Kathleen Farrell, "Modes of Judicial Discourse: The Search for Argument Fields," in *Argument: Analysis and Practices*, ed. Frans H. van Eemeren, Rob Grootenborst, J. Anthony Blair, and Charles A. Willard (Dordrecht, The Netherlands: Foris, 1987), and Thomas J. Hynes, Jr., "Interpretation, Law and Argument: Prospects for Cross-fertilization," in the same volume. See also Vivian I. Dicks, "Courtroom Rhetorical Strategies: Forensic and Deliverative Perspectives," *Quarterly Journal of Speech* 67 (1981): 178–92, and Richard Rieke, "Argumentation in the Legal Process," in *Advances in Argumentation Theory and Research*, ed. J. Robert Cox and Charles A. Willard (Carbondale: Southern Illinois University Press, 1982), 363–78.

18. This approach is represented by much of the work listed in the preceding references, and conducted masterfully by Schuetz and Snedaker, *Communication and Litigation.*

19. As Schuetz and Snedaker also demonstrate, the conventional work in legal communication can culminate in a synoptic perspective on a trial, as is evident in the structure of their book and particularly in their concluding chapter, "Courtroom Drama: The Trial of the Chicago Eight." But their perspective remains constrained powerfully by its assumptions of the rightful primacy of legal practice in the conduct and interpretation of any trial.

20. See the Free Speech Yearbooks published annually by the Speech Communication Association, especially the bibliography in each of articles, books, and Supreme Court decisions; Peter Kane, comp., "Table of Contents and Index to Free Speech Yearbook, Volumes I–XXV, 1962–1986," *Free Speech Yearbook* (Speech Communication Association, 1986): 144–54; Janice Schuetz, "Political Trials and Free Speech," *Free Speech Yearbook* (Speech Communication Association, 1985): 38–50; Franklyn S. Hairman, *Speech and Law in a Free Society* (Chicago: University of Chicago Press, 1981); Thomas L. Tedford, *Freedom of Speech in the United States* (Carbondale: Southern Illinois University Press, 1985); Peter Kane, *Murder, Courts, and the Press: Issues in Free Press/Fair Trial* (Carbondale: Southern Illinois University Press, 1986). The reception of Kane's book illustrates the range of interest in popular trials: Reviews have appeared in both the *Quarterly Journal of Speech* 73 (1987): 511–12, and the *Village Voice* 31: (26 August 1986): 48.

21. See, for example, Forston, *Legal Communication;* Symposium: The Use of Videotape in the Courtroom, *Brigham Young University Law Review*

(1975, no. 2); Herbert E. Rollings and Jim Balscovich, "The Case of Patricia Hearst: Pre-trial Publicity and Opinion," *Journal of Communication* 27 (1977): 58–65; Bert Pryor, David U. Strawn, Raymond Buchanan, and Milan D. Meeske, "The Florida Experiment: An Analysis of On-The-Scene Responses to Cameras in the Courtroom," *Southern Speech Communication Journal* 45 (1979):12–26; Susanna Barber, *News Cameras in the Courtroom* (Norwood, N.J.: Ablex, 1987); Gerald R. Miller and Norman E. Fontes, *Real Versus Reel: What's the Verdict? The Effects of Videotaped Court Materials on Juror Response* (National Science Foundation, n.d.).

22. Admittedly, this consensus seems valid if we focus solely on the media's effect on the legal process. See Renata Adler, *Reckless Disregard: Westmoreland v. CBS et al., Sharon v. Time* (New York: Knopf, 1986).

23. For paradigmatic portraits of legal orators, see William Norwood Brigance, ed., *The History and Criticism of American Public Address*, vol. 1 (New York: McGraw-Hill, 1943), 434–500.

24. Some studies do come closer to our approach to examining the trials as forms and forums of communication: Timmis, *Thine Is the Kingdom*; David Grover, *Debaters and Dynamiters: The Story of the Harwood Trial* (Corvalis: Oregon State University Press, 1965); Akira Sambonmatsu, "Darrow and Rourke's Use of Burkeian Identification Strategies in *New York* v. *Gitlow*," *Communication Monographs* 38 (1971): 36–48; Milton Dickens and Ruth E. Schwartz, "Oral Argument Before the Supreme Court: Marshall v. Davis in the School Segregation Cases," *Quarterly Journal of Speech* 57 (1971): 32–42; David Bezayiff, "Legal Oratory of John Adams: An Early Instrument of Protest," *Western Journal of Speech Communication* 40 (1976):63–71; Stephen L. Wasby, Anthony D'Amato, and Rosemary Metrailer, "The Functions of Oral Argument in the U.S. Supreme Court," *Quarterly Journal of Speech* 62 (1976): 410–22; Vivian I. Dicks, "Courtroom Controversy: A Stasis/Stock Issues Analysis of the Angela Davis Trial," *Journal of the American Forensic Association* 13 (1976); David M. Hunskar, "The Rhetoric of *Brown vs. Board of Education:* Paradigm for Contemporary Social Protest," *Southern Speech Communication Journal* 43 (1978): 91–109; David Kaufer, "Analyzing Philosophy in Rhetoric: Darrow's Mechanism in the Defense of Leopold and Loeb," *Southern Speech Communication Journal* 45 (1980): 363–77; Carol White, "Scapegoating of Bruno Richard Hauptmann: The Rhetorical Process in Prejudicial Publicity," *Central States Speech Journal* 32 (1981): 100–10; Robert A. Francesconi, "James Hunt, The Wilmington 10, and Institutional Legitimacy," *Quarterly Journal of Speech* 69 (1982): 47–59; Celeste Michelle Condit and J. Ann Selzer, "The Rhetoric of Objectivity in the Newspaper Coverage of a Murder Trial," *Critical Studies in Mass Communication* 2 (1985): 197–216; Kurt Ritter, "Drama and Legal Rhetoric: The Perjury Trials of Alger Hiss," *Western Journal of Speech Communication* 49 (1985): 83–102; Charles Alan Taylor and Celeste Michelle Condit, "Objectivity and Elites: A Creation Science Trial," *Critical Studies in Mass Communication* 5 (1988): 293–312.

25. See Christenson, Appendix B: "Possible Political Trials," in *Political Trials*, 268–84.

Chapter One

1. Plato, *Laws* 817b–c, in *The Collected Dialogues of Plato*, ed. Edith Hamilton and Huntington Cairns, trans. A. E. Taylor (Princeton, N.J.: Princeton University Press, 1961).

2. 817d.

3. The general social theory presented here will be familiar to some as "dramatism," particularly as it has been articulated by Kenneth Burke, and to others as the "social construction of reality," particularly as it has been presented by Peter Berger and Thomas Luckmann.

4. Thomas Farrell, "Knowledge, Consensus, and Rhetorical Theory," *Quarterly Journal of Speech* 62 (1976): 1. The study of popular trials is an economical way to reach Farrell's goal of articulating a "functional relationship between a fully developed art of rhetoric and a generally accepted body of knowledge pertaining to matters of public concern."

5. Thomas Conley, "The Linnaean Blues: Thoughts on the Genre Approach," in *Form, Genre, and the Study of Political Discourse*, ed. Herbert W. Simons and Aram A. Aghazarian (Columbia: University of South Carolina Press, 1986).

6. Here I am drawing upon Michael Halloran, "Doing Public Business in Public," in Karlyn Kohrs Campbell and Kathleen Hall Jamieson, eds., *Form and Genre: Shaping Rhetorical Action* (Falls Church, Va.: Speech Communication Association, n.d.). Halloran discusses the genre of the public proceeding, which can be read as the larger category including the popular trial, or as a similar and related genre.

7. Ronald Dworkin puts the matter succinctly when he states that a practice "has some point." *Law's Empire* (Cambridge: Belknap Press of Harvard University Press, 1986), 47. See also Alasdair MacIntyre's discussion of the concept of a practice in chapter fourteen of *After Virtue*, 2nd ed. (Notre Dame: University of Notre Dame Press, 1984), 181–203.

8. The metaphor of the "container," as well as its methodological development, comes from Kenneth Burke, *A Grammar of Motives* (Berkeley: University of California Press, 1969), 3 ff. Strictly speaking, the container of the scene expresses "in fixed properties the same quality that the action expresses in terms of development" (3). But things quickly become more complicated; the important qualification to remember is that "the ratios may often be interpreted as principles of selectivity rather than as thoroughly causal relationships" (18). Furthermore, the container metaphor itself obscures an essential quality of Burke's thinking, for as the genre organizes material toward an end it is operating more as a mode of action than as a formal constraint. Carolyn R. Miller captures these ideas when she argues that the genre represents "typified rhetorical action" ("Genre as Social Action," *Quarterly Journal of Speech* 70 [1984]:151).

9. Willard B. Gatewood, Jr., *Preachers, Pedagogues, and Politicians: The Evolution Controversy in North Carolina, 1920–1927* (Chapel Hill: University of North Carolina Press, 1966), 4.

10. Farrell, "Knowledge, Consensus, and Rhetorical Theory," 2.

11. This definition of the political function comes from the work of Murray Edelman. For its integration with rhetorical analysis, see W. Lance Bennett, "Political Scenarios and the Nature of Politics," *Philosophy and Rhetoric* 8 (1975): 23–42.

12. For a recent example of how the popular trial can become a forum for evaluating the discourse of the law and of other institutions, see Renata Adler, *Reckless Disregard: Westmoreland v. CBS et al., Sharon v. Time* (New York: Knopf, 1986).

13. James Boyd White, "Is Cultural Criticism Possible?" *Michigan Law Review* 84 (1986): 1373. This perspective is elaborated in *Heracles' Bow* (Madison: University of Wisconsin Press, 1985).

14. For an extended presentation of this argument, see the essay by Bernabo and Condit in this volume.

15. Richard M. Weaver, "Dialectic and Rhetoric at Dayton, Tennessee," in *The Ethics of Rhetoric* (Chicago: Henry Regnery, 1953), 30. Weaver is articulating three discourses in the trial: scientific, theological, and legal. Although Weaver's intuitions are refracted through his heavy Aristotelian language and toward his objective of justifying the legal outcome of the trial, they anticipate my perspective. Interestingly, he locates the rhetorical advantage gained for the scientific discourse in "the embarrassment to which Darrow brought Bryan in questioning him about the Bible and the theory of evolution" (53), but Weaver dismisses this performance because it is outside the legal definition of the case.

16. The negotiations regarding the use of expert testimony in the trial neatly demonstrate how the popular trial exceeds its judicial regulation. The defense's strategy to feature testimony by scientific and theological authorities was obstructed by Judge Raulston's denial of its admissibility, but that ruling did not stop them from distributing written statements by the experts to the press, which published them along with additional commentary on the question of their appropriateness to the judgment. Nor did it matter that Bryan's testimony was stricken from the legal record.

17. See William Lewis's analysis of the Hinckley trial in this volume.

18. As the Chicago Seven demonstrated, the participants in the courtroom can be highly aware of how the trials shape perceptions. My reference to Baby M recognizes how commentators can attempt to influence this process. See Murray Kempton, "The Contract for 'Baby M,' " *New York Review of Books* (9 April 1987): 44.

19. See Murray Edelman, "Political Settings as Symbolism," in *The Symbolic Uses of Politics* (Urbana: University of Illinois Press, 1964), 95–113. Also, on legal language, 138–42.

20. For illustration of the range of issues and opportunities available here, see Brenda Danet, "Language in the Legal Process," *Law & Society Review* 14 (1980): 445–564.

21. Max Lerner, "Constitution and Court as Symbols," *Yale Law Journal* 46 (1937): 1290–1319. Lerner demonstrates how this perspective on the law need not be considered either extraneous to legal scholarship or wholly derived from contemporary social theory.

22. For a discussion of media use of the trial as a symbol, see the essay by Juliet Dee in this volume.

23. See the essay by Justin Gustainis in this volume.

24. See, for example, Natalie Zemon Davis, *The Return of Martin Guerre* (Cambridge: Harvard University Press, 1983).

Chapter Two

The author would like to thank Robert Hariman and James R. Andrews for their encouragement and suggestions at different stages in the development of this study.

1. Dr. Henry Sacheverell, "In Perils Among False Brethren," *A Complete Collection Of State Trials And Proceedings For High Treason And Other Crimes And Misdeamenors From The Earliest Period To The Present Time* (hereafter *State Trials*), Vol. XV, A.D. 1710–19, comp. T. B. Howell (London: Hansard, 1812), 70–94.

2. The best current evidence indicates that there were close to 100,000 copies of the sermon in pamphlet form in circulation by the end of the trial in March 1710, although it is important to keep in mind that popular estimates of its circulation used *at the time of the trial* kept the number at 40,000. In either case, this pamphlet was to have far more dissemination and readership than any other pamphlet in the first half of the eighteenth century. The most likely source for the 40,000 number is Gilbert Burnet, *History of His Own Time* (London: T. Ward, 1724–34), Vol. II, 237. See also J. R. Jones, *Country and Court: England, 1658–1714* (Cambridge: Harvard University Press, 1978), 334–38; and G. A. Trevelyan, *England Under Queen Anne*, 3 vols. (New York: Longmans, Green and Co., 1934), 3:48. For various editions of the sermon published prior to and during the trial see W. A. Speck, ed., *F. F. Madan, A Critical Bibliography of Dr. Henry Sacheverell* (Lawrence: University of Kansas Libraries, 1978), 17–25.

3. The possible exception to this claim would be the trial of Thomas Wentworth, Earl of Strafford in 1641. The difference between the two trials is contained in the fact that the proceedings of the Strafford impeachment were closed to the non-Parliamentary public, whereas they were purposefully opened to and displayed before the non-Parliamentary public in the Sacheverell trial. As I shall argue in this essay, this difference was considerable, having a significant effect on the rhetorical relationship between the Whig prosecution and the Tory defense of Sacheverell, as each side gradually tempered its view of the other as an adversary vying for popular endorsement, and implicitly recognized the need to negotiate a prudent settlement that accommodated their common interests in opposition to what they increasingly perceived to be a potentially violent and adversarial non-Parliamentary public. For a discussion of the impeachment of Strafford see John H. Timmis III, *Thine Is The Kingdom: The Trial For Treason of Thomas Wentworth, Earl of Strafford, First Minister of King Charles I, and Last Hope of the English Crown* (University, Ala.: University of Alabama Press, 1974).

4. The most complete source on the Sacheverell affair from beginning to end, to which my own understanding is heavily indebted, is Geoffrey Holmes, *The Trial Of Doctor Sacheverell* (London: Eyre Metheun, 1973). See also Albert Turner Scudi, *The Sacheverell Affair* (New York: Columbia University Press, 1939).

5. Holmes, *The Trial,* 124–26. See also *A Description of the High Court of Judicature for the Tryal of Dr. Henry Sacheverell* (n.p., n.d.), 125.

6. The list of pamphlets and sermons published on the Sacheverell Affair is considerable. The most complete bibliography of such sources is contained in Scudi, *The Sacheverell Affair,* 143–60. See also Holmes, *The Trial,* 289–95; and Speck, *F. F. Madan,* 61–136.

7. See Geoffrey Holmes, "The Sacheverell Riots: The Church and The Crowd in Early Eighteenth-Century London," in *Politics, Religion and Society in England 1678–1742,* ed. Geoffrey Holmes (London: Hambledon Press, 1986), 217–47; and Trevelyan, *England Under Queen Anne,* 3:55–6.

8. Holmes, "Sacheverell Riots," 218.

9. The charge of impeachment was actually based upon two sermons that Sacheverell had delivered and published. The 5 November sermon was the primary concern to the managers of the impeachment, but consideration was also given to the dedication to "The Communication of Sin," preached at the Assizes held at Derby on 15 August 1709 and included as part of the indictment. For editions of the Derby sermon see Speck, *F. F. Madan,* 17–18. For the general Whig sentiment regarding possible punishments see Holmes, *The Trial,* 227–28.

10. See "The Queen's Speech At The Close of the Session," 5 April 1710 in *The Parliamentary History of England* (London: T. C. Hansard, 1810), 6:897–99.

11. See Holmes, *The Trial,* 233–55. Much of the pressure placed on the Queen to change her ministry came in the form of "Addresses to the Queen" from counties and boroughs throughout England and Wales. Madan reports that in all there were 140 such "Addresses," running seven to one in favor of the Tory principles emphasized in the trial, including the hereditary title to the throne, passive obedience, condemnation of dissenters and occasional conformists, etc. See Speck, *F. F. Madan,* 211–34.

12. See Basil Williams, *The Whig Supremacy, 1714–1760* (Oxford: Clarendon Press, 1962).

13. See, for example, the discussion of "resistance" in relationship to the Glorious Revolution in 1688 in William Blackstone, *Commentaries on the Laws of England,* 4 vols. (1769; Chicago: University of Chicago Press, 1979), 4:429–33. See also Edmund Burke, "Reflections on The Revolution in France," *The Works of the Right Honourable Edmund Burke,* 8 vols. (London: C. & J. Rivington, 1826), 5:49–81; and Idem, "An Appeal From The New To The Old Whigs," *Works,* 6:145–84.

14. Michael Calvin McGee, "The 'Ideograph': A Link Between Rhetoric and Ideology," *Quarterly Journal of Speech* 66 (1980): 1–16.

15. I use angle brackets (⟨⟩) to set off the ideographic usage of a term such as "liberty" from its more ordinary or philosophic usages. Hence, I would say that Patrick Henry urges revolution in the name of ⟨liberty⟩,

insofar as the word liberty here functions as a primary commitment of the community, but that sailors go on "liberty" when they arrive in port. See John Louis Lucaites, "Flexibility and Consistency in Eighteenth-Century Anglo-Whiggism: A Case Study of The Rhetorical Dimensions of Legitimacy," diss., University of Iowa, 1984, 25.

16. For specific examples of this process in operation see Michael Calvin McGee, " 'Not Men, But Measures': The Origins and Import of an Ideological Principle," *Quarterly Journal of Speech* 64 (1978): 141–54; and Idem, "The Origins of 'Liberty': A Feminization of Power," *Communication Monographs* 47 (1980): 23–45.

17. See Celeste Michelle Condit, "The Rhetorical Limits to Polysemy," *Critical Studies in Mass Communication* (1989): 103–22.

18. See Michael C. McGee, "The Rhetorical Process in Eighteenth-Century England," in *Rhetoric: A Tradition in Transition,* ed. Walter R. Fisher (East Lansing: Michigan State University Press, 1974), 99–121; and James R. Andrews, " 'Charting Cultural Paths': Towards a Method for Investigating Rhetorical-Cultural Interaction," in *Rhetoric in Transition: Studies in the Nature and Uses of Rhetoric,* ed. Eugene E. White (University Park: Pennsylvania State University Press, 1980), 101–14.

19. See, for example, the group of statutes known collectively as the Clarendon Code, including "Act Restoring the Temporal Power of the Clergy," *Statutes of The Realm* (hereafter *SR*), V, 259 f.: 12 Charles II, c.24; "Corporation Act," *SR*, V, 321 f.: 13 Charles II, st. 2, c.1; "Act of Uniformity," *SR*, V, 364, f.: 14 Charles II, c. 4; "Act To Relieve The Poor," *SR*, V, 401 f.: 14 Charles II, c. 12; "Conventicle Act," *SR*, V, 516 f.: 16 Charles II, c. 4; and "Five Mile Act," *SR*, V, 575: 17 Charles II, c. 2. See also "Test Act," *SR*, V, 782 f.: 25 Charles II, c. 2; and "Second Test Act," V, 894 f.: 30 Charles II, st. 2, c. 1.

20. "Bill of Rights," *SR*, VI, 142 f.: 1 William & Mary, st. 2, c. 2; and "Act of Settlement," *SR*, VII, 636 f.: 12–13 William III, c. 2.

21. See "Act for exempting their majesties' Protestant subjects, dissenting from the Church of England, from the penalties of certain law. . . . " *SR*, VI, 74 f.: 1 William & Mary, c. 18.

22. See George Every, *The High Church Party, 1688–1718* (London: SPCK, 1956), 61–104; Geoffrey Holmes, "Religion and Party in Late Stuart England," in *Politics, Religion and Society in England,* 201–203; and G. V. Bennett, "Conflict in the Church," in *Britain After The Glorious Revolution, 1689–1714,* ed. Geoffrey Holmes (London: Macmillan Press, 1969), 165–68.

23. *The Parliamentary History of England* (London: T. C. Hansard, 1810), 6:509.

24. Holmes, *The Trial*, 45–46.

25. Bennett, "Conflict in the Church," 168–69.

26. Sacheverell, "In Perils Among False Brethren," 72.

27. Ibid., 77–78.

28. Ibid., 79.

29. Ibid., 84.

30. Ibid., 88.

31. His reference here to men of "character" and "stations" seems aimed rather directly at the members of the Queen's Whig Ministry, a point which is reinforced a bit later as he underlines the "crafty insidiousness of such wiley Volpones," Volpone being a popular (and unflattering) nickname of Lord Godolphin. Sacheverell, "In Perils Among False Brethren," 90.

32. Ibid., 93.

33. See, for example, *The Political Union, A Discourse Shewing the Dependence of Government on Religion in General: and of the English Monarchy on the Church of England in Particular* (n.p., 1702); *The True Character of a Church-Man, Shewing the False Pretences to That Name* (n.p., 1702); and *The Rights of the Church of England Asserted and Prov'd* (n.p., 1705).

34. See Holmes, *The Trial*, 70–75.

35. Sacheverell, "In Peril Among False Brethren," 70.

36. C. H. S. Stephenson and E. A. Marpler, *Law In The Light of History: England In The Middle Ages*, 4 vols. (London: Williams and Nargate, 1940), 2:294. See also Peter Charles Hoffer and N. E. H. Hull, *Impeachment in America, 1635–1805* (New Haven: Yale University Press, 1984), 3–8; and Colin G. C. Tite, *Impeachment and Parliamentary Judicature in Early Stuart England* (London: Athlone Press, 1974).

37. The second article accused Sacheverell of attacking the Toleration as "unreasonable and unwarrantable" and with encouraging the clergy to "thunder out their ecclesiastical anathema" against dissenters; the third article accused him of insinuating that "the Church was in Danger" under her majesty's administration; and the fourth article accused him of falsely and maliciously indicting "men of characters and stations," (i.e., the Whig Junto) as False Brethren in Church and State, tending towards a "general mal-administration" and "the destruction of the constitution," as well as inciting her majesty's subjects to "distinctions of factions and parties," "groundless jealousies," and "arms and violence." See *State Trials*, 38–39. For Jekyl's comments see ibid., 96.

38. See ibid., 95–134, and 380–418.

39. See J. G. A. Pocock, *The Ancient Constitution and The Feudal Law* (Cambridge: The University Press, 1957), 30–55; and Christopher Hill, "The Norman Yoke," *Democracy and The Labour Movement*, ed. John Saeville (London: Laurence and Wishart, 1954), 11–66.

40. See William Petyt, "Notes of a Speech Delivered Before the House of Lords," *Historical Manuscripts Commission, XIIth Reports*, Appendix VI, p. 14 ff. Cited in Pocock, *The Ancient Constitution*, 229.

41. See, for example, William Petyt, *Jus Parliamentarium: Or, The Ancient Power, Jurisdiction, Rights and Libertie of the Most High Court of Parliament, revived and asserted* (n.p., 1739); and James Tyrrell, *Patriarcha Non Monarcha* (n.p., 1681).

42. "Coronation Oath," *SR*, I, 12:2 Edward II, C. 1.

43. *Parliamentary History*, 5: 46. Emphasis added.

44. See J. Weston, *Monarchy and Revolution* (Totowa, N.J.: Rowman and Littlefield, 1972), 37–45; and George L. Cherry, *Early English Liberalism:*

Its Emergence Through Parliamentary Action, 1660–1702 (New York: Bookman Assoc., 1962), 79–129.

45. William Jones, *Parliamentary History*, 4:1255. Emphasis added.

46. See, for example, *State Trials*, 214–22.

47. See ibid., 41–44, 195–295.

48. Robert Filmer, "Patriarch, Or The Natural Power of Kings," *Patriarch, and Other Political Works of Sir Robert Filmer*, ed. Peter Laslett (Oxford: Basil Blackwell, 1949), 62, 96.

49. *The Whole Duty of Man*, from which this quotation comes, was a widely read "manual of devotion" of the Church of England. Quoted in H. T. Dickinson, *Liberty and Property: Political Ideology in Eighteenth-Century Britain* (New York: Holmes and Meir, 1977), 20.

50. "The Invitation To William, 1688," in *The Eighteenth-Century Constitution, 1688–1815*, ed. Neville Williams (Cambridge: The University Press, 1960), 8–10.

51. See *State Trials*, 80–81 and 95–134.

52. Ibid., 98.

53. See, for example, ibid., 63, 111, 115, 130.

54. Ibid., 115.

55. See ibid., 244–92. The entire sixth day of the trial was devoted to the entry of this testimony, each piece of evidence being read aloud in its entirety by a clerk of the court.

56. Ibid., 201–202.

57. Ibid., 196.

58. Ibid., 220.

59. Christine Oravec has developed the intriguing thesis that contemporary theories of mass audiences as "passive" and "inert" receptors of messages can be traced back to the rhetorical criticism of Whig oratory during the age of Andrew Jackson. According to Oravec, such criticism was designed to control the mass enthusiasm for participation in the political process by constructing the audience as passive spectators located in the scenic background of a sublime event. If my speculative analysis here can be sustained, we might be able to trace the roots of such a conception of audience to the development of the ideological commitment to ⟨popular sovereignty⟩. This should give us pause to wonder about the extent to which liberal democracy itself "relies" upon such a theory, at least in practice. See Christine Oravec, "The Sublimation of Mass Consciousness in the Rhetorical Criticism of Jacksonian America," *Communication* 11 (1989) 291–314.

Chapter Three

1. Despite its historical prominence, the Scopes trial has been pretty much ignored by rhetorical scholars. Richard M. Weaver considers the *Scopes* trial in his exploration of "Dialectic and Rhetoric at Dayton, Tennessee," for the purpose of showing how a grasp of rhetorical theory could have made the issues in this celebrated public controversy clearer. *The Ethics of Rheto-*

ric (Chicago: Henry Regnery, 1953), 27–54; Ray Ginger's book on the trial, *Six Days or Forever? Tennessee v. John Thomas Scopes*, relies on Kenneth Burke's writings on symbolic action to analyze the meaning of the Butler Act (New York: Oxford University Press, 1958), 1–21, 244; Kathleen Hall Jamieson uses the Scopes trial as the prime example of "Incapacitating the Eloquent Speaker," in her study of the transformation of political oratory during this century of electronic media. Jamieson argues that Bryan "was a tragic figure propelled by his own past rhetoric into entering a rhetorical forum that magnified Darrow's rhetorical strengths and his own weaknesses." In the courtroom Bryan was faced with a "rhetorical form he could not control," and Jamieson contends that Bryan's defeat was preordained. *Eloquence in an Electronic Age: The Transformation of Political Speechmaking* (New York: Oxford University Press, 1988), 31–42. Of these three examples, Ginger limits his use of rhetorical theory to a consideration of the Butler Act, while Weaver and Jamieson focus on just specific parts of the trial. Weaver focuses primarily on the legal debate prior to Darrow's cross-examination of Bryan, reducing that confrontation to a single retort by both parties, while Jamieson's analysis is essentially confined to the actual cross-examination.

2. Several recent trials have challenged the Scopes-established balance between science and religion, but even they do so upon the discursive grounds that are the legacy of the popular understandings of the Scopes trial. The defendants of religion in cases such as that of *McLean* v. *Arkansas Board of Education* argue that their religious discourses are scientifically valid. See Charles Alan Taylor and Celeste Michelle Condit, "Objectivity and Elites: A Creation Science Trial," *Critical Studies in Mass Communication* 5 (1988): 293–312. Note that the "dominant American consensus" is not constituted by the majority of the population, but by the most powerful and active political agents.

3. This is not the place to argue the relationship between the "forces of production" and the "ideology." Whatever the causal tensions between the two, we suggest that it is important to examine the way in which the public discourse develops because that discourse shapes the particular forms of public power. For a further discussion see David Zarefsky, *President Johnson's War on Poverty* (Tuscaloosa: University of Alabama Press, 1986), or Celeste Condit Railsback, "The Contemporary American Abortion Controversy: A Case Study of Public Argumentation," diss., University of Iowa, 1982.

4. Michael Calvin McGee, "The Rhetorical Process in 18th Century England," in *Rhetoric: A Tradition in Transition*, ed. Walter R. Fisher (East Lansing: Michigan State University Press, 1974), 99–121; Michael Calvin McGee, "Edmund Burke's Beautiful Lie: An Exploration of the Relationship Between Rhetoric and Social Theory," diss., University of Iowa, 1974.

5. We use the term *presence* after Chaim Perelman and L. Olbrechts-Tyteca, *The New Rhetoric: A Treatise on Argumentation* (Notre Dame: Notre Dame University Press, 1971). They appear to mean by *presence* the salience or impact imparted to a term merely by its having been spoken before a given audience. They say of it "by the very fact of selecting certain

elements and presenting them to the audience, their importance and pertinency to the discussion are implied. Indeed, such a choice endows these elements with a presence, which is an essential factor in argumentation" (116).

6. We borrow from Kenneth Burke's concept that "motive accounts" always include elements of scene (place), agent, purpose, tools, and acts. See "Part I: Ways of Placement," *A Grammar of Motives* (Berkeley: University of California Press, 1969).

7. We accept Hariman's definition (see introduction) of a popular trial as a "judicial proceeding receiving sustained coverage by the mass media." We would divide up the types of popular trials by suggesting there are at least three: (1) "sensational" trials, where the primary focus is upon the individuals and their immediate acts (particularly gruesome multiple murders by deranged individuals); (2) "political" trials, where the primary focus derives from the broadly based partisan affiliations of the individuals (most often in America, the communists vs. the capitalists); and (3) "paradigmatic" trials, where paradigms of discourse (e.g., science and religion) come into conflict. We might expect generalizations from one type to another to be problematic.

8. "2,000,000 Words Wired to the Press," *New York Times*, 22 July 1925, 2; "The Conviction of John T. Scopes, Science Teacher," *School and Society* 22 (1 August 1925): 138–39; Bynum Shaw, "Scopes Reviews the Monkey Trial," *Esquire* 74 (November 1970): 88ff; John T. Scopes, "The Trial That Rocked the Nation," *Reader's Digest* (March 1961): 142.

9. *The World's Most Famous Court Trial: State of Tennessee v. John Thomas Scopes* (1925; New York: Da Capo Press, 1971), "Complete Stenographic Report of the Court Test of the Tennessee Anti-Evolution Act at Dayton, July 10 to 21, 1925, Including Speeches and Arguments of Attorneys"; Leslie H. Allen, ed., *Bryan and Darrow at Dayton: The Record and Documents of the "Bible Evolution Trial"* (New York: Russell and Russell, 1925); William Jennings Bryan and Mary Baird Bryan, *Memoirs*, Dayton ed. (Philadelphia: John C. Winston Company, 1925). See also Robert S. Keebler, *The Tennessee Evolution Case* (Memphis, Tenn.: Davis Printing Company, 1925).

10. For an explanation of the character of different fields of discourse see Stephen Toulmin, *The Uses of Argument* (Cambridge: Cambridge University Press, 1958); Charles Willard, *Argumentation and the Social Grounds of Knowledge* (University, Ala.: University of Alabama Press, 1983); and several papers on the issue from George Ziegelmueller and Jack Rhodes, eds., *Dimensions of Argument: Proceedings of the Second Summer Conference on Argumentation* (Annandale, Va.: Speech Communication Association, 1981).

11. Chapter 17, House Bill 185 (By Mr. Butler) Public Acts of Tennessee for 1925.

12. "Protest-Law," *Time* 5 (6 April 1925): 16; George F. Milton, "Can Minds Be Closed By Statute?" *World's Work* 50 (July 1925): 323–28; Kenneth K. Bailey, "The Enactment of Tennessee's Anti-Evolution Law," *Southern Journal of History* 16 (1950): 472–90; Ginger, *Six Days or Forever?*, 2–8.

13. "Author of the Law Surprised at Fuss," *New York Times*, 18 July 1925, 2.

14. "Plan Assault on State Law on Evolution," *Chattanooga Daily Times*, 4 May 1925, 5; Lucille Milner, *Education of an American Liberal* (New York: Horizon Press, 1954), 161–63; Roger N. Baldwin, "Dayton's First Issue," in *D-Day at Dayton: Reflections on the Scopes Trial*, ed. Jerry R. Tompkins (Baton Rouge: Louisiana State University Press, 1965), 55–56.

15. Ginger, *Six Days or Forever?*, 18–21; John T. Scopes and Thomas Presley, *Center of the Storm: Memoirs of John T. Scopes* (New York: Holt, Rinehart and Winston, 1967), 55–60.

16. Charles Francis Potter, "Ten Years After the Monkey Show I'm Going Back to Dayton," *Liberty* 12 (28 September 1935): 36–38; Charles Francis Potter, *The Preacher and I* (New York: Crown, 1951), 292–93; Ginger, *Six Days or Forever?*, 179–80.

17. In his memoirs, Scopes maintained that during the meeting in Robinson's Drugstore, he had really not remembered whether he had taught evolution or not. However, Scopes agreed with the consensus that since science teachers were required to use state-approved textbooks, which included sections on evolution, teachers in Tennessee were compelled to violate the law. More importantly, Scopes agreed that the Butler Act needed to be challenged in court. Scopes and Presley, *Center of the Storm*, 58–60; Shaw, "Scopes Reviews the Monkey Trial," 88.

18. L. M. Aldridge, for the World's Christian Fundamentalist Association to Bryan, 12 May 1925; Sue K. Hicks to Bryan, 14 May 1925. Cited in Palo E. Coletta, *William Jennings Bryan: Political Puritan, 1915–1925*; Vol. III (Lincoln: University of Nebraska Press, 1969), 235. See L. Sprague de Camp, *The Great Monkey Trial* (Garden City, N.Y.: Doubleday, 1968), 73–74. Hicks, named for the mother who died giving him birth, was one of the few lawyers at the trial who was actually from Dayton (p. 1).

19. Harry P. Harrison as told to Karl Detzer, *Culture Under Canvas: The Story of Tent Chautauqua* (New York: Hastings House, 1958), 158; William Jennings Bryan, "The Prince of Peace," *William Jennings Bryan: Selections*, ed. Ray Ginger (Indianapolis: Bobbs-Merrill, 1967), 138–41.

20. Coletta, *William Jennings Bryan*, 199–200.

21. Ibid., 219–20.

22. Bryan to Rev. O. W. Baylor, 28 April 1922; R. B. Spangler to Bryan, 29 April 1922, Bryan papers.

23. Alonzo W. Fortune, "The Kentucky Campaign Against the Teaching of Evolution," *Journal of Religion* 2 (1922): 229–30; "The Vote on the Evolution Bill in the Kentucky State Legislature," *Science* 55 (1922): 317.

24. Elbert L. Watson, "Oklahoma and the Anti-Evolution Movement of the 1920's," *Chronicles of Oklahoma* 42 (Winter 1964–65): 396–401.

25. Maynard Shipley, *The War on Modern Science: A Short History of the Fundamentalist Attacks on Evolution and Modernism* (New York: Alfred A. Knopf, 1927): 89–90, 127–29, 138–41; Coletta, *William Jennings Bryan*, 231–32.

26. Bryan and Bryan, *Memoirs*, 481–82; Harbor Allen, "The Anti-Evo-

lution Campaign in America," *Current History* 24 (September 1926): 893–97; Coletta, *William Jennings Bryan*, 232.

27. The states considering anti-evolution legislation on the eve of the Scopes trial were Mississippi, Georgia, West Virginia, Arkansas, Iowa, Illinois, North Dakota, Minnesota, Oregon, and Arizona. Miriam Allen De Ford, "The War Against Evolution," *Nation* 120 (20 May 1925): 565–66.

28. William Manchester, *Disturber of the Peace: The Life of H. L. Mencken* (New York: Harper & Brothers, 1950), 164; William Manchester, *The Sage of Baltimore: The Life and Riotous Times of H. L. Mencken* (New York: Andrew-Melrose, 1952), 140.

29. Kevin Tierney, *Darrow: A Biography* (New York: Thomas Y. Crowell, 1979), 127.

30. In October 1921, Birge had denounced a Bryan lecture as being more likely to make atheists than believers of the students. Bryan had initially limited his rebuttal to letters to his friends, to the editors of papers published in Madison, and to his own magazine, the *Commoner*. In July 1923, Bryan had sent a series of questions to Birge. When Bryan's questions were published in the *Tribune,* Darrow presented his own list of questions. Bryan to Editor, *Capital Times,* 23 February 1922, 5 April 1922; Bryan, "Dr. Birge Autocrat," *Commoner,* May 1922, 2; Coletta, *William Jennings Bryan*, 228–39, 259; Wayne C. Williams, *William Jennings Bryan* (New York: G. P. Putnam's Sons, 1936), 456; Irvin G. Wylie, "Bryan, Birge and the Wisconsin Evolution Controversy, 1921–1922," *Wisconsin Magazine of History* 35 (Winter 1951): 294–301.

31. Irving Stone, *Clarence Darrow for the Defense* (Garden City, N.Y.: Doubleday, Doran & Company, 1941), 426–27; Coletta, *William Jennings Bryan*, 259; Williams, *William Jennings Bryan,* 456.

32. In spite of the dramatic, and hence, legitimating importance of Bryan and Darrow's biographical entwinement with each other and the issues, we should not overlook the fact that the clash between religion and science was, at the time, being conducted in a wide variety of forums, with a wide variety of agents. Prior to the Dayton trial, for instance, the most momentous clash between science and religion involved neither Bryan nor Darrow. On 28 January 1924, in old Carnegie Hall in New York City, Modernist Unitarian minister Charles Francis Potter debated the Fundamentalist Baptist minister John Roach Straton on the question, "Resolved, that the Earth and Man Came by Evolution." The debate was carried on radio and widely reported in print. See Potter, *Preacher,* 180–92; John Roach Straton, *The Famous New York Fundamentalist-Modernist Debates* (New York: George H. Doran, 1925).

33. The character of the local jury men—farmers and religious fundamentalists—is evident from the voir dire. The judge's position is evident in his reply to objections and rulings.

34. Arthur Garfield Hays, "The Strategy of the Scopes Defense," *Nation* 121 (5 August 1925): 157.

35. Page citations in parentheses are from the published transcript, *The World's Most Famous Court Trial.*

36. We do not mean to imply that public discourse is always consistent.

However, the avoidance of the appearance of inconsistency is nonetheless widely held to be a key standard of public discourse.

37. "Darrow Scores Ignorance and Bigotry, Seeking to Quash Scopes Indictment; State Argues for its Police Power," *New York Times* 14 July 1925, 102; "Darrow Flays Bryan in Withering Attack on Fundamentalists," *New Orleans Times-Picayune* 14 July 1925, 1 +; "The Great Trial," *Time* 6 (20 July 1925): 17.

38. Potter, *Preacher*, 266.

39. For a more detailed analysis of Malone's role in Dayton see Lawrance M. Bernabo, "Dudley Field Malone, Christian 'Evil-utionist': From Reconciliation to Ridicule at the Scopes Trial," paper presented to the Southern Speech Communication Association, Hot Springs, Arkansas, 9 April 1982.

40. The applause following Malone's statement compelled the bailiff to rap for order and remind the audience: "people, this is no circus. There are no monkeys here. This is a lawsuit, let us have order" (281–82).

41. A fact ignored by Richard Weaver, who argues (with his usual conservative slant) that the defense was inherently disadvantaged because they chose a rhetorical (hence factual and actual) position against the dialectical position of the prosecution. In fact, had Darrow chosen to use the ultimate factual position, he could easily have won the case, but at the cost of abdicating the opportunity for the larger battle. Dialectic and rhetoric are thus not absolute, inherent positions, but choices to achieve given goals. Weaver, "Dialectic and Rhetoric at Dayton," 27–54.

42. H. L. Mencken, *Baltimore Evening Sun*, 17 July 1925, rpt. in Tompkins, *D-Day at Dayton*, 47–49; H. L. Mencken, *Heathen Days, 1890–1936* (New York: Alfred A. Knopf, 1943); Joseph Wood Krutch, *More Lives Than One* (New York: William Sloane, 1962), 152–53; de Camp, *The Great Monkey Trial*, 335–36. Cf. Bryan and Bryan, *Memoirs*, 484; Mary B. Bryan, Journal, 20 July 1925, "Bulletin No. 2," Mrs. Ruth Bryan Rohde Papers, rpt. in Coletta, *William Jennings Bryan*, 255–56.

43. The account of the trial provided by the 1961 and 1962 editions of the *Encyclopaedia Britannica* calls Malone a "liberal Catholic and one of the great courtroom orators of the time." "The Scopes Trial," *Encyclopaedia Britannica*, v. 20 (New York: Encyclopaedia Britannica, 1961, 1962), 132–33. See also Richard B. Morris, *Encyclopedia of American History* (New York: Harper & Brothers, 1953), 554.

44. Scopes and Presley, *Center of the Storm*, 155–56.

45. Ibid., 154–55.

46. Mencken, *Heathen Days*, 236–27; de Camp, *The Great Monkey Trial*, 346; Potter, *Preacher*, 275.

47. de Camp, *The Great Monkey Trial*, 350.

48. *New York Times*, 18 July 1925, 1.

49. Offering testimony on translating and interpreting the Bible were Rabbi Herman Rosenwasser and Dr. Herman E. Murkett, pastor of the First Methodist Church of Chattanooga. The scientists who had come to Dayton to testify for the defense and whose statements were filed into the record were Charles Hubbard Judd, Director of the School of Education, University of Chicago; Jacob G. Lipman, Dean of the College of Agriculture, University

of New Jersey; Dr. Fay-Cooper Cole, Anthropologist, University of Chicago; Wilbur A. Nelson, State Geologist of Tennessee; Kirtley F. Mather, Chairman of the Department of Geology, Harvard University; Dr. Maynard M. Metcalf, Zoologist, Johns Hopkins University; Dr. Winterton C. Curtis, Zoologist, University of Missouri; and Prof. Horatio Hackett Newman, Zoologist, University of Chicago. The multigraphed statements were published in some newspapers, for example, "Scientists Present Case," *New York Times*, 21 July 1925, 1, 3.

50. Weaver finds that "The remarkable aspect of this trial was that almost from the first the defense, pleading the cause of science, was forced into the role of rhetorician; whereas the prosecution, pleading the cause of the state, clung stubbornly to a dialectical position. This development occurred because the argument of the defense, once the legal technicalities were got over, was that evolution is 'true.' The argument of the prosecution was that its teaching was unlawful. These two arguments depend upon rhetoric and dialectic respectively."

From this perspective, Weaver concludes, "Of those who spoke for the defense, Mr. Dudley Field Malone seems to have had the poorest conception of the nature of the contest." Weaver cites Malone's plea as clear indication of the trap from which the defense was never able to extricate itself. Malone, in Weaver's estimation, confuses the two different kinds of inquiry and is oblivious that facts are never determinative of dialectic in the sense Malone seems to presume.

However, in his consideration of the Scopes trial, Weaver fails to take into account either the distinction between the early rhetoric of reconciliation and the final rhetoric of ridicule employed by the defense, or the difference between the conflict of evolution and the Bible and the non-conflicting relationship between evolution and Christianity. Because Malone presents an "ambiguous" sense of truth, Weaver contends that the defense had impaled itself upon a dilemma. Although this might be true in terms of dialectic and argumentation, the critique is ultimately irrelevant for the consideration of the rhetorical dimensions of the trial, which was the predominant dimension. Certainly Weaver would not wish to be put in a position whereby he would be compelled to claim that if Malone had indeed understood the "two different kinds of inquiry which the Greeks were well cognizant of," the judge would have declared the Butler Act invalid and allowed the expert testimony. After all, Judge Raulston was up for re-election the following year. He would be defeated. Weaver, "Dialectic and Rhetoric at Dayton," 29–30, 47–49; de Camp, *The Great Monkey Trial*, 481.

51. "Scopes Already Convicted Says Darrow; Bryan Warns of 'Anti-Christian Plot,' " *New Orleans Times-Picayune*, 19 July 1925, 1 +.

52. H. L. Mencken, *Baltimore Evening Sun*, 18 July 1925, rpt. in Tompkins, *D-Day at Dayton*, 43.

53. Arthur Garfield Hays, *Let Freedom Ring* (New York: Liveright, 1937), 71–72; Potter, *Preacher*, 275–76.

54. de Camp, *The Great Monkey Trial*, 364–65; Kirtley F. Mather, "Creation and Evolution," in *Science Ponders Religion*, ed. Harlow Shapley (New York: Appleton-Century-Crofts, 1960), 32–45.

55. Scopes and Presley, *Center of the Storm*, 156; George F. Milton, "A Dayton Postscript," *Outlook* 140 (19 August 1925): 550–52.

56. Bryan graduated from Union College Law School in 1883. Richard L. Metcalf, *Life and Patriotic Services of Hon. William J. Bryan: The Fearless and Brilliant Leader of the People and Candidate for President of the United States* (N.p.: Edgewood Publishing Company, 1896), 238–45.

57. "Evolution Battle Rages Out of Court," *New York Times*, 22 July 1925, 2.

58. "Text of Bryan's Nine Questions on Religion And Darrow's Replies to the Commoner," *New York Times*, 22 July 1925, 2.

59. "W. J. Bryan Dies in His Sleep at Dayton, While Resting in Evolution Battle; Had Spoken Continuously Since Trial," *New York Times*, 27 July 1925, 1–2; Louis W. Koenig, *Bryan: A Political Biography of William Jennings Bryan* (New York: G. P. Putnam's Sons, 1981), 652–58; Coletta, *William Jennings Bryan*, 274. See also, Frank A. Pattie, ed., "The Last Speech of William Jennings Bryan" (Winchester, Tennessee, 25 July 1925), *Tennessee Historical Quarterly* 6 (1947): 265–83.

60. The *New York Times* provided verbatim transcripts of Darrow's speech on the motion to quash the indictment, Bryan's speech against admission of scientific experts as well as Malone's reply, and Darrow's cross-examination of Bryan. Additionally, they printed transcriptions of both the scientific statements entered by the defense into the record, and Darrow's replies to Bryan's questions concerning Christianity after the trial. See the paper for 11–22 July 1925.

61. de Camp, *The Great Monkey Trial*, 447.

62. E. S. Martin, *Life* 86 (16 July 1925): 16.

63. Samplings of editorial cartoons reprinted from papers across the nation during the trial include: "Tennessee's Coming Battle on Evolution," *Literary Digest* 86 (6 June 1925): 36; "Summer Topics, in Cartoons," *American Review of Reviews* 72 (July 1925): 31; "Give the people Scope," *Outlook* 140 (22 July 1925): 413; "Topics of the Month in Cartoons," *American Review of Reviews* 72 (August 1925): 140; "Cartoon Sidelights on Current Topics," *American Review of Reviews* 72 (September 1925): 257. There are also fourteen cartoons reprinted in de Camp, *The Great Monkey Trial*. A rich source of original cartoons is *Life* magazine, which in 1925 was concerned primarily with humor and golf: *Life* 85 (11 June 1925): 22; 85 (18 June 1925): 22; 85 (25 June 1925): 11, 21; 86 (2 July 1925): 5, 15; 86 (9 July 1925): 4–5, 8–9; 86 (16 July 1925): 7, 28; 86 (23 July 1925): 6; 86 (30 July 1925): 15; 86 (20 August 1925): 8.

64. "Life Lines," *Life* 85 (18 June 1925): 10; 85 (25 June 1925): 6; 86 (2 July 1925): 8; 86 (9 July 1925): 6; 86 (30 July 1925): 6; "Life's Encyclopedia," *Life* 85 (25 June 1925): 23; Kile Croak, "My School in Tennessee," *Life* 86 (2 July 1925): 4; Arthur Guiterman, "Notes for a Tennessee Primer," *Life* 86 (16 July 1925): 5; "Topics in Brief," *Literary Digest*, for 86 (4 July 1925): 18; 86 (11 July 1925): 15; 86 (18 July 1925): 15; 86 (25 July 1925): 15; 86 (1 August 1925): 17; 86 (8 August 1925): 13.

65. Martin, *Life* 86 (16 July 1925): 16.

66. *Life* 86 (9 July 1925): 7.

67. Both *Life* and the *New York* magazines had to stop the presses to replace attacks. *Judge* apologized for its Bryan "Monkey Edition," which was already in the mails. In New York City, "The Garrick Gaities," "The Follies" and a dozen other vaudeville acts had to be changed as well. Williams, *William Jennings Bryan*, 483–84. See also "The Great Trial," *Time* 6 (3 August 1925): 18.

68. Bryan had made arrangements for his speech to be printed in a telephone conversation right before he took the nap from which he would never awaken. The speech was published posthumously in numerous places, including newspapers across the nation. See "Text of Bryan's Evolution Speech, Written for the Scopes Trial," *New York Times*, 29 July 1925, 1, 8; "Mr. Bryan's Posthumous Speech," *Outlook* 140 (12 August 1925): 510–11; *World's Most Famous Court Trial*, 308–19; Leslie Allen, *Bryan and Darrow*, 172–98; Bryan and Bryan, *Memoirs*, 529–56. The *New York World* observed (29 July 1925) that although the speech was of "a partisan and an advocate" it "appeared as if it had come from the author's grave, hence endowed with superhuman wisdom." Coletta, *William Jennings Bryan*, 277 fn. Bryan's last published essay was William Jennings Bryan, "The Bible is Good Enough for Me," *Collier's* 76 (1 August 1925): 8 +.

69. "Tennessee Goes Fundamentalist," *New Republic* 42 (29 April 1925): 258–60; Howard K. Hollister, "In Dayton, Tennessee," *Nation* 121 (8 July 1925): 61–62; Dixon Merritt, "Smoldering Fires," *Outlook* 140 (22 July 1925): 421–22.

70. We rely here on Kenneth Burke's account of the scene/act ratio, cited above.

71. Martin, *Life* 86 (16 July 1925): 16. See also "Commoner's Plea Sways Plain Folk," *New York Times*, 12 July 1925, 5; "Two Apes and 'Link' Arrive at Dayton," *New York Times*, 15 July 1925, 1; "Mountaineers Won't Hear Arguments on Evolution," *New York Times*, 12 July 1925: 16; "Dayton Hospitable to Critical Guest," *New York Times*, 19 July 1925: 2.

72. "The Great Trial," *Time* 6 (20 July 1925): 17.

73. "Rappelyea's Razzberry," *Time* 5 (1 June 1925): 18, 20 (Note: George W. Rappelyea was the key instigator of the discussion in Robinson's Drugstore that led to Scopes being tried); "Ballyhoo," *Time* 5 (22 June 1925): 18–19; "The Great Trial," *Time* 6 (6 July 1925): 15–16; "The Great Trial," *Time* 6 (27 July 1925): 15.

74. "Dayton's Police Suppress Skeptics," *New York Times* 12 July 1925, 1.

75. The journalists appear to have been somewhat surprised when their initial expectations about Dayton's "backwardness" were confounded. In several instances they were driven to write about the apparent moderation in Dayton: Joseph Wood Krutch, "Tennessee: Where Cowards Rule," *Nation* 121 (15 July 1925): 88–89; Joseph Wood Krutch, "Tennessee's Dilemma," *Nation* 121 (22 July 1925): 110; Forrest Davis, "Tennessee—State of Brave Men," *Commonweal* 2 (29 July 1925): 283–85; Lindsay Dennison, "The Holy Rollers," *Commonweal* 2 (29 July 1925): 290; Allene M. Sumner, "The Holy Rollers on Sin Bone Ridge," *Nation* 121 (29 July 1925): 137–38; W. O.

McGeehan, "Why Pick on Dayton?" *Harper's* 151 (25 October 1925): 623–27.

76. H. L. Mencken, "The Sahara of the Bozart," *New York Evening Mail*, 13 November 1917; Hobson points out that "it is generally acknowledged that the essay did much to shock young Southern writers into an awareness of this poverty and thus played a seminal role in the revival of Southern letters which followed." Fred C. Hobson, Jr., *Serpent in Eden: H. L. Mencken and the South* (Chapel Hill: University of North Carolina Press, 1974), 2–8. See also William H. Nolte, "Mencken on the South," *Menckeniana* No. 69 (Spring 1979): 1–4; Christopher Clausen, "Mencken and the Bible Belt," *Menckeniana* No. 70 (Summer 1979): 7–11.

77. H. L. Mencken, "In Tennessee," *Nation* 121 (1 July 1925): 21–22; H. L. Mencken, *Prejudices (Fifth Series)* (New York: Alfred A. Knopf, 1926), 76. Manchester considers Mencken's essay to be an exercise in sarcasm, insisting that "Bryan swallowed it for what it was not." Manchester, *Sage of Baltimore*, 167. In contrast, Kemler argues the essay was the objective expression of the legal reality of the case. Edgar Kemler, *The Irreverent Mr. Mencken* (Boston: Little, Brown and Company, 1948), 183.

78. Kemler, *The Irreverent Mr. Mencken*, 175–90. For excerpts from Mencken's reports see Manchester, *Sage of Baltimore*, 143–45, and Tompkins, *D-Day at Dayton*, 35–51.

79. Mencken, *Heathen Days*, 231–34; Michael Williams, "Sunday In Dayton," *Commonweal* 2 (29 July 1925): 285–88.

80. "In Memoriam: W. J. B." was first printed in the *Baltimore Evening Sun*, 27 July 1925, rpt. by Mencken in the *American Mercury* 5 (October 1925): 158–60 and in his *Prejudices (Fifth Series)*, 64–74.

81. Mencken, *Heathen Days*, 280–87. In the course of his recollections on "Beaters of Breasts," Mencken did allow as how he had "heard all the famous rhetoricians of his generation . . . and it is my sober judgment, standing on the brink of eternity, that [Bryan] was the greatest of them all." As evidence Mencken stoutly declared that the speech Bryan gave at the 1904 Democratic National convention, where the Gold Democrats rejected Bryan in favor of Alton B. Parker, was a greater speech than the celebrated "Cross of Gold" oration of 1896.

82. "Mencken Epithets Rouse Dayton's Ire," *New York Times*, 17 July 1925, 3; Manchester, *Sage of Baltimore*, 143; Hobson, *Serpent in Eden*, 147–55.

83. Manchester, *Sage of Baltimore*, 152.

84. *Menckeniana: A Schimflexikon* (New York: Alfred A. Knopf, 1928).

85. See D. Schiller, *Objectivity and the News: The Public and the Rise of Commercial Journalism* (Philadelphia: University of Pennsylvania Press, 1981).

86. "Topics in Brief," *Literary Digest* 86 (11 July 1925): 15; 86 (25 July 1925): 15; 86 (8 August 1925): 13.

87. "Europe Amazed by the Scopes Case," *New York Times*, 11 July 1925, 1–2; "Foreign Amazement at Tennessee," *Literary Digest* 86 (25 July 1925): 18–19; "Delirium in Dayton," *Spectator* (London) 135 (18 July 1925): 94–95; "O Liberty, What Crimes—!" *New Statesmen* (London) 25 (18 July 1925):

388–89; "Foreign Amazement at Tennessee," *Literary Digest* 86 (25 July 1925): 18–19. Nor was the humor restricted to England. The Scopes trial was seen as an excuse to poke fun at Dayton and the South in other European countries as well. Dr. Heinrich Hermelink, "Darwin and the Bible Abroad," *Living Age* 326 (22 August 1925): 393–94; "French Scientists and Dayton Verdict," *Times* (London), 23 July 1925, 13; Lorenzo Piazza, *Nell America del Nord per l'esposizione di Chicago* (Lentini: Tip. F. Circirata, 1934), 333; Louis Pierard, *Rimouski-Puebla: du Canada au Mexique* (Paris: Librarie Valois, 1931), 60–88. It should be noted that these last two efforts were based on hearsay information and second-hand accounts, which would explain various errors; Pierard locates the Scopes trial in Dayton, Ohio.

88. "The Tennessee Trial: Scientific Evidence for the Defense," *Times* (London), 17 July 1925, 13; "The Tennessee Trial: Propagandists Busy," *Times* (London), 20 July 1925, 12. As the trial reached its climax, the *Times*, one of the few foreign papers to find anything of value in the Tennessee trial, wryly noted: "Meanwhile, all the United States, except the jury trying Mr. Scopes, can read in this morning's newspapers the evidence of eight competent scientists in regard to the validity of the theories of evolution. Despite its tragic-comic interludes, the trial has had the effect of arousing wide-spread interest in books on evolution, this accomplishing the main purpose of the defense." "The Tennessee Trial: Mr. Scopes Found Guilty," *Times* (London), 22 July 1925, 14.

89. "Europe and Tennessee," *Outlook* 140 (22 July 1925): 416–17.

90. George McCready Price, "The Evolution Trial," *Times* (London), 16 July 1925, 10; E. Ray Lankester, "The Evolution Trial," *Times* (London), 22 July 1925, 15. See also George McCready Price, *The New Geology* (Mountain View, Calif.: Pacific Pr. Pub. Assn., 1923); George McCready Price, *The Phantom of Organic Evolution* (New York: Revell, 1924); Henry Fairfield Osborn, *The Earth Speaks to Bryan* (New York: Charles Scribner's Sons, 1925).

91. *Life* 86 (9 July 1925): 7. The placement of monkeys in cartoons and passing references to them was commonly ambiguous. One recurring theme was the disavowal of evolutionary theory by apes wishing to deny their offspring. The most famous cartoon was perhaps Ireland's *Columbus Dispatch* portrayal of Mother Columbia worrying that her other children would catch "monkey-phobia." This cartoon also reflects the concern of the tainting of the national idiom by the local. In general, the cartoons indicate not only that Bryan's definitions of the relation of culture/humans versus nature/monkeys were rejected, but more profoundly, a realignment in which humans were to be judged as "un-cultured" by their failure of intellect. See "The Big Worry," rpt. in *Literary Digest* 86 (1 August 1925): 11. For other editorial cartoons on the Scopes trial see note 63.

92. E. S. Martin, *Life* 86 (30 July 1925): 14.

93. "Pastors to Discuss Scopes Trial Today," *New York Times*, 12 July 1925, sec. 2, 4; "Topics Discussed in the Metropolitan Pulpits Yesterday," *New York Times*, 13 June 1925, 15.

94. "The Religious Press on the Teaching of Evolution," *American Review of Reviews* 72 (July 1925): 97–98.

95. "Editorial," *Christian Century* 42 (23 July 1925): 943.

96. "Fundamentalist Prototypes," *Christian Century* 42 (16 June 1925): 913. See similarly *Chicago Daily Tribune*, rpt. "Thought Free or In Chains?" in *School and Society* 22 (11 July 1925): 44–45; "The Inquisition in Tennessee," *Forum* 74 (July 1925): 159–60.

97. "The Commotion at Dayton, Tenn.," *Christian Century* 42 (6 July 1925): 913.

98. "Editorial," 943; "Timid Modernism," *Christian Century* 42 (9 July 1925): 883–84; Jay S. Stowell, "It's No Joke in Tennessee," *Christian Century* 42 (9 July 1925): 893–94. The press also tended to construct its own debates on the issue: William G. Shepherd, "Monkey Business in Tennessee," *Collier's* 76 (18 July 1925): 8–9; Leonard Darwin, "You Can't Make a Silk Purse . . . " *Collier's* 76 (25 July 1925): 10–11; Bryan, "The Bible"; William Hornsby, "Evolution: Is the Tide Turning?" *Commonweal* 2 (13 May 1925): 19–21; "Concerning Evolution," *Commonweal* 2 (10 June 1925): 119–21; Bertram C. A. Windle, "The Case Against Evolution," review in *Commonweal* 2 (June 1925), of George Barry O'Toole, *The Case against Evolution* (New York: Macmillan, 1925): 124–26; Henry Fairfield Osborn, "The Earth Speaks to Bryan," *Forum* 74 (June 1925): 796–803; William Jennings Bryan, "Mr. Bryan Speaks to Darwin," *Forum* 74 (July 1925): 101–107; "The Evolution Trial," *Forum* 74 (August 1925): ill. sec. xxiv–xxviii; Edward L. Rice, "Darwin and Bryan—A Study in Method," *Science* 61 (6 March 1925): 243–50; Henry Fairfield Osborn, "Evolution and Education in the Tennessee Trial," *Science* 62 (17 July 1925): 43–45; R. R. Huestis, "Dr. W. D. Riley on Evolution," *Science* 62 (4 September 1925): 220–21; "Tennessee and the Constitution," *New Republic* 43 (8 July 1925): 166–68; "Tennessee vs. Civilization," *New Republic* 43 (22 July 1925): 220–22. Such "debates" were in marked contrast to the polemical books that attacked both evolution and the anti-evolutionists being printed at the time, the epitome of which is represented by Alfred Watterson McCann's caustic *God—or Gorilla: How the Monkey Theory of Evolution Exposes Its Own Methods, Refutes Its Own Principles, Denies Its Own Inferences, Disproves Its Own Case* (New York: Devin-Adair, 1922), and Woolsey Teller's sarcastic rejoinder, *Evolution or McCann* (New York: Truth Seeker Company, 1922). McCann, a Catholic lawyer, argues at one point that there is more evidence to suggest that human beings evolved from horses than from monkeys. McCann, 166–67.

99. The court remanded the case for retrial but urged that for the "peace and dignity of the state," a *nolle prosequi* be entered. Scopes was by then happily attending the University of Chicago on a scholarship put together for him by the scientists who had come to Dayton. Scopes and Presley, *Center of the Storm*, 206–207.

100. Scopes and Presley, *Center of the Storm*, 206–207; Annual Report, ACLU, "The Fight for Civil Liberty, 1927–28," 43, and "The Fight for Civil Liberty, 1930–31," 27.

101. De Ford, "War," 565–66; Shipley, *War on Modern Science*, 63; Harbor Allen "Anti-Evolution Campaign," 893–94; Watson, "Oklahoma," 397; R. Halliburton, Jr., "Kentucky's Anti-Evolution Controversy," *Kentucky Historical Register* 66 (April 1968): 97–98; Virginia Gray, "Anti-Evolution

Sentiment and Behavior: The Case of Arkansas," *Journal of American History* 57 (September 1970): 353; Ferenc M. Szasz, "William B. Riley and the Fight Against Teaching of Evolution in Minnesota," *Minnesota History* 41 (Spring 1969): 201–16.

102. Ferenc M. Szasz, "The Scopes Trial in Perspective," *Tennessee Historical Quarterly* 30 (Fall 1971): 290–91.

103. Shipley, *War on Modern Science*, 296–97; Szasz, "Scopes Trial," 290.

104. de Camp, *The Great Monkey Trial*, 474.

105. Shipley *War on Modern Science*, 63, 162; Harbor Allen, "Anti-Evolution Campaign," 893–94; Gray, "Anti-Evolution Sentiment," 353; R. Halliburton, Jr., "The Adoption of Arkansas' Anti-Evolution Law," *Arkansas Historical Quarterly* 23 (Autumn 1964): 280; Ginger, *Six Days or Forever?*, 212. The Supreme Court's ruling on *Epperson* v. *Arkansas* declared the state's anti-evolution law, the Rotenberry Act, unconstitutional. However, it was not until 21 December 1970 that the Mississippi Supreme Court finally got around to declaring the last remaining anti-evolution law unconstitutional (de Camp, *The Great Monkey Trial*, 486).

106. Szasz, "Scopes Trial," 290; Harbor Allen, "Anti-Evolution Campaign," 895–96; Miriam Allen De Ford, "Letter to the Editor," *Nation* 121 (29 July 1925): 143.

107. Harbor Allen, "Anti-Evolution Campaign," 893–94; Scopes and Presley, *Center of the Storm*, 233; "In Fundamentalland," *Time* 6 (24 August 1925): 16.

108. *Epperson* v. *Arkansas*, 393 U.S. 109. In its brief, the State readily admitted that the Arkansas statute was passed with the holding of the Scopes case in mind. Patterned on the Butler Act, the Rotenberry bill had adopted less explicit language than its Tennessee counterpart, consequently removing linguistically and legally from the dispute the "and" that the Scopes defense had argued required the state to prove the defendant had both taught evolution *and* denied Genesis. See Brief for the Appellee 1.

109. Donald Brod, "The Scopes Trial: A Look at Press Coverage After Forty Years," *Journalism Quarterly* 42 (1965): 219. A whole series of new trials on the subject, including the McLean trial, have occurred recently. See note 2.

110. Clarence Darrow, *The Story of My Life* (New York: Grosset and Dunlap, 1932), 244–78; Scopes and Presley, *Center of the Storm*, 45–232; Mencken, *Heathen Days*, 214–38; Hays, *Let Freedom Ring*, 25–92; Potter, *Preacher* 258–92. Mencken wrote to Sara Haardt on 1 January 1930: "There are four or five books on it, but all of them are full of nonsense. The real facts of history are always lost. Only balderdash survives." Mencken and Malone contemplated a history of the Scopes trial, but nothing ever came of their conversations. *The New Mencken Letters*, ed. Carl Bode (New York: Dial Press, 1977), 241.

111. Ginger, *Six Days or Forever?*, 243; Hays, *Let Freedom Ring*, 71–72; Darrow, *Story of My Life*, 244–78; Arthur Weinberg, ed., *Attorney for the Damned* (New York: Simon and Schuster, 1957), 174–228. Bryan's biographers were no tighter with the truth. Charles Morrow Wilson's biography,

for example, arranges the entrance of the attorneys to give the impression that Bryan was invited in only after Hays, Darrow, and Malone had volunteered. *The Commoner: William Jennings Bryan* (Garden City, N.Y.: Doubleday and Co., 1970), 420–21.

112. Coletta, *William Jennings Bryan*, 296 fn. For example, compare the following: Stone, *Clarence Darrow for the Defense*, 422–65, with Paul W. Glad, *The Trumpet Soundeth: William Jennings Bryan and His Democracy, 1896–1912* (Lincoln: University of Nebraska Press, 1960), Kendrick A. Clements, *William Jennings Bryan: Missionary Isolationist* (Knoxville: University of Tennessee Press, 1982), 141–42, and David D. Anderson, *William Jennings Bryan* (Boston: Twayne, 1981). Clements's account devotes less than three paragraphs to the trial. Anderson treats Darwinism and the Scopes Trial as one aspect of Bryan's "Decline and Fall," along with prohibition, Woodrow Wilson, and the First World War; Anderson devotes five paragraphs to the trial, and four pages to Bryan's undelivered speech.

113. de Camp, *William Jennings Bryan*, 367.

114. An entry on "The Scopes Trial" first appeared in the 1957 edition of the *Encyclopaedia Britannica*, v. 20 (Chicago: Encyclopaedia Britannica, 1957), 134. The entry, which concludes with a reference to *Inherit the Wind*, begins with the observation that the trial "seems to have been rather the trial of a religious movement, Fundamentalism, than that of an individual."

115. Jerome Lawrence and Robert E. Lee, *Inherit the Wind* (1955; New York: Bantam, 1975), 103, 112.

116. Whereas Fredric March's portrayal of Brady in the 1960 film version was modeled on Bryan, with padded stomach and balding wig, Kirk Douglas modeled his characterization in NBC's 1988 (20 March) version of *Inherit the Wind* on Jimmy Swaggart, Pat Robertson, and Oral Roberts. Douglas fostered the comparison between Bryan and Robertson, noting the latter's unsuccessful run for the Republican nomination for President in 1988. In the television movie, Brady collapses while arguing for the adoption of a school prayer amendment to the U.S. Constitution. Jerry Buck, "Actor: Play still causes controversy," *Champaign-Urbana News-Gazette*, 13 March 1988, F1 +; Jay Bobbin, "NBC airs remake of 'Inherit the Wind,' " *Champaign-Urbana News-Gazette TV Week*, 19 March 1988, 3. NBC's production of *Inherit the Wind* won the Emmy for Outstanding Drama/Comedy Special, while Jason Robards, Jr., won the Emmy for Outstanding Lead Actor in a Miniseries or Special for his portrayal of Drummond/Darrow.

117. Lawrence and Lee, *Inherit the Wind*, 69.

118. Richard N. Current, T. Harry Williams, and Frank Freidel, *American History: A Survey, Volume II: Since 1865*, 5th ed. (New York: Alfred A. Knopf, 1979), 620–21.

119. Lawrence and Lee, *Inherit the Wind*, 84–87; cf. *World's Most Famous Court Trial* 298–99, 302–303.

120. Lawrence and Lee, *Inherit the Wind*, vii. Add to this dramatic legacy the one-character plays of Clarence Darrow and H. L. Mencken, which also dealt with the Scopes trial. Henry Fonda toured in David W. Rintels, *Clarence Darrow*, which was based on Irving Stone's biography of Darrow, *Clarence Darrow for the Defense*. Fonda's portrayal aired as *IBM Presents*

Clarence Darrow, on 4 September 1974, on NBC. The drama's section on the trial prominently featured the more humorous moments of the cross-examination. David W. Rintels, *Clarence Darrow* (Garden City, N.Y.: Doubleday, 1975).

An Unpleasant Evening with H. L. Mencken, adapted by Paul Shyre, with David Wayne impersonating Mencken, premiered at Ford's Theater in Washington, D.C., on 7 March 1972. Shyre performed his revised version of the one-person drama, *Blasts and Bravos—An Evening with H. L. Mencken*, off Broadway in 1974. Shyre wrote that he was "amazed" at Mencken's coverage of the Scopes trial and particularly Mencken's protrait of Bryan. Shyre declared "I know of no other writer who was able to penetrate the character of Bryan as well as Mencken," and tried to portray that in his play. Paul Shyre, "Mencken on Stage," *Menckeniana* No. 56 (Winter 1975): 7–8.

121. The comments here are confined to the fundamentalist religions. Clearly, the "accommodationists" retained some ground, although it is not clear from this study what terms they have operated upon. In addition, the "accommodationists" did not argue for the inclusion of "morality" in national definitions of progress. Instead, they created a separation of the public value of progress from the private realm of morality. The consequences to national morality on a host of fronts—nuclear weapons proliferation, business without ethics, environmental destruction, etc.—may have been profound. The fundamentalists have recently launched a new attack that largely corrects (in some cases, overcorrects) the shortcomings cited here.

Chapter Four

1. Todd Gitlin, *The Whole World Is Watching: Mass Media in the Making and Unmaking of the New Left* (Berkeley: University of California Press, 1980), 4.

2. James Ely, "The Chicago Conspiracy Case," in *American Political Trials*, ed. Michael R. Belknap (Westport, Conn.: Greenwood Press, 1981), 263–65.

3. Ibid., 266.

4. 472 F.2d 340 (7th Cir. 1972), cert. denied 410 U.S. 970 (1973).

5. "The Chicago Trial: A Loss for All," *Time* (23 February 1970): 38–39.

6. Daniel Walker, *Rights in Conflict: A Report Submitted to the National Commission on the Causes and Prevention of Violence* (New York: Bantam Books, 1968), 228.

7. J. Anthony Lukas, *The Barnyard Epithet and Other Obscenities: Notes on the Chicago Conspiracy Trial* (New York: Harper & Row, 1970), 5.

8. Jason Epstein, *The Great Conspiracy Trial: An Essay on Law, Liberty and the Constitution* (New York: Random House, 1970).

9. Lukas, *The Barnyard Epithet*, 5.

10. David J. Danelski, "The Chicago Conspiracy Trial," in *Political Trials*, ed. Theodore L. Becker (New York: Bobbs-Merrill, 1971), 156.

11. Ibid., 159.

12. W. Lance Bennett and Martha Feldman, *Reconstructing Reality in the Courtroom: Justice and Judgment in American Culture* (New Brunswick, N.J.: Rutgers University Press, 1981), 3.

13. Ibid.; Celeste Michelle Condit and J. Ann Selzer, "The Rhetoric of Objectivity in the Newspaper Coverage of a Murder Trial," *Critical Studies in Mass Communication* 2 (1985): 197–216.

14. Kenneth Burke, *A Grammar of Motives* and *A Rhetoric of Motives* (Berkeley: University of California Press, 1969).

15. This idea of general frames of reference within which interpretations can be crystallized has become a central construct in cognitive psychology and sociology. See Erving Goffman, *Frame Analysis* (New York: Harper & Row, 1974).

16. Bennett and Feldman, *Reconstructing Reality in the Courtroom*, 68.

17. Ibid., 90.

18. Robert Enstad and Robert Davis, "Tells Abbie's Advice: Arm Against Cops," *Chicago Tribune*, 4 October 1969, 1.

19. Danelski, "The Chicago Conspiracy Trial," 172.

20. Judy Clavir and John Spitzer, *The Conspiracy Trial* (New York: Bobbs-Merrill, 1970).

21. Lukas, *The Barnyard Epithet*, 15–16.

22. Clavir and Spitzer, *The Conspiracy Trial*, 16.

23. Lukas, *The Barnyard Epithet*, 12.

24. Ibid., 73.

25. Ibid., 73–74.

26. Lukas, *The Barnyard Epithet*.

27. Ibid., 23.

28. Ibid., 98.

29. Ibid., 58.

30. Hugh Dalziel Duncan, *Communication and Social Order* (London: Oxford University Press, 1970), 340–41.

31. Walker, *Rights in Conflict*, 228.

32. Danelski, "The Chicago Conspiracy Trial," 175.

33. Helene Schwartz, *Lawyering* (New York: Farrar, Straus and Giroux, 1976), 149.

34. Janice Schuetz and Kathryn Holmes Snedaker, *Communication and Litigation: Cases Studies of Famous Trials* (Carbondale: Southern Illinois University Press, 1988), 245.

35. David O. Sears and Jonathan L. Freedman, "Selective Exposure to Information: A Critical Review," in *The Process and Effects of Mass Communication*, ed. Wilbur Schramm and Donald F. Roberts (Urbana: University of Illinois Press, 1971), 209–11.

36. Bernard Berelson and Gary A. Steiner, *Human Behavior* (New York: Harcourt, Brace & World, 1964), 529–30.

37. Paul Lazarsfeld, Bernard Berelson, and Hazel Gaudet, *The People's Choice* (New York: Columbia University Press, 1948), 164.

38. S. M. Lipset, Paul Lazarsfeld, A. Barton, and J. Linz, "The Psychology of Voting: An Analysis of Political Behavior," in *Handbook of Social Psychology*, vol. 2, ed. G. Lindzey (Cambridge, Mass.: Addison-Wesley, 1954), 1158.

39. Behavior Sciences Subpanel, President's Science Advisory Committee, "Report to the President," *Behavioral Science* 7 (1962): 277.

40. James Halloran, *Control or Consent? A Study of the Challenge of Mass Communication* (London: Sheed & Ward, 1963), 158.

41. Ibid., 309.

42. Stuart Hall, "Encoding/Decoding," in *Culture, Media, Language*, ed. Stuart Hall, D. Hobson, A. Lowe, and P. Willis (London: Hutchinson, 1980), 128–38.

43. *U.S.* v. *Dellinger*, 472 F.2d 340 (7th Cir. 1972) at 371.

44. Schwartz, *Lawyering*, 105.

45. Ibid., 106–107.

46. Schwartz, *Lawyering*.

47. Ibid.

48. *U.S.* v. *Dellinger*, 472 F.2d 340 (7th Cir. 1972) at 372.

49. Schwartz, *Lawyering*, 109.

50. Ibid., 155.

51. *U.S.* v. *Dellinger*, 472 F.2d 340 (7th Cir. 1972) at 372.

52. Ibid. at 375.

53. *Chicago Tribune*, 29 February 1970, 12

54. Ibid., 27 February 1970, 16; 6 March 1970, 18.

55. Ibid., 25 September 1969, 24.

56. Ibid.

57. William Kunstler, "Introduction," *The Conspiracy Trial* (New York: Bobbs-Merrill, 1970), xiv.

58. *Chicago Tribune*, 3 October 1969, 22.

59. Ibid., 25 September 1969, 24.

60. Ibid., 9 October 1969, 1.

61. Ibid., 17 February 1970, 1.

62. Ibid., 20 February 1970, 14.

63. Ibid., 26 February 1970, 12.

64. Ibid.

65. Ibid., 1 March 1970, 1.

66. Paul Lazarsfeld, *Radio and the Printed Page* (New York: Duell, Sloan and Pearce, 1940), 26–28.

67. *Chicago Tribune*, 18 February 1970, 16.

68. William F. Buckley, "Assault on the Courts," *National Review* (24 February 1970): 190.

69. Ibid.

70. William F. Buckley, "After Chicago," *National Review* (10 March 1970): 273.

71. Ibid., 246.

72. *Chicago Tribune*, 23 November 1972.

73. Alexander Bickel, "Judging the Chicago Trial," *Commentary* (January 1971): 40.

74. Lukas, *The Barnyard Epithet*; Danelski, "The Chicago Conspiracy Trial"; Ely, "The Chicago Conspiracy Case."

75. "Verdict on the Chicago Seven," *Time* (2 March 1970): 11.

76. *New York Times*, 20 February 1970.

77. "Verdict on the Chicago Seven," *Time* (2 March 1970): 11.

78. "The Chicago Trial: A Loss for All," *Time* (23 February 1970): 39.

79. "Verdict on the Chicago Seven," *Time* (2 March 1970): 11.

80. Ibid., 27.

81. "The Judicial Process on Trial," *Newsweek* (2 March 1970): 22.

82. Ely, "The Chicago Conspiracy Case," 266.

83. Ibid., 281.

84. Ibid., 282.

85. Tom Wicker, "The Place Where All America Was Radicalized," *New York Times Magazine* (24 August 1969): 91.

86. "Who Is on Trial in Chicago?" *Newsweek* (16 February 1970): 27.

87. "Lucky Seven," *Newsweek* (4 December 1972): 32.

88. "Poor Climate for Weathermen," *Time* (17 October 1969): 24.

89. Ibid., 25.

90. Ibid.

91. Lukas, *The Barnyard Epithet*, 10.

92. Wicker, "The Place Where All America Was Radicalized," 90.

93. "Verdict on the Chicago Seven," *Time* (2 March 1970): 9.

94. "Who Is on Trial in Chicago?" *Newsweek* (16 February 1970): 27.

95. Raymond A. Sokolov, "Perspectives on Chicago," *Newsweek* (16 November 1970): 118.

96. *New York Times*, 13 November 1972, 39.

97. Danelski, "The Chicago Conspiracy Trial," 149.

98. "Lucky Seven," *Newsweek* (4 December 1972): 31.

99. Bernard Cohen, *The Press and Foreign Policy* (Princeton: Princeton University Press, 1963), 13.

100. Ibid.

101. "Verdict on the Chicago Seven," *Time* (2 March 1970): 8.

102. Ibid.

103. "End of a Futile Case?" *Time* (4 December 1972): 16.

104. "Verdict on the Chicago Seven," 10.

105. "End of a Futile Case?" 16.

106. Ibid., 15.

107. "Who Is on Trial in Chicago?" *Newsweek* (16 February 1970): 26.

108. "End of a Futile Case?" 16.

109. Clavir and Spitzer, *The Conspiracy Trial*; Schwartz, *Lawyering*; Tom Hayden, *Trial* (New York: Holt, Rinehart and Winston, 1970).

110. "Jailing Hayden?" *Commonweal* (20 December 1968): 393.

111. Ralph Whitehead, "Daley vs. the Guerrilla Theatre," *The Nation* (7 April 1969): 422.

112. Ibid.

113. "The Conspiracy in Chicago," *Nation* (13 October 1969): 365.

114. "Political Trial, U.S. Style," *Nation* (2 March 1970): 226

115. "Repression and the Chicago Eight," *Ramparts* (January 1970): 10.

116. Larry David Nachman, "The Political Meaning of Chicago," *Nation* (23 March 1970): 326.

117. Jon R. Waltz, "This Worn-Out Piece of Tyranny," *Nation* (10 May 1971): 589.

118. Ibid.

119. "Repression and the Chicago Eight," *Ramparts* (January 1970): 7, 10.

120. Nachman, "The Political Meaning of Chicago," 327.

121. Ibid.

122. "Repression and the Chicago Eight," 10.

123. Lukas, *The Barnyard Epithet*, 5.

124. "Repression and the Chicago Eight," 40.

125. "Judge Hoffman—Reversed," *Washington Post*, 13 December 1972, A31.

126. "Notes and Comment," *The New Yorker* 46 (7 March 1970): 29.

127. "Judge Hoffman—Reversed," *Washington Post*, 13 December 1972, A31.

128. "Political Trial, U.S. Style," *Nation* (2 March 1970): 226.

129. Clavir and Spitzer, *The Conspiracy Trial*, 92.

130. *New York Times*, 16 October 1969, 18.

131. Clavir and Spitzer, *The Conspiracy Trial*, 389.

132. Lukas, *The Barnyard Epithet*, vi.

133. Clavir and Spitzer, *The Conspiracy Trial*, 467–68.

134. Lukas, *The Barnyard Epithet*, 80.

135. Abe Peck, *Uncovering the Sixties: The Life and Times of the Underground Press* (New York: Pantheon, 1985), 232–33.

136. Paul Lazarsfeld and Robert Merton, "Mass Communication, Popular Taste and Organized Social Action," in *The Communication of Ideas*, ed. Lyman Bryson (New York: Institute for Religious and Social Studies, 1948), 95–118.

137. Gitlin, *The Whole World Is Watching*, 3.

138. Ibid., 171.

139. Ibid.

140. Ibid., 172.

141. Ibid., 176.

142. Ibid., 286.

143. Danelski, "The Chicago Conspiracy Trial," 164.

144. Murdock, "Political Deviance," 172.

145. "Who Is on Trial in Chicago?" *Newsweek* (16 February 1970): 27.

146. Nachman, "The Political Meaning of Chicago," 326.

147. Gitlin, *The Whole World Is Watching*, 270–71.

148. Ibid.

149. Murdock, "Political Deviance," 164.

150. John Kifner, " 'Occupation' of Atomic Plant Site Scheduled Today," *New York Times*, 30 April 1977, 8.

151. John Kifner, "2000 Occupy Nuclear Plant Site in New Hampshire, Vow to Stay," *New York Times*, 1 May 1977, 26.

152. Gitlin, *The Whole World Is Watching*, 292.

Chapter Five

1. Daniel N. Robinson, *Psychology and Law* (New York: Oxford University Press, 1980), 45.

2. Jacques M. Quen, "Psychiatry and the Law: Historical Relevance to Today," in *"By Reason of Insanity,"* ed. Lawrence Z. Freedman (Wilmington, Del.: Scholarly Resources, 1983), 163.

3. Both Quen and Robinson note that the Justices changed their interpretation of the law between the time of the trial and the time that they provided their answers to the questions asked by the House of Lords. Quen calls the answers "a regressive and simplistic interpretation of the common law of England" (Ibid., 163).

4. For a full account of the case, see Richard Moran, *Knowing Right from Wrong: The Insanity Defense of Daniel McNaughtan* (New York: Free Press, 1981).

5. Moran reached exactly this conclusion about the McNaughtan case: "The British Victorians believed so strongly in the legitimacy of their government and the impartiality of their legal institutions that even if an investigation had revealed that McNaughtan had been persecuted by the Tories, he might still have been judged insane by the court and dismissed as a lunatic by the established press" (Ibid., 111; also, 41).

6. Mary Douglas, among others, concludes that the places of ambiguity—the gaps and overlaps—in the cultural structures of language and knowledge are most likely to be perceived both as sacred and as threatening. See *Purity and Danger* (London: Routledge & Kegan Paul, 1970).

7. Michel Foucault, *Discipline and Punish: The Birth of the Prison,* trans. Alan Sheridan (New York: Vintage Books, 1977), 27.

8. David W. Carrithers, "The Insanity Defense and Presidential Peril," *Society* 22 (July/August 1985): 24.

9. Janice Schuetz and Kathryn Holmes Snedaker show how the narrative structure of understanding was prefigured in press reports preceding the trial. They suggest that the fit of the story line presented in the *Washington Post* before the trial with that presented by the defense at the trial could have had a significant impact on the outcome. "The Press Coverage of the Hinckley Case: A Case Study of a Crime News Serial," in *Communication and Litigation: Case Studies of Famous Trials* (Carbondale: Southern Illinois University Press, 1988), 1–32.

10. See the "Closing Argument by Mr. Adelman for the Government," in *The Trial of John W. Hinckley, Jr.: A Case Study in the Insanity Defense* by Peter W. Low, John Calvin Jeffries, Jr., and Richard J. Bonnie (Mineola, N.Y.: Foundation Press, 1986), 84–93.

11. "Closing Argument by Mr. Fuller for the Defense" in *Trial of John W. Hinckley, Jr.,* by Low, et al., 101.

12. Ibid., 103.

13. Stuart Taylor, Jr., "Jury Finds Hinckley Not Guilty, Accepting His Defense of Insanity," *New York Times,* 22 June 1982, D27.

14. "Is the System Guilty?" *Time* (5 July 1982): 26–27.

15. "Shrinking from Justice," *New York Times*, 23 June 1982, A27. Joseph Kraft wrote: "The not-guilty verdict in the trial of John Hinckley does violence to common sense, so it is easy to join the outcry of protest." "Trials shouldn't deal with social issues," *Des Moines Register*, 24 June 1982, 14A. Also, Joseph Sobran, "Where is common sense?" *Des Moines Register*, 24 June 1982, 14A.

16. "A Controversial Verdict," *Newsweek* (5 July 1982): 30.

17. "Insane on All Counts," *Time* (5 July 1982): 22. This description of the public reaction has continued to dominate accounts of the Hinckley trial and discussions of the law on insanity. A case study of the Hinckley trial begins by stating that: "The general reaction to Hinckley's acquittal was outrage and disbelief." *Trial of John W. Hinckley, Jr.*, by Low et al., 1. Psychiatrist Alan Stone opens his assessment of the case with a similar observation: "The trial of John Hinckley was a bleak experience for American psychiatry, and the verdict shook public confidence in the American criminal justice system. Criticism went in two directions: outrage against the law and outrage against psychiatry." *Law, Psychiatry, and Morality* (Washington, D.C.: American Psychiatric Press, 1984), 77. Rita Simon and David Aaronson begin their recent book on the insanity defense by stating that "when the [Hinckley] jurors returned a verdict of 'not guilty by reason of insanity,' the American public was stunned . . . ; the verdict was received with disbelief and bitter criticism." *The Insanity Defense: A Critical Assessment of Law and Policy in the Post-Hinckley Era* (New York: Praeger, 1988), vii.

18. "Hinckley Acquittal Brings Moves to Change Insanity Defense," *New York Times*, 24 June 1982, D21; Steven V. Roberts, "High U.S. Officials Express Outrage, Asking for New Law on Insanity Plea," *New York Times*, 23 June 1982, B6.

19. Valerie P. Hans and Dan Slater, "John Hinckley, Jr. and the Insanity Defense: The Public's Verdict," *Public Opinion Quarterly* 47 (1983): 202.

20. Ibid., 206.

21. Stephen Cohen, "It's a Mad, Mad Verdict," *New Republic* (12 July 1982): 14. Similarly, the *National Review* reported that "common sense would agree that Hinckley had a screw loose. . . . But common sense would also say that John Hinckley knew what he was doing. That is why he did it." "Crazy and Guilty," *National Review* (9 July 1982): 12–13.

22. "In the days that followed, outrage swept Washington and the nation: how could anyone—even a deeply disturbed sociopathic loner like Hinckley—be found *not guilty* of a carefully planned and meticulously photographed attempt on the President's life?" ("A Controversial Verdict," 30).

23. "Insane on All Counts," 23.

24. "Too Much Justice," *Harper's* (September 1982): 56.

25. "Insane on All Counts," 23.

26. These, or very similar words, were reported widely following the verdict. See, "Abolish the Insanity Defense?" *US News and World Report* (5 July 1982): 15; Roberts, "High U.S. Officials," B6; Sen. Orrin Hatch, "The Insanity Defense Is Insane," *Reader's Digest* (October 1982): 199–204. Also see, Cohen, "It's a Mad, Mad Verdict," 13; Taylor, "Too Much Justice," 58.

27. Irving Kaufman, "The Insanity Plea on Trial," *New York Times Magazine* (8 August 1982): 17.

28. "Is the System Guilty?" *Time* (5 July 1982): 27.

29. "The Insanity Plea on Trial," *Newsweek* (24 May 1982): 56.

30. Marvin Stone, "Who Bears the Blame?" *US News and World Report* (13 April 1981): 76.

31. See "The Unanswered Questions," *Newsweek* (20 April 1981): 40; "Answers From John Hinckley," *Newsweek* (12 October 1981): 50–51.

32. Stewart W. Taylor, Jr., "Jury Finds Hinckley Not Guilty, Accepting His Defense of Insanity," *New York Times*, 22 June 1982, D27.

33. Ibid. A similar portrayal is provided by Lincoln Caplan in his book about the Hinckley trial, *The Insanity Defense and the Trial of John W. Hinckley, Jr.* (Boston: David R. Godine, 1984), 9–10.

34. "JoAnn Hinckley's Story," *Newsweek* (17 May 1982): 54.

35. "The Insanity Plea on Trial," *Newsweek* (24 May 1982): 57. Also: " 'It's Just Gonna Be Insanity,' " *Time* (24 May 1982): 31.

36. "Hinckley's Life," *Time* (28 March 1983): 21.

37. See Jack and Jo Ann Hinckley, "Illness Is the Culprit!" *Reader's Digest* (March 1983): 77–81; Jack and Jo Ann Hinckley with Elizabeth Sherrill, "The Secret Life of John Hinckley, Jr.," *Redbook* (May 1985): 118–20; "The Father of Reagan's Assailant Devotes His Life to Combating Mental Illness," *Christianity Today* (14 June 1985): 42–44.

38. "The Secret Life of John Hinckley, Jr.," *Redbook* (May 1985): 118. The article is an excerpt from the Hinckleys' book, *Breaking Points*.

39. *Christianity Today* quotes John Hinckley, Sr., as saying: "Many expect me to feel deep guilt about John, but I don't. I don't feel any more guilt than if he had been born with a birth defect. I honestly feel that Jo Ann and I did the best we could. . . . If I am guilty of anything, it is ignorance about mental illness" (44).

40. The textual guide to this "relationship" was the repeated reference to the "romance" or "marriage" between medicine and the law. The metaphor makes sense structurally better than it makes sense substantively.

41. "The Insanity Plea on Trial," 56.

42. "Pre-empting the Mental Defense," *National Review* (28 May 1982): 108.

43. Caplan, *The Insanity Defense*, 79–86.

44. "To Alan Stone, professor of law and psychiatry at Harvard, the sight of competing psychiatrists testifying for and against a defense of insanity is like 'clowns performing in a three-ring circus.' " "Is the System Guilty?" *Time* (5 July 1982), 26.

45. *Wall Street Journal*, 24 June 1982 in *Editorials on File, 1982*, 696.

46. "The Insanity Plea on Trial," 61.

47. 23 March 1982, in *Editorials on File, 1982*, 696.

48. 23 June 1982, in *Editorials on File, 1982*, 697. Carrithers, "The Insanity Defense," 25: "Insanity, after all, is a legal concept, not a psychiatric one."

49. Chuck Lane, "Measuring Madness," *New Republic* (31 December 1984): 41.

50. An Associated Press-NBC News poll taken shortly after the beginning of the Hinckley trial found "that 87 percent of Americans believe too many accused murderers plead insanity to avoid prison." "The Insanity Plea is on Trial Again," *US News and World Report* (10 May 1982): 7. The same sentiment was cited as a cause of the negative reaction to the Hinckley verdict: "The cascade of public outrage after John W. Hinckley, Jr.'s acquittal Monday on the ground of insanity reflects a widespread suspicion that law and psychiatry have combined in a way that confuses juries and almost presumes that people cannot be held responsible for even the most bizarre and heinous crimes." Stuart Taylor, Jr., "The Hinckley Riddle," *New York Times*, 24 June 1982, D21.

51. "Picking Between Mad and Bad," *Time* (12 October 1981): 68. Joseph Sobran, "Where is common sense?" *Des Mines Register*, 24 June 1982, 14A: "Hinckley's acquittal comes as a shock, but not a surprise. It will be no shock, only a mild surprise, if he is soon a free man."

52. Wallace Turner, "New Law on Insanity Plea Stirs Dispute in Alaska," *New York Times*, 22 June 1982, A16.

53. "Interview with Julius Hunter of KMOX-TV in St. Louis, Missouri," *Weekly Compilation of Presidential Documents*, 22 July 1982, 964–65.

54. For a theoretical discussion of the status relationships between forms of discourse see, Robert Hariman, "Status, Marginality, and Rhetorical Theory," *Quarterly Journal of Speech* 72 (1986): 38–54.

55. "Enactment of Crime Package Culmination of 11-Year Effort," *Congressional Quarterly* (20 October 1984): 2752–54; Carrithers, "The Insanity Defense," 25–26.

56. See, for example, Garland DeNelsky, "How Psychiatry Can Aid Courts," *New York Times*, 21 June 1982, A19.

57. American Psychiatric Association, "American Psychiatric Association Statement on the Insanity Defense," *American Journal of Psychiatry* 140 (1983): 681–88.

58. National Commission on the Insanity Defense and the National Mental Health Association, *Myths and Realities: A Report of the National Commission on the Insanity Defense* (Alexandria, Va.: National Mental Health, 1983), 24.

59. Stone, "Who Bears the Blame," 93.

60. *Jones* v. *US*, 463 U.S. 354, 366 (1983).

61. Richard Singer, "The Aftermath of an Insanity Acquittal: The Supreme Court's Recent Decision in *Jones* v. *United States*," *Annals*, 477 (January 1985): 117, 118.

62. Leslie Maitland Werner, "Request for Hinckley Leave Withdrawn," *New York Times*, 16 April 1987, A8.

63. Caplan, *The Insanity Defense*, 114.

64. Hence, in a letter to *Newsweek*, Hinckley himself reflected the general understanding when he opposed the guilty but mentally ill plea, writing that "we would be in the sorry position of wanting to punish a mentally ill person for his sickness." "The insanity defense and me," *Newsweek* (20 September 1982): 30. Also quoted in Caplan, *The Insanity Defense*, 106–107.

65. Both anthropologists and political analysts have noted that a society's categories of understanding must appear to be immutable if they are to have the necessary social power. As anthropologist Mary Douglas wrote, "the moral order and the knowledge which sustains it are created by social conventions. If their man-made origins were not hidden, they would be stripped of some of their authority." *Rules and Meanings* (Baltimore: Penguin Books, 1973), 15.

Steven Lukes asks: "is not the supreme and most insidious exercise of power to prevent people, to whatever degree, from having grievances by shaping their perceptions, cognitions and preferences in such a way that they accept their role in the existing order of things, either because they can see or imagine no alternative to it, or because they see it as natural and unchangeable, or because they value it as divinely ordained and beneficial?" *Power: A Radical View* (London: Macmillan, 1974), 24.

66. The same themes have also been applied in the commentary on the possibility of granting Hinckley temporary leaves. After quoting U.S. Attorney Joseph diGenova, who opposed Hinckley's leave on the grounds that "we do not believe that anyone who tries to nullify a national election with a bullet deserves the privilege of moving freely in a civilized society," syndicated columnist Roger Simon countered: "But I guess he must have forgotten John Hinckley is an innocent man. Hinckley may never be cured. But if he is, he will be allowed to move freely among us civilized people because our civilized law says so. . . . As tough as it sometimes is to take, maybe that's what makes us civilized." Roger Simon, " 'Civilized' law includes Hinckley, too," *Des Moines Register*, 8 April 1987, 8A.

Chapter Six

1. William Wright, *The von Bulow Affair* (New York: Dell Publishing, 1983), 19–56.

2. Alan Dershowitz, *Reversal of Fortune: Inside the von Bulow Case* (New York: Random House, 1986), xvii.

3. Ibid., xvii.

4. Tony Burton, "Puccio: The Guilt Rests With Sunny," *Daily News*, 30 May 1985, 12.

5. Tony Burton, "Stepchildren Dare Claus to Take the Stand," *Daily News*, 31 May 1985, 2.

6. Marilyn Goldstein, "Hottest Ticket in Town," *Newsday* (5 June 1985): II, 3.

7. Michael Ryan, "A Shattered Family," *People Magazine* (17 June 1985): 108.

8. Dominick Dunne, "Fatal Charm: The Social Web of Claus von Bulow," *Vanity Fair* (August 1985): 41.

9. Dershowitz, *Reversal of Fortune*, xviii.

10. Ibid., 204.

11. Barbara Walters, Interview With Claus von Bulow, *20/20*, ABC, New York (13 June 1985).

12. Ted Koppel, *Nightline*, ABC, New York (10 June 1985).

13. Dershowitz, *Reversal of Fortunes*, 123.

14. Dunne, "A Fatal Charm," 56.

15. Tony Burton, "How Claus Case Adds Up," *Daily News*, 16 June 1985, 5.

16. Ibid.

17. Koppel (10 June 1985).

18. Dershowitz, *Reversal of Fortune*, xviii.

19. Daniel J. Boorstin, *The Image: A Guide to Pseudo-Events in America* (New York: Atheneum, 1971), 48.

20. J. G. Cawalti, "With the Benefit of Hindsight: Popular Culture Criticism," *Critical Studies in Mass Communication* 2 (1985): 363–79; Lance Strate, "Heroes, Fame and the Media," *Et Cetera* (1985): 44.

21. The manner in which the coverage of the von Bulow retrial conferred celebrity suggests how the popular trial differs from trials that do not receive publicity in at least four significant ways:

1) The celebrities need not participate *in* courtroom activities. Cosima von Bulow, born to Claus and Sunny, was neither a witness nor a courtroom observer but was often included in media coverage of the trial and characterized as the daughter who remained loyal to her father. Andrea Reynolds, von Bulow's love interest during the retrial, appeared regularly in media coverage but not in the courtroom.

2) Information available to the public audience about participants in a popular trial displaced the facts relevant to the determination of the verdict in the trial. For example, in the von Bulow trial, the defendant, who never took the witness stand, told Barbara Walters on ABC's national televised *20/20* that he "loved his wife." Magazines reported gossip which was not part of the evidence presented in court.

3) The *situs* of the popular trial extends beyond the carefully regulated environment of a physical courtroom. The popular trial includes the courtroom, the courthouse steps which provide photo opportunities and serve as the scene for press conferences, the scene of the crime, and the television studio for interviews. Von Bulow's retrial took place in the Providence, Rhode Island courthouse; Clarendon Court in Newport, the mansion in which the comatose Sunny was found; Sunny's exclusive Manhattan apartment; and the campus of Brown University (the school Cosima attended).

4) The functions of popular trials include providing both public information about the administration of justice and social control, and entertainment.

22. Goldstein, "Hottest Ticket in Town," 3.

23. Susan Drucker and Robert Cathcart, "Media Relationships: The Celebrity and the Fan" (Paper presented at the Speech Communication Association of Puerto Rico conference, San Juan, Puerto Rico, December 1986).

24. Boorstin, *The Image*, 65.

25. Karlyn Kohrs Campbell, *The Rhetorical Act* (Belmont, Calif.: Wadsworth Publishing Co., 1982).

26. "Von Bulow Closing Arguments," *Newsday* (7 June 1985): 11.

27. Dershowitz, *Reversal of Fortunes*, 244.

28. "The Second Trial: What the Jurors Heard . . . ," *Daily News*, 11 June 1985: 40.

29. Ibid.

30. *CBS Evening News*, New York (10 June 1985).

31. *CNN Coverage* (15 May 1985).

32. Dershowitz, *Reversal of Fortunes*, 242.

33. David Doret, "Trial by Videotape—Can Justice Be Seen to Be Done?" *Temple Law Quarterly* 47 (1974): 228–68.

34. Dominick Dunne, *Fatal Charms and Other Tales of Today* (New York: Crown Publishers, 1987), 203.

35. David L. Altheide and Robert P. Snow, *Media Logic* (Beverly Hills: Sage Publications, 1979).

36. Bernard Timberg, "The Rhetoric of the Camera in Television Soap Opera," in *Television: The Critical View*, 2nd ed., ed. Horace Newcomb (New York: Oxford, 1979), 15.

37. Peter W. Kaplan, "Should Televising of Rape Trials be Permitted?" *New York Times*, 30 June 1984, 48.

38. Karlyn Kohrs Campbell and Kathleen Hall Jamieson, *Form and Genre: Shaping Rhetorical Action* (Falls Church, Va.: Speech Communication Association Publications, n.d.), 19.

39. Ibid., 21. This study follows the notions of genre criticism articulated by Campbell and Jamieson. Their perspective defines genre study as a process of classification based on recorded observations which indicate that one group of entities shares some important characteristic which differentiates it. They have established a general definition for genre as a "classification based on the fusion and interrelation of elements in such a way that a unique kind of rhetorical act is created" (ibid., 25). Thus, part of the meaning of a work is derived from its traditions of production and use (25).

40. *TV Guide* (September 1987).

41. Susan J. Drucker and Janice Platt Hunold, "The Debating Game," *Critical Studies in Mass Communication* 4 (1987): 202–207.

42. Robert K. Tiemens, Susan A. Hellweg, Phillip Kipper, and Steven L. Phillips, "An Integrative Verbal and Visual Analysis of the Carter-Reagan Debate," *Communication Quarterly* 33 (1985): 34–42.

43. Altheide and Snow, *Media Logic*.

44. Percy H. Tannenbaum, ed., *The Entertainment Functions of Television* (Hillsdale, N.J.: Lawrence Erlbaum Assoc., 1980).

45. Major features appearing in current television programming were derived from suggestions of Ronald Primeau in *The Rhetoric of Television* (New York: Longman, 1979). The authors had approximately thirty-five undergraduate students view several hours of representative samples of each genre. This produced an exhaustive analysis of situation comedy, nightly news programs, dramatic prime time programs, daytime soap operas, game shows, and talk shows.

46. Dennis Porter, "Soap Time: Thoughts on a Commodity Art Form," in *Television: The Critical View,* 2nd ed., ed. Horace Newcomb (New York: Oxford, 1979), 139.

47. Ibid., 89.

48. Mary Cassata and Thomas Skill, *Life on Daytime Television: Tuning-In American Serial Drama* (Norwood, N.J.: Ablex Publishers, 1983), 143.

49. Ibid., xxiii.

50. Porter, "Soap Time," 88.

51. L. Bogart, "Television News as Entertainment," in *The Entertainment Function of Television,* ed. Tannenbaum.

52. In an effort to measure perception of lawyer credibility, witness credibility, and perception of guilt or innocence of defendants, the authors began initial experimentation in July 1985. Three videotapes were made of reenacted trials using different structural features in taping the identical content of a fictional trial. Tapes were shown to sixty undergraduate students. A semantic differential scale was used to measure perception of two attorneys, two witnesses, the judge, and a verdict preference of guilt or innocence. All responses were averaged for each set of attribute scales by model taped. Averages were compared to reach the following tentative conclusions. Verdicts of "innocent" or "guilty" were tabulated and the talk show tape resulted in the most favorable response as to credibility. Overall, the talk show and the soap opera yielded the most favorable responses as to credibility. In all tapes the defendant received a majority of innocent verdicts. The highest percentage of innocent verdicts came from the talk show tape and followed closely by the soap opera.

53. John Langer, "Television's 'Personality System,' " *Media, Culture and Society* 4 (1981): 351–65.

54. Wright, *von Bulow Affair,* 326.

55. Dunne, *Vanity Fair,* 107.

56. *Live at Five,* NBC, New York (10 June 1985).

57. Langer, "Television's 'Personality System,' " 363.

58. Ibid., 355.

59. Tony Burton, "Stepchildren Dare Claus to Take Stand," *Daily News,* 31 May 1985, 2.

60. Goldstein, "Hottest Ticket in Town," 3.

61. Drucker and Cathcart, "Media Relationships."

62. Koppel (10 June 1985).

63. Susanna Barber, *News Cameras in the Courtroom* (Norwood, N.J.: Ablex, 1986), 118.

Chapter Seven

1. "Top Story of the Night," *News,* Ch. 8, CBS, San Diego, 10 December 1984.

2. Ibid.

3. "The Hedgecock Story," *News*, Ch. 39, ABC, San Diego, 18 November 1985.

4. I recently served as an expert witness for the defense of Nancy Hoover/Hunter (she has remarried since the trials). In this more quantitative analysis I employed a content analytic scheme—a hybrid version of Osgood's Contingency Methodology. For a discussion of this method, see Ithiel de Sola Pool, ed., *Trends in Content Analysis* (Evanston, Ill.: Northwestern University Press, 1963), and Klaus Krippendorf, *Content Analysis: An Introduction to Its Methodology* (Beverly Hills, Calif.: Sage, 1980).

5. "Grand Jury Probes Hedgecock Funds," *San Diego Union*, 20 April 1984, 1. (Hereafter, the *Union* will be referred to as *SDU*.)

6. "Hedgecock on Trial," *L.A. Times: San Diego Edition*, 23 May 1984, 1.

7. "Reaction: Mayor Says DA Should Quit Vendetta," *SDU*, 14 February 1985, A6.

8. "Reaction," A3.

9. Ibid.

10. "Grand Jury Probes Hedgecock Funds," *SDU*, 20 April 1984, 1.

11. Celeste Michelle Condit and J. Ann Selzer, "The Rhetoric of Objectivity in the Newspaper Coverage of a Murder Trial," *Critical Studies in Mass Communication* 2 (1985): 210–11; See David L. Altheide, *Creating Reality: How T.V. News Distorts Events* (Beverly Hills, Calif.: Sage, 1976), 6–7, 17. These authors offer very useful discussions of what "objectivity" means in terms of the American news industry. For a neo-Marxist treatment see Michael Parenti, *Inventing Reality: The Politics of Mass Media* (New York: St. Martin's Press, 1986), 50–57. Parenti discusses the "myth of objectivity."

12. Robert MacNeil, *The People Machine* (New York: Harper & Row, 1968), 21.

13. Altheide, *Creating Reality*, 173–78.

14. Paul Weaver, "Newspaper News and T.V. News," in *T.V. as a Social Force*, ed. Douglas Cater (New York: Praeger, 1975), 86.

15. Dan Nimmo and James E. Combs, *Nightly Horrors* (Knoxville: University of Tennessee Press, 1985), 8.

16. Mark Fishman, *Manufacturing the News* (Austin: University of Texas Press, 1980), 5.

17. Lance Bennett and Martha Feldman, *Reconstructing Reality in the Courtroom: Justice and Judgment in American Culture* (New Brunswick, N.J.: Rutgers University Press, 1981), 49.

18. Fishman, *Manufacturing the News*, 5.

19. Condit and Selzer, "Rhetoric of Objectivity," 210–11.

20. Robert Drechsel, *News Making in the Trial Courts* (New York: Longman, 1983), 78–79.

21. Interview with a reporter from the *San Diego Union*.

22. "Cast of Courtroom Drama Profiled," *SDU*, 2 December 1984, B1, B3. This article offers a good example of this formula in action.

23. "Hedgecock: His Whole Future is on the Line," *SDU*, 21 November 1984, A7.

24. Vladimir Propp, *The Morphology of a Folktale* (Austin: University of Texas Press, 1968).

25. Nimmo and Combs, *Nightly Horrors*, 26.

26. "Hedgecock Fights on," *Tribune*, 20 September 1984, 1.

27. "Hedgecock Always Wanted to be in Charge," *L.A. Times: San Diego Edition*, 14 February 1985, B1.

28. *Evening News*, Ch. 39, San Diego, 10 December 1985. One call-in radio talk show asked its listeners, "What sentence would you give Roger Hedgecock?" *KFMB, AM*, San Diego, 11 December 1985.

29. *Evening News*, Ch. 39, ABC, 10 December 1985.

30. "Dominelli Leads DA on Wild Goose Chase," *SDU*, 21 April 1985, 10.

31. "To Goodman Mobsters are Citizens Too," *SDU*, 25 June 1985, A1.

32. "Cast of Courtroom Drama," B3.

33. "Hedgecock's Second Trial, More than Just a Rerun," *Tribune*, 26 July 1985, A12.

34. "Goodman's Approach is Aggressive," *Tribune*, 21 August 1985, A8.

35. This stumbling incident was aired on the *Evening News*, Ch. 39, ABC, San Diego, 4 September 1985.

36. *Evening News*, Ch. 39, ABC, 18 November 1985.

37. *Evening News*, Ch. 39, ABC, 15 February 1985.

38. "Jury's Voice is 11 to 1 in Favor of Conviction," *SDU*, 14 February 1985.

39. "Politics: Mayor will Fight, but Indictment Could be the Kiss of Death," *SDU*, 20 September 1984, A11.

40. "Hedgecock's not the First Indicted San Diego Mayor," *Tribune*, 20 September 1984, A3.

41. "Politics," A1.

42. Ibid.

43. "Hedgecock's Silence a Dramatic Gamble," *Tribune*, 25 September 1985, A12.

44. *Evening News*, Ch. 39, ABC, San Diego, 19 December 1985.

45. Dreschel, *News Making*, Chapter 1.

46. Parenti, *Inventing Reality*, Chapter 1.

Chapter Eight

1. Cited in Anthony Towne, "Reflections on Two Trials: A Plea for Anarchy in the Name of Christ," *Christian Century* 85 (December 1968): 1535.

2. Ibid.

3. Jack Nelson and Ronald J. Ostrow, *The FBI and the Berrigans* (New York: Coward, McCann & Geoghegan, 1972), 54.

4. John F. Bannan and Rosemary S. Bannan, *Law, Morality and Vietnam: The Peace Militants and the Courts* (Bloomington and London: Indiana University Press, 1974), 125.

5. Nancy Zaroulis and Gerald Sullivan, *Who Spoke Up? American Protest against the War in Vietnam 1963–1975* (Garden City, N.Y.: Doubleday & Co., 1984), 233.

6. The press statement has been reprinted in Charles Anthony Wilkinson, "The Rhetoric of Movements: Definition and Methodological Approach, Applied to the Catholic Anti-War Movement in the United States," diss., Northwestern University, 1975, pp. 221–28. The quotation is taken from p. 223.

7. For a discussion of the rhetorical aspects of the Catonsville Nine action, see John H. Patton, "Rhetoric at Catonsville: Daniel Berrigan, Conscience, and Image Alteration," *Today's Speech* 23 (Winter 1975): 3–12. Patton analyzes the symbolic dimensions of the burning of draft files at Catonsville but does not discuss the trial that resulted from it.

8. See Carl Cohen, *Civil Disobedience: Conscience, Tactics, and the Law* (New York and London: Columbia University Press, 1971), 52–75, for a detailed explanation of the distinction between direct and indirect civil disobedience, as well as discussion of the Catonsville Nine incident as an example of indirect civil disobedience.

9. Wilkinson, "Rhetoric of Movements," 189.

10. Quoted in Charles A. Meconis, *With Clumsy Grace: The American Catholic Left 1961–1975* (New York: Seabury Press, 1979), 33.

11. Zaroulis and Sullivan, *Who Spoke Up?*, 233.

12. *United States of America* v. *Philip Berrigan, Daniel Berrigan, Thomas Lewis, James Darst, John Hogan, Marjorie Melville, Thomas Melville, George Mische, and Mary Moylan,* United States District Court for the District of Maryland, Criminal Trial #28111, 225. Hereafter referred to as "Trial Transcript."

13. Quoted in Bannan and Bannan, *Law, Morality and Vietnam,* 129.

14. Quoted in ibid., 130.

15. Trial Transcript, 781–82.

16. Sidney E. Zion, "Another 'No' to a Challenge on the Vietnam War," *New York Times,* 13 October 1968, 8E.

17. Trial Transcript, 667.

18. Ibid., 798.

19. Zaroulis and Sullivan, *Who Spoke Up?*, 233.

20. Trial Transcript, 226–27.

21. Thomas M. Gannon, "Trial of the Catonsville Nine," *America* 119 (26 October 1968): 379.

22. Daniel Boorstin, *The Image* (New York: Atheneum, 1971), 11–12.

23. Paul Velde, "Guerrilla Christianity," *Commonweal* 85 (13 December 1968): 372.

24. Stephen J. Lynton, "Peace Group Foils Arrest of 2 on Trial," *Baltimore Sun,* 7 October 1968, C20 and C10.

25. Bart Barnes, "2000 Protest at Draft File Trial of Nine," *Washington Post,* 8 October 1968, A12.

26. Dierdre C. Carmody, "9 War Foes Begin Baltimore Trial," *New York Times,* 8 October 1968, 13.

27. Barnes, "2000 Protest," A12.

28. Stephen J. Lynton, "Vietnam Foes Carry Coffin to Baltimore's Draft Offices," *Baltimore Sun*, 9 October 1968, C26.

29. "City's Largest Anti-War March; '9' Found Guilty," *Baltimore Sun*, 13 October 1968, D18.

30. Gordon C. Zahn, "The Berrigans—A Catholic Pacifist's View," *Dissent* 18 (June 1971): 202.

31. Ibid.

32. Meconis, *With Clumsy Grace*, 35.

33. Ibid., 153–66.

34. Robert McAfee Brown, "The Berrigans: Signs or Models?" in *The Berrigans*, ed. William Van Etten Casey and Philip Nobile (New York: Avon Books, 1981), 60.

35. J. Justin Gustainis, "The Catholic Ultra-Resistance: Rhetorical Strategies of Anti-War Protest," *The Communicator* 12 (Spring 1983): 37–42.

36. J. Justin Gustainis, "Daniel Berrigan and the Catholic Ultra-Resistance: The Roots of a Rhetorical Genre," diss., Bowling Green State University, 1981, 34–52.

37. Sarah A. Fahy, "The Catonsville Nine Action, A Study of An American Catholic Resistance Action," Diss., Temple University, 1975, 54.

38. Towne, "Reflections," 1536.

39. Wilkinson, "Rhetoric of Movements," 94.

40. Karlyn Kohrs Campbell, "The Rhetoric of Women's Liberation: An Oxymoron," *Quarterly Journal of Speech* 59 (February 1973): 75.

41. "Has the Church Lost Its Soul?" *Newsweek* (4 October 1971): 188–89.

42. Michael Novak, " 'Blue-Bleak Embers . . . Fall, Gall Themselves . . . Gash Gold-Vermillion,' " in *Conspiracy: The Implications of the Harrisburg Trial for the Democratic Tradition*, ed. John C. Raines (New York: Harper & Row, 1974), 44.

43. Elliot R. Siegel, Gerald Miller, and C. Edward Wotring, "Source Credibility and Credibility Proneness: A New Relationship," *Speech Monographs* 36 (June 1969): 118.

44. Don A. Schweitzer, "The Effect of Presentation on Source Evaluation," *Quarterly Journal of Speech* 56 (February 1970): 33–39.

45. This was a problem not only for the Catonsville Nine, but for anti-war protestors generally. See J. Justin Gustainis and Dan F. Hahn, "While the Whole World Watched: Rhetorical Failures of Anti-War Protest," *Communication Quarterly* 36 (1988): 203–16.

46. "Has the Church Lost Its Soul?" 188.

Chapter Nine

1. M. S. Piccirillo, "On the Authenticity of Televisual Experience: A Critical Exploration of Para-Social Closure," *Critical Studies in Mass Communication* 3 (1986): 344.

2. David Porter, "Soap Time: Thoughts on a Commodity Art Form," in

Television: The Critical View, 3rd ed., ed. Horace Newcomb (New York: Oxford University Press, 1982), 122; John Fiske, "Television and Popular Culture: Reflections on British and Australian Critical Practice," *Critical Studies in Mass Communication* 3 (1986): 213.

3. John Fiske and John Hartley, *Reading Television* (New York: Methuen, 1978), 17.

4. Ibid., 38.

5. Aristotle, *Rhetoric and Poetics of Aristotle*, trans. W. Rhys Roberts (New York: Modern Library, 1954), 167 (1404b. 18–20).

6. Dick Hebdige, *Subculture: The Meaning of Style* (New York: Methuen, 1979), 11.

7. Douglas Kellner, "TV, Ideology, and Emancipatory Popular Culture," in *Television: The Critical View*, 3rd ed., ed. Newcomb, 388–89; Farrell Corcoran, "Television as Ideological Apparatus: The Power and the Pleasure," *Critical Studies in Mass Communication* 1 (1984): 134; Hebdige, *Subculture*, 84–85.

8. Stuart Hall, "Signification, Representation, Ideology: Althusser and the Post-Structuralist Debates," *Critical Studies in Mass Communication* 2 (1985): 103–104.

9. Jay G. Blumler and Michael Gurevitch, "The Political Effects of Mass Communication," in *Culture, Society and the Media*, ed. Michael Gurevitch, Tony Bennett, James Curran, and Janet Wollacott (New York: Methuen, 1982), 263.

10. Harold A. Innis, *The Bias of Communication* (Toronto: University of Toronto Press, 1951); Walter Ong, *The Presence of the Word* (New York: Clarion, 1967).

11. Joshua Meyrowitz, *No Sense of Place: The Impact of Electronic Media on Social Behavior* (New York: Oxford University Press, 1985); Neil Postman, *Amusing Ourselves To Death: Public Discourse in the Age of Show Business* (New York: Viking, 1985).

12. James W. Chesebro, "The Media Reality: Epistemological Functions of Media in Cultural Systems," *Critical Studies in Mass Communication* 1 (1984): 123–24, 120.

13. Gary Gumpert and Robert Cathcart, eds., *Inter/Media* (New York: Oxford University Press, 1982), 9–10; Gary Gumpert and Robert Cathcart, "Media Grammars, Generations, and Media Gaps," *Critical Studies in Mass Communication* 2 (1985): 25.

14. David L. Altheide and Robert P. Snow, *Media Logic* (Beverly Hills, Calif.: Sage, 1979), 15.

15. Ibid., 23.

16. Ibid., 22–23.

17. David L. Altheide, *Media Power* (Beverly Hills, Calif.: Sage, 1985).

18. Peter L. Berger and Thomas Luckmann, *The Social Construction of Reality: A Treatise in the Sociology of Knowledge* (New York: Doubleday, 1966).

19. Robert A. Hackett, "Decline of a Paradigm? Bias and Objectivity in News Media Studies," *Critical Studies in Mass Communication* 1 (1984): 236.

20. Michael Calvin McGee, "A Materialist's Conception of Rhetoric," in *Explorations in Rhetoric: Studies in Honor of Douglas Ehninger*, ed. Ray E. McKerrow (Chicago: Scott, Foresman, 1982), 23–48.

21. Louis Althusser, *Lenin and Philosophy and Other Essays*, trans. B. Brewster, (New York: Monthly Review Press, 1971), 166.

22. Hebdige, *Subculture*, 13.

23. Michael Novak, "Television Shapes the Soul," in *Television: The Critical View*, 3rd ed., ed. Newcomb, 340.

24. See Lawrence Grossberg, "Strategies of Marxist Cultural Interpretation," *Critical Studies in Mass Communication* 1 (1984): 392–421, on the dangers of "vulgar" Marxism.

25. Altheide and Snow, *Media Logic*, 236–37.

26. Fredric Jameson, *The Political Unconscious: Narrative as a Socially Symbolic Act* (Ithaca, N.Y.: Cornell University Press, 1981).

27. Tony Bennett, "Theories of the Media, Theories of Society," in *Culture, Society and the Media*, ed. Gurevitch, et al., 51; James Curran, Michael Gurevitch, and Janet Wollacott, "The Study of the Media: Theoretical Approaches," in *Culture, Society and the Media*, ed. Gurevitch, et al., 22; Todd Gitlin, "Prime Time Ideology: The Hegemonic Process in Television Entertainment," in *Television: The Critical View*, ed. Newcomb, 429–30; Stuart Hall, "The Rediscovery of 'Ideology': Return of the Repressed in Media Studies," in *Culture, Society and the Media*, ed. Gurevitch, et al., 64, 67; Marina Camargo Heck, "The Ideological Dimension of Media Message," in *Culture, Media, Language*, Stuart Hall, D. Hobson, A. Lowe, eds. (London: Hutchinson, 1980), 122; James Monaco, *Media Culture* (New York: Delta Books, 1978), 5.

28. Ian Connell, "Television News and the Social Contract," in *Culture, Media, Language*, Hall et al., eds. 140.

29. Gaye Tuchman, *Making News: A Study in the Construction of Reality* (New York: The Free Press, 1978).

30. Stuart Hall, "Recent Developments in Theories of Language and Ideology: A Critical Note," in *Culture, Media, Language*, Hall et al., eds., 159; Chesebro, "The Media Reality," 112.

31. Dennis Mumby and Carole Spitzack, "Ideology and Television News: A Metaphoric Analysis of Political Stories," *Central States Speech Journal* 34 (1983): 162.

32. Michael Kerbel, "The Golden Age of Television Drama," in *Television: The Critical View*, 3rd ed., ed. Newcomb, 53; Douglas Antin, "Video: The Distinctive Features of the Medium," in *Television: The Critical View*, ed. Newcomb, 467.

33. Chesebro, "The Media Reality," 119.

34. David Sohn and Jerzy Kosinski, "A Nation of Videots," in *Television: The Critical View*, ed. Newcomb, 364; Martin Esslin, "Aristotle and the Advertisers: The Television Commercial Considered as a Form of Drama," in *Television: The Critical View*, ed. Newcomb, 260; Gitlin, "Prime Time Ideology," 432.

35. Altheide and Snow, *Media Logic*, 238.

36. Fiske, "Television and Popular Culture," 212.

37. Postman, *Amusing Ourselves*; Altheide and Snow, *Media Logic*, 54.

38. Richard Corliss, "Happy Days Are Here Again," in *Television: The Critical View*, ed. Newcomb, 70.

39. Fiske, "Television and Popular Culture," 212.

40. Arthur Asa Berger, *Media Analysis Techniques* (Beverly Hills, Calif.: Sage, 1982).

41. Altheide and Snow, *Media Logic*, 38, 53; Newcomb, ed., *Television: The Critical View*, 480; David Thorburn, "Television Melodrama," in *Television: The Critical View*, ed. Newcomb, 534, 542; Raymond Williams, *Television: Technology and Cultural Form* (New York: Schocken Books, 1974), 47, 56.

42. Meyrowitz, *No Sense of Place*, 99.

43. Fiske and Hartley, *Reading Television*, 160–65.

44. Gitlin, "Prime Time Ideology," 447.

45. Meyrowitz, *No Sense of Place*.

46. Michael Schudson, "The Ideal of Conversation in the Study of Mass Media," in *Inter/Media*, ed. Gumpert and Cathcart, 46–47.

47. Meyrowitz, *No Sense of Place*; Newcomb, *Television: The Critical View*, 169.

48. Corcoran, "Television as Ideological Apparatus," 135.

49. Klaus Bruhn Jensen, "Qualitative Audience Research: Toward an Integrative Approach to Reception," *Critical Studies in Mass Communication* 4 (1987): 25.

50. Fiske and Hartley, *Reading Television*, 88.

51. Corcoran, "Television as Ideological Apparatus," 139.

52. Ibid., 141.

53. Antin, "Video," 470; Esslin, "Aristotle and the Advertisers," 264–65; Williams, *Television*, 69, 70.

54. Gitlin, "Prime Time Ideology," 434.

55. Paul M. Hirsch, "The Role of Television and Popular Culture in Contemporary Society," in *Television: The Critical View*, 3rd ed., ed. Newcomb, 280; Fiske and Hartley, *Reading Television*, 86.

56. Altheide and Snow, *Media Logic*, 24.

57. Curran, Gurevitch, and Wollacott, "Study of Media," 227.

58. Fiske and Hartley, *Reading Television*, 157.

59. Kenneth Burke, *A Grammar of Motives* (Berkeley: University of California Press, 1969); Frank Lentricchia, *Criticism and Social Change* (Chicago: University of Chicago Press, 1983).

60. John Fiske, *Television Culture* (New York: Methuen, 1987).

61. Hirsch, "Role of Television," 292.

Select Bibliography

Adler, Renata. *Reckless Disregard: Westmoreland v. CBS et al., Sharon v. Time.* New York: Knopf, 1986.

Altheide, David L. *Creating Reality: How T.V. News Distorts Events.* Beverly Hills, Calif.: Sage, 1976.

———. *Media Power.* Beverly Hills, Calif.: Sage, 1985.

Altheide, David L., and Robert P. Snow. *Media Logic.* Beverly Hills, Calif.: Sage, 1979

Althusser, Louis. *Lenin and Philosophy and Other Essays.* Translated by B. Brewster. New York: Monthly Review Press, 1971.

Aymer, Brandt. *A Pictorial History of the World's Great Trials.* New York: Crown, 1967.

Aymer, Brandt, and Edward Sagarin. *A Pictorial History of the World's Great Trials from Socrates to Jean Harris.* New York: Bonanza Books, 1985.

Bailey, Kenneth K. "The Enactment of Tennessee's Anti-Evolution Law." *Southern Journal of History* 16 (1950): 472–90.

Bannan, John F., and Rosemary S. Bannan. *Law, Morality and Vietnam: The Peace Militants and the Courts.* Bloomington and London: Indiana University Press, 1974.

Barber, Susanna. *News Cameras in the Courtroom.* Norwood, N.J.: Ablex, 1986.

Becker, Theodore L., ed. *Political Trials.* New York: Bobbs-Merrill, 1971.

Belknap, Michael R., ed. *American Political Trials.* Westport, Conn.: Greenwood Press, 1981.

Bennett, W. Lance. "Political Scenarios and the Nature of Politics." *Philosophy and Rhetoric* 8 (1975): 23–42.

———. "Rhetorical Transformations of Evidence in Criminal Trials: Creating Grounds for Legal Judgment." *Quarterly Journal of Speech* 65 (1979): 311–23.

———. "Storytelling in Criminal Trials: A Model of Social Judgment." *Quarterly Journal of Speech* 64 (1978): 1–22.

Bennett, W. Lance, and Martha Feldman. *Reconstructing Reality in the Courtroom: Justice and Judgment in American Culture.* New Brunswick, N.J.: Rutgers University Press, 1981.

Berelson, Bernard, and Gary A. Steiner. *Human Behavior.* New York: Harcourt, Brace & World, 1964.

Berger, Arthur Asa. *Media Analysis Techniques.* Beverly Hills, Calif.: Sage, 1982.

Berger, Peter L., and Thomas Luckmann. *The Social Construction of Reality: A Treatise in the Sociology of Knowledge.* New York: Doubleday, 1966.

Bernabo, Lawrance M. "Dudley Field Malone, Christian 'Evil-utionist': From Reconciliation to Ridicule at the Scopes Trial." Southern Speech Communication Association, Hot Springs, Arkansas, 9 April 1982.

Bezayiff, David. "Legal Oratory of John Adams: An Early Instrument of Protest." *Western Journal of Speech Communication* 40 (1976): 63–71.

Bitzer, Lloyd. "The Rhetorical Situation." *Philosophy and Rhetoric* 1 (1968): 1–14.

Boorstin, Daniel J. *The Image: A Guide to Pseudo-Events in America.* New York: Atheneum, 1971.

Bormann, Ernest G. "Fantasy and Rhetorical Vision: The Rhetorical Criticism of Social Reality." *Quarterly Journal of Speech* 58 (1972): 396–407.

Brigance, William Norwood, ed. *The History and Criticism of American Public Address*, vol. 1. New York: McGraw-Hill, 1943.

Brod, David. "The Scopes Trial: A Look at Press Coverage After Forty Years." *Journalism Quarterly* 42 (1965): 219.

Brooks, Alexander D. "The Merits of Abolishing the Insanity Defense." *Annals* 477 (January 1985): 125–36.

Burke, Edmund. *The Works of the Right Honourable Edmund Burke.* 8 vols. London: C & J. Rivington, 1826.

Burke, Kenneth. *A Grammar of Motives.* Berkeley: University of California Press, 1969.

———. *A Rhetoric of Motives.* Berkeley: University of California Press, 1969.

———. *The Philosophy of Literary Form: Studies in Symbolic Action*, 3rd ed. Berkeley: University of California Press, 1973.

Campbell, Karlyn Kohrs. "The Rhetoric of Women's Liberation: An Oxymoron." *Quarterly Journal of Speech* 59 (1973): 74–86.

———. *The Rhetorical Act.* Belmont, Calif.: Wadsworth Publishing Co., 1982.

Campbell, Karlyn Kohrs, and Kathleen Hall Jamieson. *Form and Genre: Shaping Rhetorical Action.* Falls Church, Va.: Speech Communication Association, n.d.

Caplan, Lincoln. *The Insanity Defense and the Trial of John W. Hinckley, Jr.* Boston: David R. Godine, 1984.

Carrithers, David W. "The Insanity Defense and Presidential Peril." *Society* 22 (July/August 1985): 23–27.

Carroll, J., and J. Payne, eds. *Cognition and Social Behavior.* Hillsdale, N.J.: Lawrence Erlbaum, 1976.

Casey, William VanEtten, and Philip Nobile, eds. *The Berrigans.* New York: Avon Books, 1981.

Cassata, Mary, and Thomas Skill. *Life on Daytime Television: Tuning-In American Serial Drama.* Norwood, N.J.: Ablex Publishers, 1983.

Cawalti, J. G. "With the Benefit of Hindsight: Popular Culture Criticism." *Critical Studies in Mass Communication* 2 (1985): 363–79.

Chaly, Ingeborg, and Kurt Ritter. "Bibliography of Popularized Trials." Unpublished.

Cherry, George L. *Early English Liberalism: Its Emergence Through Parliamentary Action, 1660–1702.* New York: Bookman Assoc., 1962.

Chesebro, James W. "The Media Reality: Epistemological Functions of Media in Cultural Systems." *Critical Studies in Mass Communication* 1 (1984): 111–30.

Christenson, Ron. *Political Trials: Gordian Knots in the Law.* New Brunswick, N.J.: Transaction Books, 1986.

Clavir, Judy, and John Spitzer. *The Conspiracy Trial.* New York: Bobbs-Merrill, 1970.

Cohen, Bernard. *The Press and Foreign Policy.* Princeton: Princeton University Press, 1963.

Cohen, Carl. *Civil Disobedience: Conscience, Tactics, and the Law.* New York and London: Columbia University Press, 1971.

Cohen, Stanley, and Jock Young, eds. *The Manufacture of News: A Reader.* Beverly Hills, Calif.: Sage, 1973.

Coletta, Palo E. *William Jennings Bryan: Political Puritan, 1915–1925.* Vol. III. Lincoln: University of Nebraska Press, 1969.

Condit, Celeste Michelle. *Decoding Abortion Rhetoric: Communicating Social Change.* Urbana: University of Illinois Press, 1990.

———. "The Rhetorical Limits to Polysemy." *Critical Studies in Mass Communication* 6 (1989), 103–22.

Condit, Celeste Michelle, and J. Ann Selzer. "The Rhetoric of Objectivity in the Newspaper Coverage of a Murder Trial." *Critical Studies in Mass Communication* 2 (1985): 197–216.

Corcoran, Farrell. "Television as Ideological Apparatus: The Power and the Pleasure." *Critical Studies in Mass Communication* 1 (1984): 131–45.

Danet, Brenda. "Language in the Legal Process." *Law & Society Review* 14 (1980): 445–564.

Darrow, Clarence. *The Story of My Life.* New York: Grosset and Dunlap, 1932.

Davis, Natalie Zemon. *The Return of Martin Guerre.* Cambridge: Harvard University Press, 1983.

de Camp, L. Sprague. *The Great Monkey Trial.* Garden City, N.Y.: Doubleday, 1968.

Dershowitz, Alan. *Reversal of Fortune: Inside the von Bulow Case.* New York: Random House, 1986.

Dickens, Milton, and Ruth E. Schwartz. "Oral Argument Before the Supreme Court: Marshall v. Davis in the School Segregation Cases." *Quarterly Journal of Speech* 57 (1971): 32–42.

Dickinson, H. T. *Liberty and Property: Political Ideology in Eighteenth-Century Britain.* New York: Holmes and Meir, 1977.

Dicks, Vivian I. "Courtroom Controversy: A Stasis/Stock Issues Analysis of the Angela Davis Trial." *Journal of the American Forensic Association* 13 (1976).

———. "Courtroom Rhetorical Strategies: Forensic and Deliberative Perspectives." *Quarterly Journal of Speech* 67 (1981): 178–92.

Dietz, Park Elliott. "Why the Experts Disagree: Variations in the Psychiatric Evaluation of Criminal Insanity." *Annals* 477 (January 1985): 84–95.

Doret, David. "Trial by Videotape—Can Justice Be Seen to Be Done?" *Temple Law Quarterly* 47 (1974): 228–68.

Douglas, Mary. *Purity and Danger.* London: Routledge & Kegan Paul, 1970.

———. *Rules and Meanings.* Baltimore: Penguin Books, 1973.

Drechsel, Robert. *News Making in the Trial Courts.* New York: Longman, 1983.

Drucker, Susan, and Robert Cathcart. "Media Relationships: The Celebrity and the Fan." Paper presented at Speech Communication Association of Puerto Rico, San Juan, Puerto Rico, December 1986.

Drucker, Susan J., and Janice Platt Hunold. "The Debating Game." *Critical Studies in Mass Communication* 4 (1987): 202–207.

Duncan, Hugh Dalziel. *Communication and Social Order.* London: Oxford University Press, 1970.

Dunne, Dominick. *Fatal Charms and Other Tales of Today.* New York: Crown Publishers, 1987.

Dworkin, Ronald. *Law's Empire.* Cambridge: Belknap Press of Harvard University Press, 1986.

Edelman, Murray. *The Symbolic Uses of Politics.* Urbana: University of Illinois Press, 1964.

Eemeren, Frans H. van, Rob Grootenborst, J. Anthony Blair, and Charles A. Willard. *Argument: Analysis and Practices.* Dordrecht, The Netherlands: Foris, 1987.

Ennis, Bruce J. "Straight Talk About the Insanity Defense." *Nation* (24–31 July 1982): 70–72.

Epstein, Jason. *The Great Conspiracy Trial: An Essay on Law, Liberty and the Constitution.* New York: Random House, 1970.

Fahy, Sarah A. "The Catonsville Nine Action: A Study of an American Catholic Resistance Action." Diss. Temple University 1975.

Farrell, Thomas. "Knowledge, Consensus, and Rhetorical Theory." *Quarterly Journal of Speech* 62 (1976): 1–14.

Fingarette, Herbert. "Mental Disabilities and Criminal Responsibility." *The Center Magazine* 15 (November/December 1982): 8–16.

Fish, Stanley. "Fish v. Fiss." *Stanford Law Review* 36 (1984): 1325–47.

Fisher, Walter R., ed. *Rhetoric: A Tradition in Transition.* East Lansing: Michigan State University Press, 1974.

Fishman, Mark. *Manufacturing the News.* Austin: University of Texas Press, 1980.

Fiske, John. "Television and Popular Culture: Reflections of British and Australian Critical Practice." *Critical Studies in Mass Communication* 3 (1986): 200–16.

Fiske, John, and John Hartley. *Reading Television.* New York: Methuen, 1978.

Fiss, Owen M. "Objectivity and Interpretation." *Stanford Law Review* 34 (1982): 739–63.

Fleming, Alice. *Trials That Made Headlines.* London: St. Martins, 1974.

Forston, Robert A. *Legal Communication: A Bibliography.* American Forensic Association, 1975.

Foucault, Michel. *Discipline and Punish: The Birth of the Prison.* Trans. Alan Sheridan. New York: Vintage Books, 1977.

Francesconi, Robert A. "James Hunt, The Wilmington 10, and Institutional Legitimacy." *Quarterly Journal of Speech* 69 (1982): 47–59.

Friendly, Fred W., and Martha J. H. Elliott. *The Constitution: That Delicate Balance.* New York: Random House, 1984.

Gatewood, Willard B., Jr. *Preachers, Pedagogues, and Politicians: The Evolution Controversy in North Carolina, 1920–1927.* Chapel Hill: University of North Carolina Press, 1966.

Geis, Gilbert, and Robert F. Meier. "Abolition of the Insanity Plea in Idaho: A Case Study." *Annals* 477 (January 1985): 72–83.

Ginger, Ray. *Six Days or Forever? Tennessee v. John Thomas Scopes.* New York: Oxford University Press, 1958.

Gitlin, Todd. *The Whole World Is Watching: Mass Media in the Making and Unmaking of the New Left.* Berkeley: University of California Press, 1980.

Glad, Paul W. *The Trumpet Soundeth: William Jennings Bryan and His Democracy, 1896–1912.* Lincoln: University of Nebraska Press, 1960.

Glasgow Media Group. "Bad News." *Theory and Society* 3 (Fall 1976): 339–63.

Goffman, Erving. *Frame Analysis.* New York: Harper & Row, 1974.

Grossberg, Lawrence. "Strategies of Marxist Cultural Interpretation." *Critical Studies in Mass Communication* 1 (1984): 392–421.

Grover, David. *Debaters and Dynamiters: The Story of the Harwood Trial.* Corvalis: Oregon State University Press, 1965.

Gumpert, Gary, and Robert Cathcart, eds. *Inter/Media.* New York: Oxford University Press, 1982.

———. "Media Grammars, Generations, and Media Gaps." *Critical Studies in Mass Communication* 2 (1985): 23–35.

Gurevitch, Michael, Tony Bennett, James Curran, and Janet Wollacott, eds. *Culture, Society and the Media.* New York: Methuen, 1982.

Gustainis, J. Justin. "Daniel Berrigan and the Catholic Ultra-Resistance: The Roots of a Rhetorical Genre." Diss., Bowling Green State University, 1981.

———. "The Catholic Ultra-Resistance: Rhetorical Strategies of Anti-War Protest." *The Communicator* 12 (1983): 37–42.

Gustainis, Justin, and Hahn, Dan F. "While the Whole World Watched:

Rhetorical Failures of Anti-War Protest." *Communication Quarterly* 36 (1988): 203–16.

Hackett, Robert A. "Decline of a Paradigm? Bias and Objectivity in News Media Studies." *Critical Studies in Mass Communication* 1 (1984): 229–59.

Haiman, Franklyn S. *Speech and Law in a Free Society.* Chicago: University of Chicago Press, 1981.

Hall, Stuart. "Signification, Representation, Ideology: Althusser and the Post-Structuralist Debates." *Critical Studies in Mass Communication* 2 (1985): 91–114.

Hall, Stuart, D. Hobson, A. Lowe, and P. Willis, eds. *Culture, Media, Language.* London: Hutchinson, 1980.

Halloran, James. *Control or Consent? A Study of the Challenge of Mass Communication.* London: Sheed & Ward, 1963.

Halloran, James, Philip Elliott, and Graham Murdock. *Demonstrations and Communication: A Case Study.* London: Penguin, 1970.

Hans, Valerie P., and Dan Slater. "John Hinckley, Jr. and the Insanity Defense: The Public's Verdict." *Public Opinion Quarterly* 47 (1983): 202–204.

Hariman, Robert. "Status, Marginality, and Rhetorical Theory," *Quarterly Journal of Speech* 72 (1986): 38–54.

Harrison, Harry P., as told to Karl Detzer. *Culture Under Canvas: The Story of Tent Chautauqua.* New York: Hastings House, 1958.

Hayden, Tom. *Trial.* New York: Holt, Rinehart and Winston, 1970.

Hays, Arthur Garfield. *Let Freedom Ring.* New York: Liveright, 1937.

Hebdige, Dick. *Subculture: The Meaning of Style.* London: Methuen, 1979.

Hermann, Donald H. J. "Assault on the Insanity Defense: Limitations on the Effectiveness and Effect of the Defense of Insanity." *Rutgers Law Journal* 14 (1983): 241–371.

Hoffer, Peter Charles, and N. E. H. Hull. *Impeachment in America, 1635–1805.* New Haven: Yale University Press, 1984.

Holmes, Geoffrey. *The Trial Of Doctor Sacheverell.* London: Eyre Metheun, 1973.

———. ed. *Politics, Religion and Society in England 1678–1742.* London: Hambledon Press, 1986.

Hunskar, David M. "The Rhetoric of *Brown vs. Board of Education:* Paradigm for Contemporary Social Protest." *Southern Speech Communication Journal* 43 (1978): 91–109.

Innis, Harold A. *The Bias of Communication.* Toronto: University of Toronto Press, 1951.

Jameson, Fredric. *The Political Unconscious: Narrative as a Socially Symbolic Act.* Ithaca, N.Y.: Cornell University Press, 1981.

Jamieson, Kathleen Hall. *Eloquence in an Electronic Age: The Transformation of Political Speechmaking.* New York: Oxford University Press, 1988.

Jensen, Klaus Bruhn. "Qualitative Audience Research: Toward an Integrative Approach to Reception." *Critical Studies in Mass Communication* 4 (1987): 21–36.

Jones v. *United States*. 463 U.S. 354, 103 S. Ct. 3043 (1983).

Kane, Peter. *Murder, Courts, and the Press: Issues in Free Press/Fair Trial.* Carbondale: Southern Illinois University Press, 1986.

————, comp. "Table of Contents and Index to Free Speech Yearbook, Volumes I–XXV, 1962–1986." *Free Speech Yearbook.* Falls Church, Va.: Speech Communication Association, 1986.

Kapis, Robert, Bruce Saunders, Jim Smith, Paul Takagi, and Oscar Williams. *The Reconstruction of a Riot: A Case Study of Community Tensions and Civil Disorder.* Waltham, Mass.: Brandeis University Lemberg Center for the Study of Violence, 1970.

Kaufer, David. "Analyzing Philosophy in Rhetoric: Darrow's Mechanism in the Defense of Leopold and Leob." *Southern Speech Communication Journal* 45 (1980): 363–77.

Kaufman, Irving R. "The Insanity Plea on Trial." *New York Times Magazine* (8 August 1982): 16–20.

Koenig, Louis W. *Bryan: A Political Biography of William Jennings Bryan.* New York: G. P. Putnam's Sons, 1981.

Krippendorf, Klaus. *Content Analysis: An Introduction to its Methodology.* Beverly Hills, Calif.: Sage, 1980.

Langer, John. "Television's 'Personality System.'" *Media, Culture and Society* 4 (1981): 351–65.

Lazarsfeld, Paul. *Radio and the Printed Page.* New York: Duell, Sloan and Pearce, 1940.

Lazarsfeld, Paul, Bernard Berelson, and Hazel Gaudet. *The People's Choice.* New York: Columbia University Press, 1948.

Lentricchia, Frank. *Criticism and Social Change.* Chicago: University of Chicago Press, 1983.

Lerner, Max. "Constitution and Court as Symbols." *Yale Law Journal* 46 (1937): 1290–1319.

Lindzey, G., ed. *Handbook of Social Psychology.* Vol. 2. Cambridge, Mass.: Addison-Wesley, 1954.

Llewellyn, Karl N. *Jurisprudence: Realism in Theory and Practice.* Chicago: University of Chicago Press, 1962.

Low, Peter W., John Calvin Jeffries, Jr., and Richard J. Bonnie. *The Trial of John W. Hinckley, Jr.: A Case Study in the Insanity Defense.* Mineola, N.Y.: Foundation Press, 1986.

Lucaites, John Louis. "Flexibility and Consistency in Eighteenth-Century Anglo-Whiggism: A Case Study of The Rhetorical Dimensions of Legitimacy." Diss., University of Iowa, 1984.

Lukas, J. Anthony. *The Barnyard Epithet and Other Obscenities: Notes on the Chicago Conspiracy Trial.* New York: Harper & Row, 1970.

Lukes, Steven. *Power: A Radical View.* London: Macmillan, 1974.

Lyon, Peter. "The Herald Angels of Women's Rights." *American Heritage* 10 (1959): 21.

McGee, Michael Calvin. "'Not Men, But Measures': The Origins and Import of an Ideological Principle." *Quarterly Journal of Speech* 64 (1978): 141–54.

———. "Edmund Burke's Beautiful Lie: An Exploration of the Relationship Between Rhetoric and Social Theory." Diss., University of Iowa, 1974.

———. "The 'Ideograph': A Link Between Rhetoric and Ideology." *Quarterly Journal of Speech* 66 (1980): 1–16.

———. "The Origins of 'Liberty': A Feminization of Power." *Communication Monographs* 47 (1980): 23–45.

MacIntyre, Alaisdair. *After Virtue.* 2nd ed. Notre Dame: University of Notre Dame Press, 1984.

McKerrow, Ray E., ed. *Explorations in Rhetoric: Studies in Honor of Douglas Ehninger.* Chicago: Scott, Foresman, 1982.

Mather, Kirtley F. "Creation and Evolution," in *Science Ponders Religion*, ed. Harlow Shapley, 32–45. New York: Appleton-Century-Crofts, 1960.

Matlon, Ronald J., and Richard J. Crawford, eds. *Communication Strategies and the Practice of Lawyering.* Speech Communication Association, 1983.

Meconis, Charles A. *With Clumsy Grace: The American Catholic Left 1961–1975.* New York: Seabury Press, 1979.

Meyrowitz, Joshua. *No Sense of Place: The Impact of Electronic Media on Social Behavior.* New York: Oxford University Press, 1985.

Miller, Carolyn R. "Genre as Social Action." *Quarterly Journal of Speech* 70 (1984): 151.

Miller, Gerald R., and Norman E. Fontes. *Real Versus Reel: What's the Verdict? The Effects of Videotaped Court Materials on Juror Response.* National Science Foundation, n.d.

Milliband, Ralph. *The State in Capitalist Society: An Analysis of the Western System of Power.* New York: Basic Books, 1969.

Monaco, James. *Media Culture.* New York: Delta Books, 1978.

Moran, Richard. *Knowing Right from Wrong: The Insanity Defense of Daniel McNaughtan.* New York: Free Press, 1981.

———, ed. "The Insanity Defense." *Annals* 477 (January 1985): 31–42.

Morley, David. *The Nationwide Audience: Structure and Decoding.* London: British Film Institute, 1980.

Morse, Stephen J. "Retaining a Modified Insanity Defense." *Annals* 477 (January 1985): 137–47.

Mumby, Dennis, and Carole Spitzack. "Ideology and Television News: A Metaphoric Analysis of Political Stories." *Central States Speech Journal* 34 (1983): 162–71.

Nelson, Jack, and Ronald J. Ostrow. *The FBI and the Berrigans.* New York: Coward, McCann & Geoghegan, 1972.

Newcomb, Horace, ed. *Television: The Critical View.* New York: Oxford, 2nd edition, 1979; 3rd edition, 1982.

Nichols, B. *Ideology and the Image.* Bloomington: Indiana University Press, 1981.

Nimmo, Dan, and James E. Combs. *Mediated Political Realities.* New York: Longman, 1983.

———. *Nightly Horrors.* Knoxville: University of Tennessee Press, 1985.

Ong, Walter. *The Presence of the Word.* New York: Clarion, 1967.

Oravec, Christine. "The Sublimation of Mass Consciousness in the Rhetorical Criticism of Jacksonian America." *Communication* 11 (1989): 291–314.

Parenti, Michael. *Inventing Reality: The Politics of Mass Media.* New York: St. Martin's Press, 1986.

Pasewark, Richard A. "A Review of Research on the Insanity Defense." *Annals* 484 (March 1986): 100–14.

Pattie, Frank A., ed. "The Last Speech of William Jennings Bryan." *Tennessee Historical Quarterly* 6 (1947): 265–83.

Patton, John H. "Rhetoric at Catonsville: Daniel Berrigan, Conscience, and Image Alteration." *Today's Speech* 23 (Winter 1975): 3–12.

Peck, Abe. *Uncovering the Sixties: The Life and Times of the Underground Press.* New York: Pantheon, 1985.

Perelman, Chaim, and L. Olbrechts-Tyteca. *The New Rhetoric: A Treatise on Argumentation.* Notre Dame: Notre Dame University Press, 1971.

Piccirillo, M. S. "On the Authenticity of Televisual Experience: A Critical Exploration of Para-Social Closure." *Critical Studies in Mass Communication* 3 (1986): 337–55.

Plato. *The Collected Dialogues of Plato.* Translated by A. E. Taylor. Edited by Edith Hamilton and Huntington Cairns. Princeton, N.J.: Princeton University Press, 1961.

Pocock, J. G. A. *The Ancient Constitution and The Feudal Law.* Cambridge: The University Press, 1957.

Postman, Neil. *Amusing Ourselves to Death: Public Discourse in the Age of Show Business.* New York: Viking, 1985.

Primeau, Ronald. *The Rhetoric of Television.* New York: Longman, 1979.

Propp, Vladimir. *The Morphology of a Folktale.* Austin: University of Texas Press, 1968.

Pryor, Bert, David U. Strawn, Raymond Buchanan, and Milan D. Meeske. "The Florida Experiment: An Analysis of On-The-Scene Responses to Cameras in the Courtroom." *Southern Speech Communication Journal* 45 (1979): 12–26.

Quen, Jacques M. "Psychiatry and the Law: Historical Relevance to Today." In *"By Reason of Insanity,"* edited by Lawrence Z. Freedman. Wilmington, Del.: Scholarly Resources, 1983.

Raines, John C., ed. *Conspiracy: The Implications of the Harrisburg Trial for the Democratic Tradition.* New York: Harper & Row, 1974.

Rieke, Richard. "Argumentation in the Legal Process," in *Advances in Argumentation Theory and Research,* edited by J. Robert Cox and Charles A. Willard, 363–78. Carbondale: Southern Illinois University Press, 1982.

Rintels, David W. *Clarence Darrow.* Garden City, N.Y.: Doubleday, 1975.

Ritter, Kurt. "Drama and Legal Rhetoric: The Perjury Trials of Alger Hiss." *Western Journal of Speech Communication* 49 (1985): 83–102.

Robinson, Daniel N. *Psychology and Law.* New York: Oxford University Press, 1980.

Rollings, Herbert E., and Jim Balscovich. "The Case of Patricia Hearst: Pretrial Publicity and Opinion." *Journal of Communication* 27 (1977): 58–65.

Ross, John M. *Trials in Collections: An Index to Famous Trials Throughout the World.* Metuchen, N.J.: Scarecrow Press, 1983.

Rubenstein, Richard E. *Great Courtroom Battles.* Chicago: Bayboy Press, 1973.

Saks, Michael J., and Reid Hastie. *Social Psychology in the Court.* New York: Van Nostrand Reinhold, 1978.

Sambonmatsu, Akira. "Darrow and Rourke's Use of Burkeian Identification Strategies in *New York* v. *Gitlow.*" *Communication Monographs* 38 (1971): 36–48.

Schiller, D. *Objectivity and the News: The Public and the Rise of Commercial Journalism.* Philadelphia: University of Pennsylvania Press, 1981.

Schramm, Wilbur, and Donald F. Roberts, eds. *The Process and Effects of Mass Communication.* Urbana: University of Illinois Press, 1971.

Schudson, Michael. *Discovering the News: A Social History of American Newspapers.* New York: Basic Books, 1978.

———. "The Ideal of Conversation in the Study of Mass Media." In *Inter/Media,* edited by G. Gumpert and R. Cathcart, 41–48. New York: Oxford University Press, 1982.

Schuetz, Janice. "Political Trials and Free Speech." *Free Speech Yearbook.* Falls Church, Va.: Speech Communication Association, 1985, 38–50.

Schuetz, Janice, and Kathryn Holmes Snedaker. *Communication and Litigation: Case Studies of Famous Trials.* Carbondale: Southern Illinois University Press, 1988.

Schwartz, Helene. *Lawyering.* New York: Farrar, Straus and Giroux, 1976.

Schweitzer, Don A. "The Effect of Presentation on Source Evaluation." *Quarterly Journal of Speech* 56 (February 1970): 33–39.

Scott, Robert L. "Rhetoric as Epistemic." *Central States Speech Journal* 18 (1967): 9–17.

Scudi, Albert Turner. *The Sacheverell Affair.* New York: Columbia University Press, 1939.

Sears, David O., and Jonathan L. Freedman. "Selective Exposure to Information: A Critical Review." In *The Process and Effects of Mass Communication,* edited by Wilbur Schramm and Donald F. Roberts, 209–34. Urbana: University of Illinois Press, 1971.

Shapley, Harlow, ed. *Science Ponders Religion.* New York: Appleton-Century-Crofts, 1960.

Shipley, Maynard. *The War on Modern Science: A Short History of the Fundamentalist Attacks on Evolution and Modernism.* New York: Alfred A. Knopf, 1927.

Siegel, Elliot R., Gerald Miller, and C. Edward Wotring. "Source Credibility and Credibility Proneness: A New Relationship." *Speech Monographs* 36 (June 1969): 118–25.

Sigman, Stuart J., and Donald L. Fry. "Differential Ideology and Language Use: Readers' Reconstructions and Descriptions of News Events." *Critical Studies in Mass Communication* 2 (1985): 307–22.

Simon, Rita, and David Aaronson. *The Insanity Defense: A Critical Assessment of Law and Policy in the Post-Hinckley Era.* New York: Praeger, 1988.

Simons, Herbert W., and Aram A. Aghazarian, eds. *Form, Genre, and the Study of Political Discourse.* Columbia: University of South Carolina Press, 1986.

Singer, Richard. "The Aftermath of an Insanity Acquittal: The Supreme Court's Recent Decision in *Jones* v. *United States." Annals* 477 (January 1985): 114–24.

Slovenko, Ralph. "The Insanity Defense in the Wake of the Hinckley Trial." *Rutgers Law Journal* 14 (1983): 373–95.

Speck, W. A., ed. *F. F. Madan, A Critical Bibliography of Dr. Henry Sacheverell.* Lawrence: University of Kansas Libraries, 1978.

Steadman, Henry J., and Joseph P. Morrissey. "The Insanity Defense: Problems and Prospects for Studying the Impact of Legal Reforms." *Annals* 484 (March 1986): 115–26.

Stewart, Charles, Craig Smith, and Robert E. Denton, Jr. *Persuasion and Social Movements.* Prospect Heights, Ill.: Waveland Press, 1984.

Stone, Alan. *Law, Psychiatry, and Morality.* Washington, D.C.: American Psychiatric Press, 1984.

Stone, Irving. *Clarence Darrow for the Defense.* Garden City, N.Y.: Doubleday, Doran & Company, 1941.

Strate, Lance. "Heroes, Fame and the Media." *Et Cetera* (1985): 44.

Straton, John Roach. *The Famous New York Fundamentalist-Modernist Debates.* New York: George H. Doran, 1925.

Symposium: The Use of Videotape in the Courtroom. *Brigham Young University Law Review* (1975, no. 2).

Szasz, Ferenc M. "The Scopes Trial in Perspective." *Tennessee Historical Quarterly* 30 (Fall 1971): 290–91.

Tannenbaum, Percy H., ed. *The Entertainment Functions of Television.* Hillsdale, N.J.: Lawrence Erlbaum Assoc., 1980.

Taylor, Charles Alan, and Celeste Michelle Condit. "Objectivity and Elites: A Creation Science Trial." *Critical Studies in Mass Communication* 5 (1988): 293–312.

Taylor, Stuart, Jr. "Jury Finds Hinckley Not Guilty, Accepting His Defense of Insanity." *New York Times,* 22 June 1982, A1.

———. "The Hinckley Riddle: Outrage on Acquittal Focuses on Confusion Created by Combining Psychiatry and Law." *New York Times,* 24 June 1982, D21.

———. "Too Much Justice." *Harper's* (September 1982): 56–60.

Tedford, Thomas L. *Freedom of Speech in the United States.* Carbondale: Southern Illinois University Press, 1985.

Tiemens, Robert K., Susan A. Hellweg, Phillip Kipper, and Steven L. Phillips. "An Integrative Verbal and Visual Analysis of the Carter-Reagan Debate." *Communication Quarterly* 33 (1985): 34–42.

Tierney, Kevin. *Darrow: A Biography.* New York: Thomas Y. Crowell, 1979.

Timmis, John H. III. *Thine Is the Kingdom: The Trial for Treason of Thomas Wentworth, Earl of Strafford, First Minister to King Charles I, and Last Hope of the English Crown.* University, Ala.: University of Alabama Press, 1974.

Tite, Colin G. C. *Impeachment and Parliamentary Judicature in Early Stuart England.* London: Athlone Press, 1974.

Tocqueville, Alexis de. *Democracy in America.* New York: Vintage, 1945.

Tompkins, Jerry R., ed. *D-Day at Dayton: Reflections on the Scopes Trial.* Baton Rouge: Louisiana State University Press, 1965.

Toulmin, Stephen. *The Uses of Argument.* Cambridge: Cambridge University Press, 1958.

Tuchman, Gaye. *Making News: A Study in the Construction of Reality.* New York: The Free Press, 1978.

Tushnet, Mark. "Critical Legal Studies and Constitutional Law: An Essay in Deconstruction." *Stanford Law Review* 36 (1984): 626.

Wasby, Stephen L., Anthony D'Amato, and Rosemary Metrailer. "The Functions of Oral Argument in the U.S. Supreme Court." *Quarterly Journal of Speech* 62 (1976): 410–22.

Watkins, B. "Television Viewing as a Dominant Activity of Childhood: A Developmental Theory of Television Effects." *Critical Studies in Mass Communication* 2 (1985): 323–37.

Weaver, Richard M. *The Ethics of Rhetoric.* Chicago: Henry Regnery, 1953.

Weber, Ronald, ed. *The Reporter as Artist: A Look at the New Journalism.* New York: Hastings House, 1974.

Weinberg, Arthur, ed. *Attorney for the Damned.* New York: Simon and Schuster, 1957.

Weston, J. *Monarchy and Revolution.* Totowa, N.J.: Rowman and Littlefield, 1972.

White, Carol. "Scapegoating of Bruno Richard Hauptmann: The Rhetorical Process in Prejudicial Publicity." *Central States Speech Journal* 32 (1981): 100–10.

White, Eugene E., ed. *Rhetoric in Transition: Studies in the Nature and Uses of Rhetoric.* University Park: Pennsylvania State University Press, 1980.

White, James Boyd. *Heracles' Bow: Essays on the Rhetoric and Poetics of the Law.* Madison: University of Wisconsin Press, 1985.

———. "Is Cultural Criticism Possible?" *Michigan Law Review* 84 (1986): 1373.

———. *When Words Lose Their Meaning: Constitutions and Reconstitutions of Language, Character, and Community.* Chicago: University of Chicago Press, 1984.

Wilkinson, Charles Anthony. "The Rhetoric of Movements: Definition and Methodological Approach, Applied to the Catholic Anti-War Movement in the United States." Diss., Northwestern University, 1975.

Willard, Charles. *Argumentation and the Social Grounds of Knowledge.* University, Ala.: University of Alabama Press, 1983.

Williams, Neville, ed. *The Eighteenth-Century Constitution, 1688–1815.* Cambridge: The University Press, 1960.

Williams, Raymond. *Television: Technology and Cultural Form.* New York: Schocken Books, 1974.

Wilson, Charles Morrow. *The Commoner: William Jennings Bryan.* Garden City, N.Y.: Doubleday and Co., 1970.

Wright, William. *The von Bulow Affair.* New York: Dell Publishing, 1983.

Zaroulis, Nancy, and Gerald Sullivan. *Who Spoke Up? American Protest against the War in Vietnam 1963–1975.* Garden City N.Y.: Doubleday & Co., 1984.

Ziegelmueller, George, and Jack Rhodes, eds. *Dimensions of Argument: Proceedings of the Second Summer Conference on Argumentation.* Annandale, Va.: Speech Communication Association, 1981.

Contributors

Lawrance M. Bernabo currently lives in Duluth, Minnesota, where he is working on *The Scopes Myth*, a book about the Scopes trial. He has taught at New Mexico, Minnesota, Iowa, Illinois, Millikin, and Minnesota-Duluth.

Barry Brummett is Associate Professor of Communication at the University of Wisconsin-Milwaukee. He has published several essays on rhetorical theory, with special attention to epistemological issues, and, more recently, on the criticism of mass media and popular culture.

Celeste Michelle Condit is Associate Professor of Speech Communication at the University of Georgia, Athens. Her academic interest in the role of rhetoric in the processes of social change has focused on several legal cases. Her co-authored articles on the Alabama creation-science trial and the Koerner murder trial appear in *Critical Studies in Mass Communication*. Her work on the role of *Roe* v. *Wade* as part of the abortion controversy appears in *Decoding Abortion Rhetoric: Communicating Social Change*.

Juliet Lushbough Dee is Assistant Professor of Communication at the University of Delaware. She is a co-author of *Mass Communications Law in a Nutshell*, and has published an article about media responsibility for stimulating real-life violence in the *Journal of*

Communication. Other articles also deal with First Amendment law.

Susan J. Drucker is an attorney and Assistant Professor of Communication at Queens College, City University of New York. She teaches media law and communication in the legal system, and she has published in the *New York State Bar Journal, Critical Studies in Mass Communication,* and *Communication Quarterly.*

J. Justin Gustainis is Associate Professor of Communication at the State University of New York, Plattsburgh. He is the author of numerous papers, chapters, and articles dealing with rhetorical criticism, public address, and popular culture. His book, *Jimmy Carter and the Rhetoric of Idealism,* will be published in 1990.

Robert Hariman is Associate Professor of Speech Communication at Drake University, where he teaches and writes about rhetorical theory and political discourse. His essays have appeared in *Quarterly Journal of Speech, Journal of the History of Ideas,* and *Rhetorica.*

Janice Platt Hunold has worked professionally in media production for several years and has taught media arts at the University of Missouri, University of Kansas, and Queens College.

William Lewis is Associate Professor of Speech Communication at Drake University. He teaches courses in argumentation and public policy, political and legal communication, and rhetorical criticism. His essays have appeared in the *Quarterly Journal of Speech* and the *Journal of Communication Inquiry.*

John Louis Lucaites is Assistant Professor of Speech Communication at Indiana University where he teaches courses in contemporary rhetorical theory. He has edited *Great Speakers and Speeches* and has published essays tracing the rhetorical development of "public trust" in seventeenth-century and eighteenth-century England. He is currently writing a book on the rhetoric of racial equality with Celeste Michelle Condit.

Larry Williamson is Associate Professor and Chair of Communication Studies at the University of San Diego. In addition to his academic research on the subject, he has acted as an expert witness on media coverage of trials. He has also authored rhetorical critiques of other facets of popular mass media.

Index

Mencken, H. L. (*Continued*)
  Sahara of the Bozart," 76; caricatured South, 76–77
Merton, Robert, 109
Metaphor, container, 21–22, 198 (n. 8)
Metcalf, Maynard M., 70
Meyrowitz, Joshua, 182, 188–89
Miller, District Attorney Edwin, 150
Mische, George, 165, 172
Mitchell, Attorney General John, 88, 103
Moylan, Mary 165

Nachman, Larry, 106, 111
Nancarrow, Loren, 148
Neal, Dean Randolph, 59
Nietzsche, Friedrich, 59
Nimmo, Dan, 155
Nixon, Richard, 88, 101, 105
Novak, Michael, 176

O'Connor, Maureen, 150
Objectivity: rhetoric of, 154; in American news industry, 231 (n. 11)
Ong, Walter, 182

Parenti, Michael, 163
Parker, Judge, 122
Peay, Governor Austin, 57
Piccirillo, M. S., 181
Plato: *Laws*, 17
Popularization of trials, 2–3, 8, 10
Porter, David, 181
Potter, Charles Francis, 70
Postman, Neil, 182–83
Power, and adjudication of discourses, 25, 115
Press, Copley, 150
Price, McCready George, 78
Propp, Vladimer: *Morphology of a Folktale*, 155; terms related to, 159
Public address, study of as background, 10–11; criticism of, 11; speaker orientation in criticism, 11
Public proceedings as genre, 198 (n. 6)
Pucinski, Congressman Roman, 96–97

Quen, Jacques M., 114

Rap Brown law, 104
Raulston, Judge, 61, 62, 65, 70, 72, 75, 80, 199 (n. 16)
Reagan, Ronald, 13, 102, 114, 116, 126–27

Robinson, Daniel N.: *Psychology and Law*, 114
Robson, Judge Edwin, 99
Roe v. Wade decision, 4
Rubin, Jerry, 88, 92, 96, 99, 103, 108–9, 109–10

Sacheverell, Dr. Henry, 12; Gunpowder Day sermon of 1709, 38–41
Sacheverell impeachment trial: hereditary monarchy in, 12, 44–52 passim; right of resistance, 12, 44–53 passim; sermons leading to, 31, 37–42, 201 (n. 9); popular response to, 32; as public spectacle, 32; and 18th-century British government, 33; liberty, 34, 35, 44, 46; rule of law, 34, 50; ideographic competition in, 42–44; consent of the governed, 43–54 passim; non-resistance, 45–47, 48, 51; passive obedience, 45–47, 49–50; passive resistance, 45–47, 48; Whig argument in, 49–50 (200 n. 3); Tory argument in, 50–52 (200 n. 3); parliamentary sovereignty, 52; popular sovereignty, 52, 54, 204 (n. 59); open proceedings of, 200 (n. 3). *See also* Ideographs
Schaller, 107–8
Schuetz, Janice, 94, 196 (nn. 16, 18, 19)
Schultz, Richard, 108
Schwartz, Helene: *Lawyering*, 94
Scopes, John Thomas, 12, 58; as inappropriate defendant, 58; 207 (n. 17)
Scopes trial, 20–21; functioning to judge discourses, 24–25; religious discourse in, 24–25, 56–57, 62–65; scientific discourse in, 24–25, 56–57, 62–65; transcript, edited version of, 56; press coverage of, 56, 69, 73–78, 211 (n. 60); action leading to, 57–58; defense objective in, 61–62; prosecution in, 61; constitutional issues in, 62–65; evolution and genesis in, 62–65; legal story of, 66; Darrow's cross-examination of Bryan in, 70–73; outcome delegitimated, 75; popularization in, 75; three discourses in trial, 199 (n. 15); and science and the accommodationists, 217–18 (n. 120); accommodationist editorial position, 79–80; rhetoricians' consideration of, 204–5 (n. 1); religion versus science in, 208 (n. 32);

About the Series

STUDIES IN RHETORIC AND COMMUNICATION
General Editors:
E. Culpepper Clark, Raymie E. McKerrow, and David Zarefsky

The University of Alabama Press has established this series to publish major new works in the general area of rhetoric and communication, including books treating the symbolic manifestations of political discourse, argument as social knowledge, the impact of machine technology on patterns of communication behavior, and other topics related to the nature or impact of symbolic communication. We actively solicit studies involving historical, critical, or theoretical analyses of human discourse.